COURTING SCIENCE

COURTING SCIENCE

Securing the Foundation for a

Second American Century

DAMON V. COLETTA

STANFORD SECURITY STUDIES

An Imprint of Stanford University Press

Stanford, California

Stanford University Press
Stanford, California

Library of Congress Cataloging-in-Publication Data

Names: Coletta, Damon V., author.
Title: Courting science : securing the foundation for a second American
    century / Damon V. Coletta.
Description: Stanford, California : Stanford University Press, 2016. | © 2016
    | Includes bibliographical references and index.
Identifiers: LCCN 2015034970 | ISBN 9780804798938 (cloth : alk. paper) |
    ISBN 9780804798945 (pbk : alk. paper)
Subjects: LCSH: Science and state—United States. | Technology and
    state—United States. | United States—Foreign relations—21st century. |
    Hegemony—United States.
Classification: LCC Q127.U6 C625 2016 | DDC 338.973/06—dc23
LC record available at http://lccn.loc.gov/2015034970

Printed in the United States of America on acid-free, archival-quality
paper. Typeset at Stanford University Press in 10/14 Minion.

ISBN 9780804798969 (electronic)

This work is dedicated to our current generation of American scientists, toiling as ever on the frontier of knowledge and carrying now the hopes for a second American Century to political frontiers at home and abroad

Contents

Acknowledgments

This academic work does not represent official views of the U.S. government or the U.S. Air Force Academy (USAFA). The kernels of ideas and chapters that make up this book, however, were developed thanks to patient funding and encouragement from several sources, including organizations within the government. Jim Smith, director of the Institute for National Security Studies (INSS) at USAFA, funded a critical research trip for interviews and substantive participation at the joint Brazilian Association of International Relations (ABRI)/International Studies Association (ISA) meeting in 2009. Later that year, he posted my report on "Science, Technology, and the Quest for International Influence" (www.usafa.edu/df/inss/researchpapers.cfm) at INSS, which boosted confidence in my line of questioning for American S&T and pushed me to expand my research on case studies mentioned in that sketch—the U.S. Office of Naval Research and the Brazilian S&T establishment. Even before that, the U.S. Office of Naval Research Global (ONRG) in London introduced me to connections between science and technology and U.S. diplomacy, sponsoring me for a short fellowship at their office in November 2007.

I owe a debt of gratitude to many individuals serving within and outside of government. First and foremost, my department head at USAFA during the writing of this book, Col. Cheryl Kearney, is our chief advocate for scholarly research as part and parcel of faculty responsibilities at a service academy. Every step of the way, she approved, endorsed, and battled for academic support in the form of special temporary duty, workshop funding, fellowships, and sabbaticals to keep me and my civilian colleagues not only recharged but also engaged in the broad discourse of our field, so we could stay sharp for our classrooms. This book simply would not have been possible without her steady determination to see all her scholars succeed.

Also in the Department of Political Science, Ambassador Roger Harrison and Deron Jackson directed the Eisenhower Center for Space and Defense Studies. Time and again, these gentlemen set aside resources to allow my participation in specialized workshops. More than that, they entrusted me with editing the Eisenhower Center's scholarly journal, *Space & Defense*. This assignment introduced me to a large, energetic network spanning government, business, and academia, working away at problems of governance as they relate to space policy. From this opportunity was born my final case study on global governance at the Final Frontier. Our band of full-time civilians at the department—Paul Bolt, Fran Pilch, Paul Carrese, and Dave Sacko—were extraordinarily supportive of this book, reading and discussing various sections of the work, sometimes more than once, over the years.

As the scope of this work expanded and encompassed more organizations—such as ONRG; Ministry of Science and Technology (MCT), Brasilia; National Space Agency (CONAE), Buenos Aires; and U.S. country teams at the embassies in Brazil and Argentina—more individuals stepped forward and gave generously of their time. From the Office of Naval Research Global, Dr. John Zimmerman, Dr. Clay Stewart, and Ms. Sharon Reeve were welcoming and supportive at the beginning. This book is dedicated to the American science enterprise, which applies to a large, diverse group, but it is with special individuals like the folks at ONRG very much in mind.

A book coming together over several years involves building blocks and many moving parts. Portions of the work were presented at a series of meetings organized by ISA in the spring and jointly by the International Security Studies Section, ISA and International Security and Arms Control section, American Political Science Association during the fall. These regular workshops were important for understanding how the field of security studies was evolving and for developing a research network, including fine editors such as Geoffrey Burn and James Holt at Stanford, eager to work with scholars in Professional Military Education. During this period I was also fortunate to receive invitations for fellowships and visiting professorships, where this book project was improved. In spring 2011, Magnus Petersson and Paal Hilde hosted me for a research fellowship with the NATO Programme at the Norwegian Institute for Defence Studies, Oslo. Erik Gartzke and Jon Lindsay were kind enough to invite me to study in summer 2014 as a visiting scholar with their project on Cross-Domain Deterrence, carried out at the storied Institute on Global Conflict and Cooperation, University of California, San Diego campus and sponsored by the U.S. Department of Defense Minerva Initiative. At present I am finishing a visiting professorship under Col. "Tank" McKinzie, with the innovative, hard-charging men and women at the Office of Science and Technology, U.S. Northern Command in Colorado Springs.

Finally, my mentor, Peter Feaver at Duke University, taught me the politics of principal-agent dilemmas when he was writing an important book, *Armed Servants: Agency, Oversight, and Civil-Military Relations* (Harvard University Press, 2003), nearly twenty years before principals and agents became the theoretical backbone for this effort. My parents, Vince and Sandy; my sister, Joelle, at the VA Hospital, University of California, San Diego; daughter, Grayce; and my wife, Jonan, can be proud and grateful, too. From the beginning they played an integral part in this enterprise.

Damon Coletta, Colorado Springs, CO

June 2015

1   A Second American Century

Toward the end of his influential *War and Change in World Politics* (1981), Robert Gilpin famously claimed that Thucydides, by virtue of his deep insight into the causes and consequences of the Peloponnesian War, would, if properly briefed about critical technologies and lead actors on the world stage, render a similarly penetrating history of contemporary international rivalries.[1] On its face, the assertion that nothing much has changed over twenty-five centuries sounds absurd, but Gilpin's idea has not lost its luster.[2] It speaks to a central and controversial ambition for universality in both the study and practice of International Relations.

Yet, something important *has* changed in the last half-century: the centrality of science and technology (S&T) for creating power in international affairs. Thucydides wrote about the implications of geography, population, democratic culture, and ship-building technology for the balance of power in ancient Greece. Many of his insights do hold in modern times, but in comparison with the factors on Thucydides' original list, science really is different. While crucial for cultivating national capability, science encompasses more than *technē* or a library of useful facts about Nature. Science is also a method of inquiry, a practice of cosmopolitan high culture, a human activity that cannot be cornered or harnessed entirely by any single government.

Thucydides wisely remained vague about whether divine or cosmic justice intervened in the power competition among states. He detailed, in protagonists' arguments for war and in his battle descriptions, which miscalculations, which misapprehensions of physical force, led to spectacular Athenian defeat in Sicily, the beginning of the end of Athenian influence. Curiously, though, Thucydides moved Sicily from its actual position in the chronological stream of events so close to Athens' barbaric destruction of tiny Melos, and so close to the end of Athenian hegemony, while Athens would fight on for years; readers

1

were left to wonder whether Athenian *injustice* ultimately frustrated Athenian imperialism.[3] When Professor Gilpin conjured Thucydides in the 1980s, he may have intended to invoke classic balance-of-power realism, but humanist critics who read Thucydides as literature would sense an opportunity to mine a more complex portrayal of hegemonic decline.

Twenty-five centuries later, science and technology have attained a stature in human affairs on the same scale with cosmic justice, only less vague. If the United States now hopes to extend its international influence and fashion a second American Century, it will have to come to terms with relatively new sources of power that operate largely outside Thucydides' history. This book argues that the United States has not done so, mainly because it conflates scientific advancement with technological development—science and technology (S&T) are hopelessly jumbled together in the rush of national policy-making. Among the consequences of this U.S. myopia are distortion of the national effort to remain the world's leading technological power and the hastening of American hegemonic decline.

Thirty years ago, Gilpin's claim for universal International Relations Theory rested on the notion that the ancients understood raison d'état and that actions of the most powerful states set basic parameters for societies caught in the international milieu—whether they remained at peace, how they prospered, and whose justice inscribed their laws and mores. Having insight as to why states acted as they did admitted one to a special fellowship spanning thousands of years.[4] Members of this circle included not only Thucydides, Machiavelli, and contemporary realists but also statesmen who went beyond studying the world and strived to shape it: Pericles of Athens, Richelieu of France, Metternich of Austria, and Kissinger of the United States. If they could all belong to the same club, if states, after all the changes in circumstance, were still states, then perhaps international politics was more of a trade—and statecraft more of a profession—than heroic biographies implied. Almost anyone who studied the cases systematically would see for themselves the governing principles, the near universal theories of political power, which shaped great questions of any age.

Contemporary opponents of realism seek to explain why the international system defies Gilpin's claim, why it is no longer what it once was, and why today's great states are fundamentally different from the creatures that fought for dominance of ancient Greece. Robert Keohane's and Joseph Nye's (1989) complex interdependence comes to mind because it so carefully dissects and reconfigures the basic assumptions of Gilpin and other realists. States are not solitary key actors determining important international outcomes; military force is not the ultima ratio in high politics; and a state's survival may be sufficiently secure to admit other national objectives as primary.[5]

If actors, instruments, and goals of international politics can change so much, the way is open for a host of new possibilities. Policies of the capitalist class, rather than the Great Powers, may decide questions of war and peace. State motivations may not be predictable across time if democratic regimes weigh options differently from autocrats.[6] The meaning of anarchy and the motivation for Great Power intervention on the seas and in lesser developed regions can change according to shifts in a global discourse.[7] Given the potential confusion, it is tempting, though by no means agreed among scholars, to do as Gilpin did in *War and Change*: place realism first, then see what sort of adjustments explain important international outcomes that do not fit the original pattern.[8] Appropriating Thucydides for our time may violate several social science criteria for reasonable counterfactuals, but Gilpin hit on something by snatching him up anyway. Contemporary theories for apprehending International Relations still do turn on how well Thucydides succeeded in applying his explanations for state behavior in the Aegean so many centuries ago. Thucydides' ideas, however, probed beyond states' differential capacity to wage war. The West's first international historian examined the wasting effect of Great Power war on civilization, which is to say, the Hellenic world's communion with the divine through human art and science.

Science and International Realism

Intriguingly, a younger, iconoclastic Robert Gilpin, well before *War and Change*, conducted groundbreaking research on why Thucydides would *not* be able to sift details and reveal underlying order in contemporary politics. Thucydides' *History of the Peloponnesian War* became a classic work of Western civilization because it memorialized the tortured fall of onetime exemplar Athens, linking hegemonic decline forever to the conditions of its assent.[9] By contrast, young Gilpin's *France in the Age of the Scientific State* boldly asserted how state development entered a qualitatively different epoch after World War II.[10] The Great Power contest midway through the twentieth century ended abruptly with the birth of new technology, the atomic bomb. Had German rather than American science developed the weapon in time, Hitler might well have recovered, even from the Allied invasion of France. Had American science failed along with the Germans in 1945, the timing and terms of Japan's surrender in the Pacific theater would have been dramatically different.

With the dawn of the Scientific State, Gilpin reported, the gap between scientific discovery and innovation in strategic technologies vital to military and economic power had shrunk from decades to a few years or months. While Thucydides could anthropomorphize his leading city-states, bequeathing them a natural cycle of rise and decline, modern science was the proverbial Fountain of Youth made real for states. It completely disrupted the old narrative of international politics. Once a Great Power partook of Science, once it unlocked the secrets of Nature at a depth and pace well beyond that of other states, other actors in the system could *never* catch up. Science, particularly in the fields of atomic energy, electronics, and computers, broke Thucydides' twenty-five-hundred-year run. The life and death of Athens as an international power was no longer a story for all time. To be sure, young Gilpin's heraldry has not panned out, at least not yet, but this book explores what it would take to bring the immortal Scientific State to life in the twenty-first century.

For a moment, the Scientific State seemed real back in the 1960s. Gilpin concluded, then, that if France did not resolve the dilemma of preserving its autonomy by pooling resources with Germany and other European powers in order to master science, it actually risked sinking to irrelevancy in what was rapidly becoming an American dominated system. Yet Gilpin also hedged his bets, noting plausible arguments that discounted links between leadership in basic science and unassailable hegemonic power, so he provided ample documentation that at all events French leaders fretted over the rise of America as a Scientific State. Perceptions of a close connection between scientific achievement and subsequent economic and military capacity—even if the precise mechanism could not be isolated—were sufficient to shape domestic policy on science and technology as well as international behavior.

Once the American debacle in Vietnam had unfolded during the 1970s, Gilpin's fallback position carried more weight. How could America bestride the world like a Colossus when it failed to protect tiny South Vietnam against radical insurgency and a communist army from underdeveloped North Vietnam? How could science and technology render the United States invincible when the Defense Department was capable of such tragic miscalculation in Southeast Asia, when American society itself appeared torn by self-doubt over everything from the war to race, poverty, and the environment? Gilpin expertly portrayed the Age of the Scientific State in the late 1960s, but this vision simply did not fit the collapse of the ensuing decade. Far more attuned and prominent were treatments like that of Robert Keohane's *After Hegemony* (1984), which asked how international order could survive once the American hegemon *declined*—the opposite of Gilpin's bullish projection in 1968.[11]

Yet, if *France in the Age of the Scientific State* did not have much to say about the 1970s, it served as an uncanny primer for the late 1990s. Tables demonstrating the U.S. lead on indicators of economic, military, and cultural influence, along with arguments about how research and development expenditures were widening the gap, appeared in Gilpin's *Scientific State* thirty-five years before updated versions arrived in fin-de-siécle reflections on American unipolarity.[12]

The old description of the French mindset, capturing both Charles De Gaulle and his domestic opposition, hit the mark decades later when Hubert Védrine and Dominique de Villepin, foreign ministers from different parties, raised comparable warnings against the American hyperpower and conjured multilateral restraints for the United States to safeguard French independence on the world stage.[13] Since de Villepin's star turn during the Iraq crisis, U.S. fortunes in the Middle East and in its mastery of the global economy have dipped. Today, many scholars return to themes of the 1970s, analyzing how the United States might best manage hegemonic decline, or teasing out distinctions between raw economic and military capacity versus effective power to organize matters abroad.[14]

Despite recent difficulties, though, now is an appropriate moment to revisit Gilpin's early themes. Writing from his mid-twentieth-century vantage point, Gilpin chose the French perspective. Could a midsize power reform its national institutions, and for some traditional functions, pool its sovereignty with other Europeans in order to retain freedom of action against the scientific behemoth across the Atlantic?

This research question presumed that (1) a lead in science was crucial for maintaining a lead in international influence, and (2) unless other state actors altered their science and technology portfolios, the United States would extend its advantage to outclass other participants in the system, including the Soviet Union and older European powers. The latter assumption has frayed only in recent years, and that does not mean that the former was any less plausible. We should indeed re-examine the old concept of the Scientific State.[15]

Surveying the link between scientific productivity and international hegemony is more interesting—more is at stake—if the pole position in the new international order remains, as realism would predict, difficult to maintain.

5

Young Gilpin and a coterie of American research university presidents may have been correct: a cluster of natural discoveries in the twentieth century, unlocking atomic energy and accessing vast information potential in particle dynamics, constituted a political big bang, with sufficient force to interrupt the cycle of Great Power rivalries from Thucydides' model. Patterns in politics, though, unlike natural laws of physics, are subject to human will, which means that Gilpin's scientific superstate, of its own accord, might misstep and fail to capitalize on an unprecedented opportunity to escape the decline phase so central to realism's tragic view of international politics. What is required, then, is an understanding of the connection between scientific achievement and power among nations that moves beyond the traditional realist focus on material resources.

In the time of Napoleon, during the last, great French bid for mastery, when European armies clashed in epic violence, moral elements were "among the most important in war."[16] Napoleon, himself, purportedly believed, "Even in war moral power is to physical as three parts out of four."[17] It is not unreasonable to imagine that in the broader competition among nations, even from a realist perspective, moral factors, legitimacy, or what is sometimes termed today as "soft power" could make the difference between success or decline in international affairs.[18] A judgment, then, on whether and how something like the Scientific State could ultimately emerge and maintain the lead role in global affairs rests on an understanding of the scientific element in the composition of state power for the twenty-first century, and respective relationships of this kind of power to polarity and more durable hegemony in the international system.

Science and Technology

Much of the conventional wisdom relating science to international affairs emphasizes what young Gilpin emphasized in the 1960s: atomic weapons, computers, and aerospace. That is, scientific knowledge forms the foundation from which superior technology springs, and technology affords the possessor, from Athens to America, certain material advantages that can be applied toward coercion of inferior states.

As the older Gilpin pointed out in *War and Change*, though, such technology is as much accoutrement as cause of power in the international system. Just as in Athens' time, technological success can breed arrogance, which inspires new coalitions among enemies until the would-be hegemon must literally conquer the world to maintain its place in the pecking order.[19] Technologies that permit one state to take the offensive sometimes have asymmetric antidotes that allow "lesser" states to create quagmires or deny access for their aspiring conqueror.[20] If it is true that necessity is the mother of invention, rising up-starts will generally be in greater need and know greater hunger than the state on top, which must feel an unrelenting temptation to enjoy privilege while resting on its laurels.

The irony of the conventional link, and it is fair to say the ultrarealist link, between science and state power in the international arena is that it excises the collective will to fight, the acceptance of risk or hardship, to see through a great national enterprise. In this narrow evaluation of science, it matters not whether the leading state values larger truths of individual dignity or human freedom, whether the method it uses to organize its union or the purposes to which it directs its power have any appeal abroad.

Yet, for arguably the greatest contest in the history of world politics, that between the United States and the Soviet Union, ideological competition *was* critical to the outcome. At the technological level, the United States may have ended up with advantages in miniaturization and precision control, but these were not sufficient to physically overthrow a Soviet Union with massive, ro-bust, and nuclear second-strike capability. Realists would point out how in the long run, economic strength underwrote military power, and economic con-cerns eventually forced the Soviet Union to discontinue its arms race with the West and release its death grip on satellite states.[21] Still, the economic defeat involved more than technology deficits. Soon after Secretary Gorbachev came to power in the 1980s, official policy attempted to restructure and open insti-tutions within the USSR. Part of the reason perestroika and glasnost came too late was that Soviet production could not compete with ever-rising standards in the global economy, led by the United States to be sure, but sustained by active cooperation from Western Europe and Japan and invigorated by rising economies from the so-called periphery in Latin America and East Asia.[22] True, U.S. science and technology outclassed all rivals, including the Soviet Union, but in tracing the many twists and turns leading toward the end of the Cold War, it is difficult to divorce the science advantage from elements of soft power, specifically the appeal of the U.S. system at home and the legitimacy of U.S. leadership abroad.[23]

Indeed, it is worth thinking about just why American grand strategy pre-vailed, given the daunting challenges after World War II. The architecture for that strategy was laid out by State Department diplomat George Kennan at the dawn of the Cold War. It hinged on the internal weakness of the Soviet system.

> Thus the future of Soviet power may not be by any means as secure as Russian capacity for self-delusion would make it appear to the men of the Kremlin . . . . [T]he hardships of their rule and the vicissitudes of international life have taken a heavy toll of the strength and hopes of the great people on whom their power rests . . . . Observing that human institutions often show the greatest outward brilliance at a moment when inner decay is in reality farthest advanced, he [novelist Thomas Mann] compared one of those stars whose light shines most brightly on this world when in reality it has long since ceased to exist. And who can say with assurance that the strong light still cast by the Kremlin on the dissatisfied peoples of the western world is not the powerful afterglow of a constellation which is in actuality on the wane?[24]

Kennan wrote these words in 1947. The "powerful afterglow" would last decades and feature stunning technological achievements buttressed by Russian science: introduction of fusion and hydrogen bombs far sooner than predicted; the first space satellite; surface-to-air missiles that shot down the American U-2 spy plane; the first man in space; and later, supersonic bombers, submarine-launched ballistic missiles, and multiple independently targetable reentry vehicles to roughly match the American nuclear arsenal. Yet, for all this brilliant armament, the fate of containment strategy ultimately rested where Kennan said it would.

> The issue of Soviet-American relations is in essence a test of the overall worth of the United States as a nation among nations. To avoid destruction the United States need only measure up to its own best traditions and prove itself worthy of preservation as a great nation.[25]

Containment required that the United States restrain itself even as it mobilized science and technology. It would have to forgo rash action, allowing the Soviet Union to recover from near destruction at the hands of Nazi Germany. Ensuing crises would push the United States to legitimize its rival, to reassure the Kremlin that despite intense political competition, U.S. nuclear, computer, and aerospace technology would remain sheathed, even if it meant some geopolitical concessions to the Soviet Union. In short, if the United States turned out not to be the worthy nation over the long haul, containment would work in the Soviet's favor. To the frustration of some on the American side, containment sloughed America's nuclear and technological edge, granting the Soviets a free hand to attack, below the nuclear threshold, U.S. values and interests worldwide. In response, Kennan noted that if the experiment in self-government was worth preserving, Americans should welcome the salutary trial of their republican virtue rather than a hot war, which would fast become a wasting duel of military and industrial strength.

> Surely, there was never a fairer test of national quality than this. In the light of these circumstances, the thoughtful observer of Russian-American relations will find no cause for complaint in the Kremlin's challenge to American society. He will rather experience a certain gratitude to a Providence which, by providing the American people with this implacable challenge, has made their entire security as a nation dependent on their pulling themselves together and accepting the responsibilities of moral and political leadership that history plainly intended them to bear.[26]

Science and Soft Power

In the wake of the 2003 invasion of Iraq, when military victory and regime change brought, instead of peace or justice, even more hemorrhaging of treasure and lives for the United States, greater attention to legitimacy and the importance of what Joseph Nye called "soft power" made sense. Unlike the case during Vietnam, there was no rival superpower for lowly Iraq to enlist in complicating intervention for the United States. Like the situation in South Vietnam, Iraq's very incoherence, its incapacity to harness massive U.S. economic and military aid, trapped the United States in a quagmire. The harder the United States struggled over there, the more continued killing and political failure in Iraq consumed American politics at home.

From his post at Harvard, former Assistant Secretary of Defense for International Affairs Joseph Nye reinvigorated his notion of soft power in several books and articles during the Bush administration.[27] For Nye, there were two analytically distinct dimensions of power in international affairs: coercion and persuasion. As inheritors of the largest economy, the largest research and development establishment, and the most powerful military, the Bush administration, in its rush to meet the urgent threat of global terrorist networks acquiring weapons of mass destruction, had neglected soft power, relying almost exclusively on economic leverage or military force to pursue its goals. The result had been some narrow military successes, but also strategic failure in Afghanistan and Iraq along with a precipitous decline in the willingness of allies to offer diplomatic support on a wide range of issues and accept sacrifices under American leadership. Accordingly, directors of U.S. foreign policy should recognize the importance of attracting support, inspiring optimism not just fear across international organizations and various regions of the globe. Smart power, most likely for successors to the first Bush administration, would combine instruments of hard and soft power to maximize America's chances for strategic success.

Smart power received a boost at the end of 2006 when Secretary of Defense Donald Rumsfeld, who sneered at the relevance of the soft power concept in 2003 during the initial stages of the Iraq conflict, was driven from office, largely because of subsequent failures to enlist foreign support or stabilize Iraq. Nye warned earlier that Rumsfeld would not be able to win without incorporating soft power. Attraction not attrition would determine whether terrorists would recruit more followers than coalition arms could kill or deter.[28] After Rumsfeld's departure, Nye noted with some satisfaction that the new secretary of defense, Robert Gates, advocated greater attention to diplomacy and more budgetary support for the State Department, in part to persuade more allies about the worthiness of America's cause.[29]

Yet, as Nye heralded the arrival of soft power for U.S. policy in 2007, the enterprise in Iraq turned on some factors that, while not technically inconsistent with "smart power," nevertheless surprised just about everyone in the U.S. Congress along with military experts inside and outside the uniformed services.[30] The Surge, spearheaded by thirty thousand troops, applied a new counterinsurgency doctrine against a relatively localized center of gravity around Baghdad. Beyond the expectations of Democratic and Republican opponents to the president's war policy, many of whom incorporated elements of soft power thinking into their critique, the Hail Mary pass succeeded. Election year 2008 featured dramatic declines in casualties for ordinary Iraqis and American troops but not because the Bush administration had dutifully followed soft power advice from the bipartisan Iraq Study Group report.[31]

The disconnect left soft power vulnerable as a concept, and shortly thereafter a high-profile critique came in the form of Leslie Gelb's surly, back-to-basics primer, *Power Rules: How Common Sense Can Rescue America's Foreign Policy*.[32] To the neoconservative triumphalists and the liberal institutionalists, Gelb called a plague down on both their houses. Sophisticated theories from both camps muddied the waters for American statesmen and contributed to policy errors, actually squandering the power advantage the United States still enjoyed early in the twenty-first century. Gelb's opening letter to the new president read less like Machiavelli to Medici and more like a drill sergeant scolding his green recruit on fundamentals: "Permit me a final admonition, then, that brings you and power together before you embark on these pages: Power is power. It is neither hard nor soft nor smart nor dumb. Only you can be hard, soft, smart, or dumb."[33]

For Gelb, nevertheless, getting back to basics meant revisiting the writings of Niccolò Machiavelli, the talented Florentine official who may have coveted power more than the once cherished republican mores of his city.[34] Gelb focused not on the republican *Discourses* but Machiavelli's briefer and more famous pamphlet, *The Prince*, in which the exiled advisor attempted to ingratiate himself with his torturers, now in possession of Florence. *The Prince* offered the ruling Medici seductive insights on the acquisition and maintenance of political power, certainly questions of interest to today's America, beset by two wars and a historic financial crisis. Gelb was especially interested in how Machiavelli, under inhospitable circumstances if not immediate peril, clarified our understanding of power by separating it from the question of whether its purposes were praiseworthy. From his intense study of Roman and Italian politics, Machiavelli found that justness of the cause did not guarantee strength in its pursuit. In short, real power is not soft. It always moves other people according to another's will.

Following Gelb, the most efficient means for staunching the hemorrhage from the Iraq conflict would be to demonstrate for relevant figures there what could happen to them if they did not bend their behavior to accommodate U.S. interests and increase their cooperation with American forces. That would involve persuasion of a sort, but it would not require that influential Iraqis grow fond of Americans or the U.S. cause. In any case, Gelb or Machiavelli might say, providential epiphany of foreigners goes against what we should expect—what "common sense" tells us about human nature.

In the afterglow of soft power's apparent triumph, then, Gelb, unimpressed, riposted with a sharp critique. It reassured those who might have smelled a hint of the old, discredited idealism when American foreign policy too eagerly embraced the concept. Could victory in Iraq or loyal allies under American leadership be made through the power of positive thinking? Gelb's unsentimental, ecumenical perspective on power seemed to fit better when explaining how the Surge could succeed and why that success registered more in the security rather than the political realm.

Still, Gelb's description, even as it rescues certain realities of power from gauzy optimism, obscures analytically distinct mechanisms by which power can move others. A traditional realist would concede that a prince's competitors could change their tune out of fear or love and that their welcome actions could be prompted using economic as well as military means. Unfortunately, this range of scenarios is not enough to solve the puzzle to fully explain how science (or some other human endeavor) might stave off hegemonic decline in the international system.

Science and Hegemony

The usual route between scientific achievement and technological superiority maps quite easily to consequent economic and military options for holding carrots or sticks over other states. These traditional levers of power, however, have not kept hegemons from suffering eventual decline. Instead, the system has periodically convulsed with power transitions as Thucydides and modern realists emphasized.[35] Nye's notion of soft power gives some idea of alternative action channels that might work in parallel with well understood technological pathways.

Nye noted that players in other states sometimes move because of attraction or admiration. A foreign official working with the United States does not have to be enamored with the American cause in order to admire American administrative skill or, it must be said, acquire contempt for American hypocrisy. Regarding scientific ideas, independent of American interest, they do not live merely within a narrow techno-innovation cycle. They also shape the societies that bore or later adopted them. This was true in the original Scientific Age that coincided with the rise of Europe, in the time of London's Royal Society and the French Royal Academy of Sciences, when scientists owed their financial stability to politically influential, aristocratic patrons. It is no less true in the Space and Information Age, when states provide a large share of scientific funding through mission agencies and indirectly via public universities. Technology production matters, of course, but it ignores the potential for scientific ethos, buttressed by outstanding discoveries, to rationalize and improve public administration. Even in a world in which "power is power," separable from the culturally laden value of its purpose, good administration helps. While great science is no guarantee, today it helps a powerful state's case for hegemony by credibly signaling its government's capacity to implement policy.

Next, Science as the methodical study of Nature produces ideas for economic development that might usefully be adopted by struggling governments around the world. Again, related technology production matters directly, but in parallel with foreign aid, there is admiration that attends Olympian performance in a cosmopolitan enterprise eagerly pursued across cultures. Many nations around the world want better science, yes, for the technology it can yield but also for the glory.[36] Because Science relentlessly unlocks Nature, a fundamental force that delimits Man and excludes him from God, great national science inspires near universal awe even before any technology blooms. One of the best ways for other nations to get better is to use available diplomatic tools in order to work with the best: joint research projects, prestigious international awards, international scholarships, and skilled migration. While these initiatives cannot directly conquer a rival state, so much of geopolitics involves weighing uncertainty and battling unknowns: Machiavelli would still appreciate the diplomatic value of science without weapons if it kept other elites in awe.[37] Thirdly, technology confines us too quickly into thinking in terms of strong hegemons holding science as a club over weaker states. For many issues related to security, prosperity, and justice, even powerful states find it in their interest to bargain under the aegis of international organizations (IOs). Collective determinations can be defied afterward by recalcitrant states, which generally have better control over *their* people and resources, but IOs open new avenues for cooperation, making it easier for members working with the hegemon to isolate a challenger. IOs do not possess their own arms, as Machiavelli advised, but their agreements can be consequential for states dealing with so-called transnational issues, distinguished by a high degree of interdependence.

Arms control, counterproliferation, climate change, deep-sea mining, financial regulation, protection of human rights—these transnational issues, in turn, create an urgent need for technical expertise.[38] Scientific knowledge, conceived broadly, may reduce uncertainty about effects from various alternative agreements. Not unlike a state that adjusts its bureaucracy in order to exploit scientific inputs, international organizations frequently institutionalize channels for receiving technical advice. Because the constitution of IOs tends toward confederalism in the sense of granting voice to all member states in order to keep from losing them, expert panels for entities like the UN's Intergovernmental Panel on Climate Change (IPCC) draw from international communities of scientists.

The example of the IPCC illustrates how difficult it is to separate technical advice from policy advocacy—or science from international politics.[39] American scientists may disagree, of course, about which sort of policies would be in the interest of the United States. At the same time it would be unusual for a scientist to build a reputation sufficient to garner policy influence, either from the perch of an IO panel or from within the collection of specialized nongovernmental interest groups, while railing openly against the well-being of his own country.

Great science by the hegemon means widely held respect for that state's consultants when they arrive to discuss transnational issues on the world stage. This form of power is not exactly technological, nor is it directive, but by Gelb's definition, it is still real: from a position of strength, the scientific lead, this form, call it civilizational, influences other states to do something different and, more likely than not, something favorable toward the leader's continued good health.

Lessons for America on the Cusp of a Second Century

If it is the case that links between scientific excellence and international leadership have been underreported or half-understood, this could make a difference in world history. For centuries scholars have argued over whether history progresses on an upward trajectory toward Heaven or humankind labors as beasts under the tyranny of cycles, predestined to encounter again and again the fate of Plato's *Republic* or Thucydides' Athens. As the modern state system matured, farsighted observers wrote down how it might be possible to achieve a lasting and just order. Immanuel Kant's essay on "Perpetual Peace" still inspires genuine optimism—and modern analytical rigor—over two hundred years later.[40]

Yet intellectuals just as talented and determined have established the opposite argument: America has had its moment in the sun, the latest in a long line of Great Powers that could credibly claim leadership of the system.[41] Now, after a century or so it must accommodate itself to the structure of that system—the iron law of history—and find, if it can, a way to retire gracefully.[42]

Recent events in the military and economic realms have stressed American hegemony even further, making the search for a way out from cycles in world politics more urgent and simultaneously more quixotic. Even after a dramatic election in 2008, completing a comprehensive change of ruling party across the House, Senate, and White House, the United States still seemed bogged down, after its two most important post-9/11 military operations, in Iraq and

Afghanistan. The wars drained the government treasury at the same time that economic growth, tax revenues, employment, and consumer confidence all suffered. The pressure to control the deficit and borrow less by allowing at least some cuts in defense mounted through President Obama's first term. Midsize countries around the world charted ways to reduce their dependence on the dollar and dethrone it as the global economy's reserve currency.[43]

> Economically, it already is doubtful that the United States is still a hegemon. At the April 2009 Group of 20 meeting in London, President Barack Obama acknowledged that the United States no longer is able to play this role, and the world increasingly is looking to China (and India and other emerging market states) to be locomotives for global recovery.[44]

Consistent with Leslie Gelb's demanding notion for what constitutes real power, a genuine system leader can use legitimacy to manipulate potential rivals—that is, to elicit their cooperation on economic or military matters without burning precious resources on direct coercion. "Real" legitimacy, though, will fade if the leading state cannot *perform* as expected to ameliorate world problems. Other states see less self-interest in deferring to a hegemon who will not or cannot act to maintain system benefits. To be fair, what species of attractive, "soft" power could withstand the embarrassment of successive failure on the world stage?[45]

Despite the unipolar moment of the United States after the Cold War, a second American Century, bestowing generations of U.S. statesmen with military, economic, diplomatic, and cultural preeminence well into the 2100s, seems right now like an increasingly shaky bet. Still, in midstream the currents of world history are hard to decipher; Robert Gilpin did much to flesh out the concept of the immortal Scientific State but then flip-flopped in the late-1980s. Not all experts joined him in endorsing the traditional life cycle of *War and Change*, possibly out of concern for the sort of risks the Reagan administration would run if it turned desperate to hold onto hegemony.[46] For related reasons, some careful studies, today, find no reason to act in haste or fear in order to protect U.S. prerogatives from a rising China.[47]

Yet the uncertain feeling—that U.S. capacity to shape events is slipping but loss of a second century is not inevitable—compels those interested in America's future to scramble to save it. There just may be a way out from Thucydides' tragic tale, which was to endure for all time, but first, a vantage point must be found where another hundred years of hegemony appears peaceful, prosperous, and sufficiently natural as a plausible evolution out of the current turbulence in international affairs.

This book investigates whether the escape route might lie with neglected links between scientific achievement and international leadership. Again, before *War and Change*, Gilpin himself challenged the notion that Thucydides could master twenty-first-century international politics merely by substituting contemporary names and places for those of ancient Greece. Young Gilpin called forth modern science and technology to broach conventional wisdom on International Relations with the prospect of a permanent hegemon, which reigned not on the basis of imperial control but through a mix of universal admiration and fear that came as a natural reaction to mastering fundamental forces in Nature. At some point, U.S. military and economic failures dissipated confidence that science and technology were sufficient to sustain world order. However, superior technology is not the only progeny of scientific leadership.

Science at its best pursues a kind of truth that lies outside nationalism and translates across cultures. Much of scientific activity may be funded out of state coffers, but scientific achievements are celebrated as boons to all civilization. They bring a certain respect and credibility to the state that discovers them, beyond what statesmen could expect from economic or military preponderance. Scientific ethos may be turned inward to rationalize public administration at home and encourage similar reforms abroad, and both of these shifts can increase the leading state's influence during international bargaining. Secondly, scientific excellence in one state excites admiration in adversaries as well as allies. There is an attractive force, a desire to work with and learn from leading lights in Science, that enters prior to the harvest of new technology and modulates the usual suspicions among statesmen toward economic and military power. Finally, Thucydides might not recognize the transnational dimensions of wealth, security, and justice questions in contemporary world politics. Many policy-makers and diplomats turn to international communities of scientists for technical advice on the likely consequences of proposals to address global problems like nuclear proliferation and climate change. Although the panels are chartered to be neutral, it matters for international leadership if one state produces a disproportionate share of the scientists qualified to serve on these councils.

Machiavelli's classical analysis of power among princes notwithstanding, the three understudied routes to international influence surveyed in the empirical chapters for this book give substance to Professor Nye's ethereal notion of soft power. Chapter 4's case study on domestic science administration in the United States after 1945; Chapter 5 on U.S. scientific diplomacy toward rising Brazil; and Chapter 6, covering U.S. attempts on the transnational level shaping global governance of earth's orbital space indicate how often hegemonic power derived from Science works on the principle of attraction rather than coercion; how it operates in the constructivist context of problem definition and preference formation rather than Machiavelli's arena of cost-benefit manipulation against implacable rivals. These chapters, in short, highlight routes to hegemonic influence Nye urged us to consider. Well, the scientific dimensions, apart from superior technology and contra Gelb, are not common sense. They require abstraction from many disparate experiences across time and space in order to be seen, which is why even young Gilpin, in his early theorizing of the Scientific State, along with subsequent policy-makers overlooked them.

The oversight actually grows out of Machiavelli's revolutionary treatment of Truth in his scientific political analysis. In the time of competing Italian city-states, as ever, moral truth was integral to tradecraft for the *consigliere*, but Machiavelli cut it away as so much underbrush obstructing the real dynamics of political power. When the exiled diplomat methodically dissected Truth and exposed its limits, though, he could not have anticipated he was, ironically, removing natural science from the formulation as well. The following chapters insert science back into the mix. Chapter 2, "Science and the Hegemon," explains how Science, as a cosmopolitan enterprise, must be courted, forever, and cannot be subordinated in fine or successfully micromanaged by the powerful state, particularly one with visions of international leadership. In Chapter 3, "Power, Polarity, and Hegemony in the Twenty-first Century," if the American Scientific State were to emerge, half a century after *France in the Age of the Scientific State*, characteristics of the international system—at domestic, international, and transnational levels—are such that a second American Century becomes significantly more plausible and, relatedly, happier for many concerned.

Admittedly, Science, next to the grand sweep of Ethics or Theology, is rather impoverished—it can provide answers to only a narrow set of questions. Nevertheless, those questions have become more relevant to International Relations over the centuries, and scientific answers, compared with moral doctrines, have gained acceptance across a wider circle of entities in the system. In the wake of the Cold War, political economist and UN special representative John Ruggie asked: "What Makes the World Hang Together?"[48] A large part of the answer, depending on which variant one uses to explain a peaceful end for the U.S.-Soviet superpower rivalry, is the success of Science as a civilizational enterprise and not just a state-owned factory for advanced technology. America just might salvage a Second Century by dint of broader appreciation for what national science can do. First, though, it appears that America, with the assistance of several partners, will have to help Science.

2   Science and the Hegemon: Speaking Truth to Power

How to govern science comes under the larger and more enduring political project in Plato's *Republic* of how powerful men should coexist with Truth. In his prize essay "Discourse on the Origin of Inequality" (1754), Jean-Jacques Rousseau's answer towered above modern critiques of Western civilization because he so seductively articulated a vision of authentic (and scientific) Man harmonious with Nature, uncorrupted by life either within state boundaries or under the yoke of government.[1] In laying bare the cravenness of kings, nobles, and bishops, their thievery cowering behind state institutions and trumped up morality, Rousseau preserved for a scientific age, from its fount at the Academy in ancient Greece, the grand tradition of dissent in the Western canon. Moreover, he crystallized the *problematique* surrounding why the Scientific State— and eternal hegemon—in this entropic world is rare, yet rarer than the miracle-inducing, short-lived Higgs-Boson recently detected in particle physics.

Rousseau's writing, contemporaneous with the philosophical Enlightenment and the development of science as a state concern, lent modern airs to Truth as iconoclasm. Centuries later, in today's formal political theory, packaged with the mathematical idiom of physics, inhabit fine descendants of the same defiant streak: states modeled, now with algebraic precision, as figments constructed by elites for efficient exploitation of mass population and natural resources within their power.[2]

To be sure, not all political theory, or search for Truth, in classical or modern times, adheres to revolutionary doctrine, but one of its main purposes has been to respond to problems at the core of the angst-ridden quest for human happiness, problems related to security, prosperity, and justice within or between human communities. In exposing how insecurity, impoverishment, and injustice come about, and in proposing reforms, truth seekers employing philosophy in general often challenge state policy along with government elites owning those decisions, the more stridently when the state has pretentions to hegemony.[3]

Since the birth of the successful state and an identifiably Western conception of politics, speaking truth to power has been one of the world's hazardous vocations. Certainly, modern democracy does not publicly execute philosophers for their teachings, nor does it send scientists to the gulag for their political or religious beliefs. Yet, scientists do risk their careers when they counsel the state. Influence over the sovereign is fleeting, and resources for future research often depend upon state approval. Realizing that the specter of revolution haunts their labors under the aegis of the state, even contemporary scientific agents hedge; they accommodate public passions and government demand for improved technology over liberating truth. Long ago, Athenians despairing after the catastrophe of their ancient world war across the Aegean and Ionian seas discovered acutely how fear for security of their *polis* banished Truth and ultimately made their hegemony less secure. Upon close inspection, constitutional democracy, today, has not, after much trial and error, mitigated this old conundrum for the hegemon, merely buried it.

The trial of Socrates, now regarded as the founder of political philosophy in the Western tradition, vividly illustrated the complex dynamic between Truth and the hegemonic state. Governing authorities in Athens prosecuted a seventy-year-old gadfly on charges of impiety and corrupting the youth. According to Plato's account, Socrates was defiant until the end, proposing to the jury that Athens should reward him rather than kill him, reserve him a place and nourish him at the public table. The ordinary citizens in democratic Athens split on whether Socrates' unbridled truth-telling threatened the state. They voted nearly unanimously, however, to reject out of hand the state's sponsorship of his scientific-philosophical mission. Socrates ended up losing both the trial and sentencing phases. As he was being led away to execution, Plato had him utter a kind of prophecy: to die may not be worse than living opposed to the Truth . . . . The city-state of Athens would come to regret its decision. In killing Socrates, Athenian democracy turned on philosophy at its own peril.[4] So too, today's great states neglect the cultivation of scientific truth at their peril, though the pursuit of Science or the content of its findings can frustrate immediate designs of those who would direct the government.

The trial of Socrates works very well as a lofty allegory for today's state-science relationship because of the epistemological status of philosophy during the time of Athens' decline. Philosophical truth covered then the range of contemporary university disciplines, integrating the study of rhetoric, ethics, and the gods, as well as mathematics and Nature. Aristotle, in the Socratic tradition, identified political philosophy as the master science. Without government and societal order, there could be no systematic inquiry into human existence: politics enabled science. At the same time, Aristotle made politics a subject of systematic investigation. Conscious efforts toward better politics demanded increased knowledge of other sciences, so political science drew upon just about everything else, including the study of Nature. As Socrates demonstrated to Athens, Truth inevitably challenged power; yet, power would not long endure unless it remained attentive to Truth.

Through centuries, from the conversion of Rome to the advent of the hydrogen bomb under President Truman, those in the West who rose to wield state power would confront the search for Truth—and erudite councilors who claimed special access to its hidden secrets. In the case of the West, moral and natural philosophy parted ways under the hegemony of Rome. The eventual result was that Western science developed within the context of a long, fraught, triangular relationship among institutions: the hegemonic state in problematic courtship with both church and academy.

The Roman Empire's embrace of Christian truth in 313 CE soon created severe contradictions for state and religion; the empire and especially the church radically revised their internal structure to accommodate the novel relation between Truth and state. Both St. Augustine and Gibbon took seriously the charge that Christianity's promise of eternal life in Heaven hastened Rome's decline.[5] Centuries later, when Christianity once again circled close to the seat of political power, religion jealously resisted independent development of the natural sciences.

Christendom's soldiers and clergy during the Middle Ages rediscovered science entombed in the libraries of the Ancient World, and the West pressed to catch up technologically after Islam found many of these same scientific records first.[6] Putting science to work for the state, though, fortified secular regimes that would grow to challenge the teachings then the primacy of the church in public affairs. During the Enlightenment period, expanding European states patronized a golden age when scientific academics advanced their theoretical enterprise while maintaining political confidence of their princes.

Democratic revolutions, which rocked European monarchs in the late eighteenth century and escorted the Industrial Revolution of the nineteenth, did not entirely benefit science.[7] On the one hand, researchers enjoyed new freedom to pursue ideas across a vast frontier, regardless of whether they appealed to arbitrary, narrow political elites. On the other, as monarchy and aristocracy declined, science lost its great patrons. While danger of fanatical persecution waned, new difficulties arose in escaping the state's benign neglect.

This polite distance lasted until the United States, in its twentieth-century bid for hegemony, needed advanced technology, based upon cutting edge science, to defeat overseas the Nazi, Japanese, and eventually Soviet empires. As with Western Christendom nearly four hundred years before, Great Powers, especially a superpower, had little choice but to pull science once again toward the bosom of state power. As in the past, this embrace was not without tension, and it aggravated dilemmas for the state, which, regardless of commitment toward transparency, accountability, or liberalism, might court but never conquer Truth.

Science as an Autonomous Profession

Over time, during volatile relations with church and state, Science consistently succeeded on its own terms, demonstrating repeatedly its value for national capabilities. As governments became directly interested in scientific progress, natural science, in order to survive intensifying political competition, loudly and frequently recused itself from philosophical questions of the good life and the best republic. While national science specialized, it professionalized, developing its own systems for administration and ethics, and naturally enough, acquiring its own taste for autonomy. Conventional wisdom in the United States has it that liberal democracy is naturally predisposed to grant this autonomy and delegate responsibility so that its professionals, including scientists, outperform counterparts in authoritarian systems. As the fate of the independent philosopher Socrates before democratic Athens implies, though, the conventional, Cold War era explanation for blissful state-science relations in the West is too simple. In fact, democracies, especially hegemonic ones, must work hard and deliberate carefully in order to court Science and maintain a healthy national scientific enterprise.

With the rise of specialized expertise and administrative bureaucracy, in both government and professional science, there emerged a new set of difficult trade-offs modern scholars dubbed the "principal-agent" problem.[8] Those elected to steer the course of government and their top assistants for implementing policy were the principals. In democracy, those officials were themselves agents representing the will of the people, but modern administration encouraged a chain of delegation from these politicians to their professional experts, including scientists who came to work for the state. The crux of the principal-agent problem was the same as it had been for Socrates and Rousseau: preferences of the academics and researchers with purchase on new knowledge often did not match those of their principal, or sponsor, in the government.

A series of questions flows from the dual gap in preferences and information separating principals from agents. As a matter of policy, the principal within the state must decide how it will verify performance of the agent—in our case scientists—without interfering too much or handcuffing the experts. For Socrates and Rousseau, of course, the government eliminated this dilemma by executing or exiling the expert. Today, the temptation for modern bureaucracy is to control risk by placing science firmly in the harness.[9]

Reducing the chance that scientists will serve their own ends rather than those of the state typically involves monitoring costs. Once shirking is detected, government officials must be willing to accept delays and political costs from replacing a specialist who may enjoy support from other leaders in his profession or other government officials seeking to change current policy. As with other professions contracted for service to the state, including the military, excessive monitoring or fear of punishment in the name of public accountability can strangle the profession. Particularly in a democracy, governments must take care not to choke off scientific inquiry with bureaucratic procedures intended to ensure productivity—or politically appealing returns—on the government's scientific investment.

Principal-agent dilemmas suffuse all three pathways we have discussed for how science could help restore American leadership in international affairs. First, rational administration of science policy would recognize fully the problem of stifling expert agents. Talented scientists would not have to fear losing their professional autonomy once the government recruited them, and sufficient funds would be reserved for basic research, not just applied efforts to develop specific technologies. Second, when it came to joint projects with foreign scientists, the American government, appraising the value of the global scientific enterprise, would distinguish between scientific research and foreign aid. U.S. sponsors of basic research such as the research offices of the armed services or the Missile Defense Agency would doggedly preserve their reputations for scouting and steadfastly supporting the best science abroad. Third, with regard to scientific advice on transnational issues, political principals back in the United States would pay attention to soft power, letting American scientists run free, so they could provide high-quality technical information to all nations, even at the cost of tabling near-term diplomatic demands.

Corresponding to each manifestation of the principal-agent dilemma for science and the state, three case studies in this book illustrate the present challenges of speaking truth to power. In the area of *science administration*, powerful arguments pressure domestic agencies to shift away from pure science to produce technology demonstrations or perform intelligence work. Some U.S. organizations for scientific outreach find their *international partnerships* reduced and access to the best science of foreign powers blocked by political-diplomatic concerns on the part of the host countries. Other states also find it hard at times to separate American scientific advice on *resolving global problems* from U.S. technical intelligence stratagems designed to ply the international community on behalf of American interests.

The past offers scant evidence that a hegemonic state can easily resolve multilevel principal-agent dilemmas with respect to Truth. For twenty-four hundred years, no Great Power has managed to break through Thucydides' iron logic linking the rise and fall of civilizations. Imperial capitals, as American theologian Reinhold Niebuhr once warned, confuse their acquired strength with virtue. They come to believe that they must be mighty because they are right.[10] At that moment, Robert Gilpin, Paul Kennedy, and others' mechanisms of deterioration kick in. The state, like ancient Athens, becomes deaf to truth without quite realizing, and hegemony slips declining leaders' grasp.[11]

Once science is recognized as one of several professions essential to operations of modern government, a large literature examines how various types of experts fare working with government bureaucracies. Finding the right mix of accountability and discretionary authority has preoccupied reformers across government. Governing science is among the state functions predestined for enduring struggle between growth for the profession and expedience for the politician-principals it serves. In order to mitigate this tension and reduce costs imposed by the principal-agent dilemma, a modern state that seeks to extend hegemony as far as a second century will have to complete the dialogue: speaking Truth to power must be accompanied by power comporting itself in order to speak appropriately back to Truth. Healthy state-science relations, not unlike civil-military relations, will have to overcome a long record of previous disappointments. Advances in democracy notwithstanding, the question remains after the first American Century whether a lead state struggling for influence in the international system can ever develop sufficient trust of science in order to benefit fully from a genuine dialog between Truth and power.

Two sea changes in the chronicle of speaking Truth to power show the difficulty of finding a balance that would preserve both Truth and power. Science helped the state break free from religion but not without complicating its own relationship to governing elites. Science also gave American democracy an edge over the Soviet Union during the early Cold War but not without creating, in the soul-searching aftermath of disaster in Vietnam, lingering popular suspicion against technocracy and establishment science.

Science, Religion, and the State

In the history of Europe, national science, before it came to aid the state, first had to negotiate a tempestuous relationship with religion. From the time of Hellenic civilization, science had been a branch of philosophy, that general mode of inquiry employing reason and example perfected at the Socratic Academy.[12] Socrates, of course, questioned authority, antagonizing its representatives by holding them accountable to a truth standard independent of political power or religious teaching.

Modern Europe's dominant religion, Christianity, actually began in parallel fashion, threatening first Jewish clerical influence then Rome's secular control. After Roman emperor Constantine issued the Edict of Thessalonica in 380 CE, the church switched modes and, in turn, courted earthly power in the West. Eventually, science would unseat this religious authority from the right hand of sovereign power but not fill in to take its fortified place. The fall of Christendom provided little respite. Scientific claims to truth would still have to compete with *other voices* before being heard, and this chore would never disappear, even when secular monarchies gave way to self-described enlightened democracy in Europe.

During the age of kings, European princes expanded their holdings from city-states like Venice or Florence to the beginnings of nation-states such as Spain, France, and England. For a while, as early modern states grew, the church in Rome grew as well. When Catholic monarchs Ferdinand and Isabel united Spain and expelled the last emir from Granada in 1492, the pope, too, acquired jurisdiction over territory and new souls. Eighty years later at the Battle of Lepanto, when Spain, now heading a grand empire, underwrote defense of the northern Mediterranean against Muslim galleys, credit for victory went not to the Holy League's gunnery as much as intercession by the Virgin Mary.[13]

In northern Europe, however, Protestantism eventually posed a more formidable threat to the shield afforded by Catholic saints. Hegemonic Spain under Philip II (1556–98) and Philip III (1598–1621) defended the orthodox cause against an ever-expanding coalition: England, the Netherlands, and principalities defecting from the Holy Roman Empire in central Europe. While Spain would substantially succeed in containing the heresy for decades, the end of Europe's Thirty Years' War (1618–48) saw Catholic France expel Catholic Spanish forces from much of the continent. French intervention and success signaled that raison d'état as political motivation diverged from and surpassed defense of a unified church under the Holy See. France and (Protestant) Sweden's victories over Spain created space around sovereigns not just for the growth of Protestantism but also for an explosion of scientific thought now unleashed from authoritative religious censorship. The Scientific Revolution of the late-seventeenth and early-eighteenth centuries reached beyond radical conceptions of Nature to new understandings of how scientific inquiry ought to interact with state administration.

The English scientist and one-time lord chancellor Francis Bacon proposed a more intimate relationship in *Novo Atlantis* (1624): in a university-like structure, learning, and scientific advice were at the seat of earthly political power "for the relief of man's estate" as bequeathed by the heavenly Creator.[14] The Thirty Years' War then the English Civil War deferred Bacon's vision. Still, after the restoration of England's Charles II, the first state-endorsed national body for science formed near the throne as London's Royal Society (1660).

Across the Channel, a young King Louis XIV was exploiting the French state's room for maneuver after 1650. Interestingly, his father, Louis XIII, had relied on Catholic clergy, Cardinal Richelieu, as his state councilor. Richelieu represented a transition figure, suppressing French Huguenot Protestant campaigns for autonomy at one point then coming about to thwart Catholic Spain toward the end of the Thirty Years' War.[15] By contrast, Louis XIV relied on his secular finance minister, Jean-Baptiste Colbert, for national security advice. While the king and Colbert maintained cordial relations with Rome, Colbert took greater interest in pursuing *la gloire* for his master's reign through fiscal and economic reform plus state investment in the fine arts, architecture, and science.[16]

Colbert was among the first statesmen to appreciate what contemporary analysts might identify as soft power consequences of nationally sponsored scientific achievement. He saw so clearly, perhaps, because there was less underbrush at the time—fewer technologies that dramatically spawned novel ways of life or shook the established order among social classes; no democracy; and a bureaucracy in flux, yet untutored by theories of rational organization that the Scientific Revolution itself would nurture.[17] In retrospect Colbert would be disappointed, but he acted on the premise that Louis XIV could invest and grow national capability without necessarily antagonizing competitors in the rest of Europe.

Unfortunately, the limitations of scientific advance as an elixir for promoting benign hegemony in Europe undercut this vision. The flourishing of the French Academy did not prevent old religious quarrels from threatening Louis's rule and in any case pushing him toward expensive policies to enforce intolerance.[18] In addition, concomitant ideas of scientific autonomy and meritocratic advancement reinforced the notions of salutary restraint on the monarchy in rival Britain and contributed to what would eventually become revolutionary sentiments—particularly regarding liberty and equality—in France as well as the New World. Ironically, the return of democracy to Western civilization would not liberate scientific inquiry or overturn the historic verdict on Socrates; rather, democracy brought mixed effects on establishment science and the progress of discovery.

Science and the U.S. Constitution

At first blush, science played the role that Hamiltonians in the American Revolution might have hoped for: handmaiden to liberal hegemony.[19] Notably, autonomy for the British Academy outlasted that of the authoritarian French system. In due course, British discoveries set the context for economic success, which roiled British society, preparing it for the ideas of John Locke and later the Scottish Enlightenment. Leading lights David Hume and Adam Smith applied natural philosophy to economic and moral questions with political effect, in a sense arranging a productive marriage between scientific achievement and state power. Not Imperial Britain's commercial, manufacturing, nor her naval achievements were conceivable without advances in science and technology (S&T).

Eventually, when Britain's star faded in terms of global science, another democracy, imbued with Anglo-Saxon culture from colonial days and liberal values from the struggle for independence, arose in Britain's place. The day arrived when the quintessential British imperialist, Prime Minister Winston Churchill, albeit reluctantly, accepted the new leadership role of an upstart power whose very birth, baptism, and constitution enshrined anticolonialist ideology.[20]

A rebel colony should have made a poor champion for spreading the ideas and order of Anglo civilization. In fact, America in the 1930s, 1970s, 1990s, and again in the second decade of the twenty-first century performed the "civilizing mission" and bore burdens of intervention in distant quarrels clumsily. Beyond fanatical adversaries willing to massacre innocents and die in the hundreds of thousands to break U.S. influence during the twentieth century, yet more formidable resistance to hegemony derived from American liberty at home. Born in successful defiance of the world's greatest empire, democratic dissent in America has shown little patience for what declining Britain in the mid-twentieth century regarded as imperial necessities. Every decade of U.S. international leadership produced profound consternation about how the accidental superpower would manage its technological, economic, and military lead abroad.[21]

At the same time, the United States set the standard for institutional innovation coming out of the Enlightenment. Under the Constitution of 1789, different domestic factions would compete across issue areas by grasping at a complex variety of countervailing levers to exercise political power. Progressive president Woodrow Wilson a century later attacked the obsolescence of this original design on the proposition that "the admirable expositions of the Federalist read like thoughtful applications of Montesquieu to the political needs and circumstances of America."[22] Since "the makers of our Constitution followed the scheme as they found it expounded in Montesquieu, followed it with genuine scientific enthusiasm," it is useful to review how Montesquieu indeed balanced relations in the eighteenth century between science, religion, and the state.[23]

In his grand treatise *The Spirit of Laws*, Montesquieu devoted as much attention to cultural as institutional foundations. To perform well in service to the state, laws must reflect the climate and the people, not just the form of government from which they issued. The people, in turn, were educated by often competing streams of religious and worldly engagements.[24] Religion, particularly of Christian denominations, supplemented purposes of state by teaching self-renunciation and a form of virtue compatible with the love of laws and love of country over self-gratification.[25]

As important as cultural predilections were, however, Montesquieu heavily circumscribed the institutional-legal space reserved for religion. Church doctrine, for example, that devoted set days on the calendar to fasting or praying should be broken if an adversary's forces could gain advantage by attacking on those days.[26] As adopted by the Framers of the U.S. Constitution, Montesquieu proposed that the rule of law could sustain order without tyranny. Since laws were what allowed the very best modern states to survive, religious practices would have to be flexible enough to harmonize with Law's organic, civil function.[27]

Civil constraints held for clergy, who would be permitted in rather narrow language to minister to the afflicted, reconcile families, and preach for justice—at the local level.[28] They could retain their lands, but in a move reminiscent of Colbert's attack on Louis's incumbent finance minister, Nicolas Fouquet, clergy would not be allowed to "acquire new inheritances" at the expense of the state.[29] Moreover, religion was contained by banishing it to a separate sphere. Montesquieu apportioned the "variable good," which is to say matters for political discussion, to the realm of policy and legislatures. Those few beliefs that were best, enduring, and stabilizing for society remained for clergy to minister.[30]

Without a massive scientific establishment of the kind that would emerge centuries later, particularly after World War II, Montesquieu nevertheless addressed science and scientists in *Spirit of Laws*. Scientists, like clergy, would work apart from the civil power, now as systematic investigators of Nature rather than interpreters of ancient faith. This new estate would de facto reverse the expectation for priests. With rare exception, religious practice, upon a confrontation, would bow to civil necessity; yet Montesquieu judged the best civil practice should rather defer to laws of Nature, or natural necessity.[31]

True, the enduring verities of Nature reflected divine will, but these natural laws mechanized both the physical and social worlds for Man's benefit through his God-given reason. In a spectacular departure from Christendom in the Middle Ages, public policy honored God when it conformed to knowledge of the physical and social sciences. A law, for example, requiring sons to betray their parents to the magistrate would erode familial bonds and, based on concepts long established in Aristotle's political science, weaken the state from the inside.[32]

Social and physical mechanics also shaped how Montesquieu arranged commerce, the beating heart of state vigor. A clarion call to large-scale cooperation, commerce also tempted the state's most talented citizens to scatter from underneath the sovereign, abandon civic virtue, and greedily pursue private profits. As a bulwark against the most severe storms of individual consumerism that might breach the constitution of a state, Montesquieu installed a high government official to monitor contracts and sales on behalf of the city.[33] Still, to encourage the innovation that would increase a state's economic strength, Montesquieu recommended government incentives such as intellectual property rights. If free individuals, for example, could harness science and technology to divert Nature's streams and create gardens from deserts, the entire country ought to have confidence that the state would reward such entrepreneurship through protection of the private benefits for years to come.[34]

Preserving individual incentive to work harder and smarter was sufficient justification to form mild and limited government. Building a long-lived state upon unforgiving geography meant that citizens would have to work the land and wring benefits from Nature, unfettered by government tyranny. Accomplishing this requirement for state survival implied knowledge of Nature that would have to come from science, not religious faith. In a passage following his discussion of industry for building states, Montesquieu remarked that the compass and navigation had "opened the universe" and transformed Europe from a loose collection of feuding empires to the hub of truly powerful worldwide commercial networks.[35] Nature's voice might be the "sweetest of all sounds," but it took human labor, scientific investigation, to translate her call from instinct to something intelligible.

Application of reason to Nature overtook revelation of God's Word as the state won ascendancy over alternative forms of political organization in Europe. State prerogative—rather than conversion of souls to one catholic faith—held out the possibility for peace within and among human communities, not least because the state diverted resources from irreconcilable religious conflicts.[36] Competent state officials rather than church clergy would sponsor the best laws. Legislation, in turn, would harness incomparable energies of a free people, uniting their labors and constituting them toward a common purpose without usurping their life stories or crushing their dignity as individuals, which were, as most religions would attest, God's greatest gifts.

Whether such claims of the philosophical Enlightenment reflected actual laws of Nature or not, they underpinned hopes of the American Founders. Science, conceived as the activity of spooling out God's plan by dint of theory and discovery, would work hand in hand with democracy to tame the bountiful New World. In time, science and democracy could also become twin heralds of a superior, benign form of international hegemony in which the United States would be a beacon to light the world rather than an empire to enslave it.[37]

Woodrow Wilson, presiding at the time of the Constitution's harvest and a great nation aborning, benefited and simultaneously bore responsibility for realizing the Founders' ambition. Ruefully, the first professor in the White House noted how assiduously the Constitution's drafters followed Montesquieu's ideas as disciples of a new political science. The French aristocrat's theories worked in the sense of providing an underlying framework for America's phenomenal growth relative to Europe during the nineteenth century. Yet, Wilson knew full well that the saga of American science, democracy, and enlightened world leadership could not be so blessedly simple. In fact, across the century that Wilson opened, the United States would struggle against fierce competition, years of uncertainty, and terrible violence from scientific totalitarian forces on both the right and left of the ideological spectrum.

Science for the Authoritarian State

Had Montesquieu's ideas played out perfectly, the U.S. Constitution would have worked exceedingly well to build a strong republic in the New World, and ideological competitors from Europe would have been unable to challenge the United States on scientific grounds. The fact that Nazi Germany and then Soviet Russia scored against the United States, rattling its perch atop the international system, reveals practical flaws in the theoretically comfortable synergy between science and democracy.

By going opposite the limited Constitution and expanding government control over citizens' lives, the Nazis and the Soviets in short order were able to produce scientific discoveries and critical technologies on behalf of the state. Even though they did not ultimately defeat the United States, the credibility of the German and Russian threats to American preeminence in the twentieth century forced Americans to rethink how scientific truth should affect political power. The competitiveness and enormous cost of these rivalries led the United States to adopt progressive science and technology policies, stretching the Constitution in a way Montesquieu might have rejected. Indeed, the rise of the American science and technology establishment ushered in boom times for American research universities but created new challenges for democracy.

In the rough and tumble of foreign affairs, contradictions of a democratic state attempting to harness science for domination over other states go underappreciated. Many Americans seem willing to tolerate government involvement in the production of science and technology. As Gilpin pointed out in the *Scientific State,* after World War II corporate research and development and private foundation grants were small on their own and too diffuse to keep rival powers at bay. On the other hand, the more the state stepped in and channeled scientific activity—the more it monitored and incentivized certain types of research—the less autonomy scientists enjoyed to investigate Nature and test original theories. The more closely scientific truth approached power in order to serve the state, the more likely science and truth parted ways. As science became an arm of the state, it became bureaucratized, ideological, politicized, and less patient with democracy.

Of course, the courtship of truth and power still benefited the United States. It inspired Gilpin and others to write of a benign and enduring *Pax Americana.* Yet, we should know better. The relationship between science and constitutional government, while unavoidable in today's Great Power politics, is riddled by barely concealed tensions. At just about any time, either touchstone of this extraordinary cooperation—the state's leadership in the discovery of knowledge or the liberal democratic character of the state—might be lost.

This, incidentally, is nearly the opposite of what Gilpin argued in the 1960s when optimism about science and the capacity of American researchers to solve social and political problems, ran high.[38] Somewhat counterintuitively, in an age when U.S. military and economic strength far exceeds that of any other state and the United States enjoys the greatest available resources for pursuit of science, we can better perceive the fragility of the U.S. position. There is less need, now, to discount German and Russian scientific achievements under totalitarian regimes and some political breathing room to criticize how highly institutionalized democracy can hijack pure science then starve basic research for public resources.

Historians of science who peer back across the decades find much to respect in Nazi and Soviet efforts despite distaste for their ideology. Although state interference and ideological orthodoxy distorted some research programs—experimentation on human subjects in Nazi camps or insistence on Lysenko's genetic theory in Soviet publications—both the German and Russian academies overall proved quite resilient.

It took years for Nazi officials, divided across several organizations and agencies competing for Hitler's favor, to break the professoriate. Many academics not openly resisting party rule retained their traditional autonomy.

During Adolf Hitler's ascent, even party leaders like SA head Ernst Röhm acknowledged the importance of free inquiry for making discoveries that could aid the national cause.[39] Several advances in physics, engineering, and medicine, at least one worthy of a Nobel Prize, continued in Germany under Nazi rule.[40] Compensating in some measure for ideological interference, the German state gained an extraordinary capacity to mobilize and concentrate societal resources. During a short span in the 1930s, the government budget for scientific research ballooned by a factor of nine. Yes, the Nazis miscalculated the potential for atomic bombs and suffered defeat at the hands of the Allied Powers, but at war's end Germany was leading in jet propulsion and rocketry. It soon became vital for the Americans to enlist German science for the next great rivalry, with authoritarian Russia.[41]

The Soviets' scientific efforts were unencumbered by a racial theory of international politics, which meant that they would have overall better access than the Nazis did to their native talent pool. Stalinist political control and a centrally planned economy made it easier for the Russian state to identify innovative minds and enlist them for the megaprojects of the mid-twentieth century. Although the Soviet lead would not endure, rocketry clearly held strategic importance at the dawn of the Nuclear Age, and Russian satellites along with Russian cosmonauts scored several firsts during the late 1950s and early 1960s.[42] A decade later, after the United States demonstrated superior guidance and control systems, the Soviets were able to compensate with larger warheads, so latter SALT and subsequent START arms control negotiations proceeded under an assumption of rough strategic parity.[43]

While Russia's commercial sector may have suffered for the lack of political and economic freedom under the Soviets, after a sweeping review, MIT's Loren Graham judged that scientifically based innovation and development for national security remained competitive under totalitarianism.[44] Respect for political and civil rights had been a crucial distinction in early assessments of whether the United States or Russia would best absorb scientific and technological lessons after victory in World War II.[45] Partisans hoping for a Western triumph in the Cold War took pride and found reassurance in Russian weakness on these terms, its unwillingness to permit dissent and the apparent constraints that would impose on free inquiry.

Yet, as in the case of Germany under the Nazis, science historians note the robustness of the scientific ethic in Russia under the Soviets. Like Nazi officials, enough Soviet apparatchiks recognized the importance of scientific discovery and engineering for the security of the state.[46] Scientific talent that posed political problems for party control could be imprisoned, it turned out, without necessarily ruining the scientists' productivity. Graham documented how dissident physicists continued to improve Soviet nuclear weapon designs while under confinement. Camp life left little alternative meaning for these driven individuals except in the progress of their life's work. Shunned and punished as political advocates, they were nevertheless respected, even privileged, in prison and highly motivated as scientists.[47]

The undeniable development of Russian arms under the Soviets presents a puzzle for traditional accounts of the relationship between scientific truth and power at the level of the nation-state. Recall that in young Gilpin's treatise on the Scientific State, France fretted that no actor in the international system could shrink the U.S. lead or maintain economic and military autonomy under U.S. scientific dominance. The Soviets nevertheless caught up as the international influence of the United States declined into the 1970s—corrupt establishment science was even seen by some on the left as part of the U.S. problem.[48]

Western statesmen and scholars predicted early that Russian ingenuity would be undone by stifling, authoritarian communism, but at the election of Ronald Reagan in 1980—and a quarter-century later during the second term of George W. Bush—expert analysts warned of declining power and fraying American leadership in the world. Civil liberties and constitutionally limited government, then, were *insufficient* to secure the lead in science, at least not in a way that secured exceptional performance and international hegemony for the United States.

Another possible explanation for U.S. escapes, albeit narrow, from German and Russian challenges during the twentieth century highlights the importance of international connections.[49] Both totalitarian and democratic systems during the twentieth century demonstrated impressive capability for pulling off megaprojects that could shift the scales in security competition. Over time, however, the United States bested both rivals at sustaining its scientific complex—the broader network of universities, laboratories, and commercial enterprises not just the military-industrial partnership. An important U.S. advantage indeed lay with its openness, but the source of new ideas encompassed more than a select group of talented and hardworking Americans; the source included knowledge imports through immigration and correspondence with researchers overseas.[50]

Greater emphasis on international connections points to a softer, more cosmopolitan side of science and technology. It invites us to revisit conventional wisdom about the optimal relation between scientific truth and state power. Traditional explanations rely on the freedom engineered into a state's political institutions. If individual scientists are free to pursue happiness, to think what they will in their daily lives, this supposedly promotes discovery and innovation during their careers, which ultimately benefits the state. Under these conditions, constitutional democracy enjoys an inherent advantage over fascism or communism because its limits on government tame Power, so it may listen and thereby gain greater access to Truth.

Bringing up international connections makes science a civilizational rather than national enterprise. It raises the importance of the structural distribution of power in the international system as the older Gilpin did in *War and Change*. Democratic or not, leading powers often struggle to maintain high levels of international cooperation; unparalleled power tends to corrupt ideological principles for the stronger, and for weaker actors it blurs the distinction between liberation and conquest at the hands of the hegemon.[51] Great power corrodes the internal compass of a polity, so it easily confuses appealing "exceptionalism" with virulent nationalism and unilateral foreign policy, the latter two of which degrade international relationships.

Regardless of the genius incorporated into its constitution, democracy is not immune from these problems occasioned by dominant power. An increase in relative power makes it more difficult to cooperate with weaker actors in part because it complicates the state's capacity for discovering and accepting the truth in many fields, including scientific ones, which are long-term resources for state power. Conventional wisdom places faith in the automatic benefits of constitutional design for limited government. While these benefits may exist, they do not secure democracy from the competition of rival, nondemocratic states. The realization of a true Scientific State in young Gilpin's terms, equipped to avoid Great Power cycles and maintain world leadership, will require a clear examination of what democracies must do to address the age-old problem of speaking truth to power.

Truth to Power in the Scientific State

Democracies are supposed to access the truth through negative means. That is, they prevent capture and manipulation of the truth in the clutches of an elite ruling class by reserving sovereignty for the people. Government officials in a democracy cannot completely control information because of incessant demands by their constituents for transparency and accountability.[52] The whole scheme rests on the goodness of the masses, their capacity to distinguish the truth from demagoguery when they hear it, and their willingness to accept civic responsibility—and private sacrifice—when their political leaders sell the false notion that the only requirement for maintaining hegemony is the people's occasional vote in a certain direction.[53] Democracy in reality has difficulty making policy choices when the truth happens to be unpopular. Unfortunately, modern science, given its highly specialized technical character, its large enabling bureaucracy, and serendipitous pathways to coveted technology, struggles to stay popular.

Under the U.S. Constitution, representatives and especially senators with their six-year terms are supposed to weigh the passions and legitimate desires of the people against a sober view of the national interest. Still, comprehending the type of government support and the balance of investments between applied and basic research for extending a particular nation's leadership in Science is more difficult than young Gilpin assumed in the *Scientific State*. Continued success for the United States demands some knowledge and experience with science among the political elite and among the *demos*, the people who periodically elect them. Under a constitution that respects popular sovereignty, it is often remarked that people will get the democracy they deserve. In similar fashion, ordinary citizens must participate to produce good science for the liberal-democratic state, but the benefits of good science are not as focused, immediate, or obvious as they are for fair elections and basic civil liberties.

When technology develops and communication systems for spanning large societies become more capable, the educational task in support of the Scientific State, unfortunately, does not get easier. Citizens, even if many of them attend college, gain more opportunities to grasp the advantages of shiny technology before they appreciate the long march of Science. Accordingly, the more responsibility a modernizing state shoulders domestically or abroad, the more tempting it is for voters to clamor for research that will lead them expeditiously to convenient devices or more powerful machines, not necessarily a better understanding of Nature. It is reasonable to expect, then, that democratic governments of such societies will respond to popular demand by steering the balance of public funds toward more technology while starving budgets in support of free scientific inquiry.[54]

Examples of the professional principal-agent problem abound in modern democratic politics. How are sovereign masses to trust their bankers, doctors, engineers, military officers, lawmakers, and scientists when these highly educated experts apprehend more of the circumstances surrounding important decisions for the country—that is, they enjoy asymmetric information advantage but do not necessarily share the preferences of the society they serve?[55] Indeed, there may be no way for successful democracy to achieve the ideal of a Scientific State and take full advantage of specialized knowledge from the professions, since giving free rein to experts rather than placing them in technology harness would abandon popular sovereignty for technocracy—the polity obeying what unelected technocrats not the people decide.

Technology-centric state control of science manifests just one aspect of a broader tension between democratic principles and good governance across several levels of political organization.[56] The same trouble bedevils any democratic power that would pursue the status of permanent hegemon, a world leader that will not succumb to the well-established cycle of decay in international affairs. Good governance across national boundaries, superior technology for projection of economic and military capabilities, and a peerless national science program in a globalized era require robust professions. Specialized technical expertise along with standards, credentials, and codes of conduct constituting robust professions, in turn, threaten control by laypeople and the bedrock principle of democracy.

Principal-agent approaches to the accountability problem with professions have become so prevalent; some texts tout this form of analysis as an alternative theoretical lens for seeing beyond U.S. frontiers and understanding how international organizations and global civil society could support benign hegemony through contributions to good governance.[57] Epistemic (knowledge rather than geography-based) communities and democratic values of transparency and accountability typically rate separate hearings from International Relations scholars, but these concepts for understanding efficient international cooperation are not so distinct in practice. Principal-agent models highlight how epistemic communities and democratic values together shape institutions and culture, among states and inside states, simultaneously. In fact, a chief task of principal-agent thinking in its application toward comparative political development has been suggesting an appropriate balance between direct external influence for better-informed epistemic communities residing within a target state and accommodation of these same scientific experts to internal democratic pressure for increased transparency and accountability.[58]

Adaptability of principal-agent models for tackling state-level concerns raises their potential for describing how a Scientific State would behave at the international and transnational levels of analysis. In the international realm, national governments, as representatives of their people, acquire characteristics of a principal actor that sponsors expert agents to conduct diplomacy on its behalf. The right balance in this application describes how freely professionals representing the Scientific State abroad would be permitted to speak the truth amid pulling and hauling of interstate bargaining, when global governance is at stake and national interests might be compromised.

Whatever autonomy the Scientific State granted its diplomats or scientists in conference halls around the globe, the choice could not be divorced from governmental arrangements the professionals faced at home. By the same token, the quality of governance agents experienced at home under the Scientific State would depend to a significant degree on whether their political masters pursued hegemony or empire abroad. Both hegemony and empire require powerful states to compromise with loyal technocrats in order to mobilize domestic power for international leadership, but as we shall see, hegemonic as opposed to imperial politics courts Truth with deeper commitment to create the right conditions, at all levels of analysis, for a resilient Scientific State.

3   Power, Polarity, and Hegemony
in the Twenty-first Century

All forms of international influence, including those that would be practiced by a Scientific State, depend on *power*. The distribution of this power, or *polarity*, in an international system affects policy interdependence of all major actors and the propensity for major war. Finally, *hegemony* connotes a status of special influence and obligation that reaches beyond what can be derived from the crudest measures of state economic and military power. On this much, most International Relations theorists would agree, but the key concepts of power, polarity, and hegemony are not used by all in the same vein, and together they do not always provide a consistent picture of what might be called the boundary conditions for International Relations.[1]

Currently, for example, most scholars would instruct that we live in a unipolar world because the United States remains far ahead in the customary indices of power. At the same time, when tens of thousands of U.S. troops were struggling in Iraq and Afghanistan and the United States faced significant defense cuts for the first time since September 11, several analysts began questioning the future of U.S. leadership in the world. Instead of confidently projecting power across every continent or stabilizing the balance among lesser powers as the British are purported to have done during the height of their empire, the United States nervously advertised exit strategies, continued its withdrawal from Europe, and pleaded for more meaningful partnerships on counterinsurgency, missile defense, counterproliferation, international development, and management of international economic affairs. In short, despite the claim about unipolarity, the United States has been neither acting nor succeeding as a hegemon, and it is not clear just where our tools for understanding International Relations have failed.

If possible, the concepts of power, polarity, and hegemony ought to be reformulated, so they may work together to tell a consistent story about the evolving order in world affairs. As in the 1970s, when the U.S. superpower was reeling after its defeat in Southeast Asia, there has been no shortage at present of efforts to cast the problems confronting international actors in global terms, beyond the difficulty that any one state or coalition of states faces in addressing transnational issues such as terrorism, economic development, human rights, or climate change.[2] At the same time, a conservative camp warns that states are still the chief actors, and the United States, barring a major policy disaster, will for some time remain the most powerful actor of the international system.[3] Given the current debate, it is futile to discern whether foreign crises are mounting because the United States no longer has the power or because it cannot find the wisdom to use its power well.

The following sections take each key term in turn. The United States may be the most powerful actor in the system, but the old sociological axiom about power being circumstantial and not just resource based still holds in the twenty-first century. Today's international system does not function as if controlled by a single pole because despite its onetime popularity among pundits, unipolar is not an appropriate descriptor. It does demand explanation, though, why simple arithmetic does not apply to the calculus of international poles: why subtracting one superpower from a bipolar world does not automatically bring about unipolarity.

Finally, if policy-makers are actually operating under asymmetric multipolarity, it has implications for hegemony. Scholars focused on international institutions have described how cooperation may continue without a leading state, but can hegemony continue without constant infusion of material resources to convince other actors of the leader's legitimacy? Historical examples of failed empires indicate that, indeed, material superiority once achieved, is still insufficient for preserving influence. The rest of the world, it seems, has a remarkable capacity to absorb coercive energy radiating from a powerful capital.[4] This resistance to hegemonic authority outpaces the pole's capacity to collect more resources and build better technologies, unless the hegemon can credibly signal that it offers uniquely effective solutions to common problems faced by different units in the system. The challenge of extending influence under conditions of asymmetric *multipolarity* actually sheds light upon a heretofore neglected civilizational role for scientific achievement, if it can be accredited to a leading power in the international system.

The Sociological Dimension of Power

Benefits and costs of hegemony are conditional on the structure of the international system, and system structure, according to Kenneth Waltz's *Theory of International Politics*, is partially defined by the distribution of power among units. In order to develop a hypothesis about sustainable hegemony, then, there has to be a solid understanding of power.

During the time when Waltz was developing his theory, he chose to emphasize power's physical dimension. Items like gross domestic product and defense spending could be easily measured and compared across sovereign states. Moreover, the distribution of power, operationalized according to its physical resources, was clearly separable from power's effects such as less interdependence and greater stability between obvious poles in the system.

It may have been the case that economic and military resources mapped well to the actual concentrations of power in the system during the late-1970s, but such indicators did not warn of the impending decline of the Soviet Union. This suggests that at other times it might be necessary to incorporate other dimensions, the psychological and especially the sociological, in order to correctly apprehend system structure.

As a baseline measure, physical resources still seem like a good place to start. In his defining work on neorealist theory, Waltz criticized the post-Vietnam tendency of analysts to confuse the loosening of superpower blocs with emergent multipolarity. In order to apply the theory, the status or ranking of states depended "on how they score on all of the following items: size of population and territory, resource endowment, economic capability, military strength, political stability and competence."[5] There is more to be said on the last two items, but the rest of the list is quite compatible with how quantitative political scientists have measured national capability over the past several decades.[6]

A few years before Waltz's *Theory*, when the United States was deeply wounded over failures in Vietnam, leading political scientist Bruce Russett, in much the same way as Waltz, marshaled the case for continued bipolarity using similar parameters such as GNP and military spending. Russett supplemented the usual size variables with indicators for development such as per capita GNP, literacy rate, and low infant mortality. He also included enlightenment and centrality factors, evaluated according to the number of scientific journals produced and number of diplomats received by the state.[7]

Russett's tables were interesting on the one hand because they showed how focused Waltz was in his subsequent and more heralded statement on physical stock when referring to power. On the other, the central theme underpinning Russett's work attempted to break up exclusive attention on resource measures. High concentration of stuff might not translate into effective power over other actors without an attempt by the leading state to invest in community.

Waltz did tack political stability and competence onto his list of size indicators. From his examples, it was clear enough how he would count population and territory, natural resources, economy, and military. While measurements for stability and competence were less obvious, Waltz did not exactly need them in the moment because most observers could agree that the United States and the Soviet Union were stable and competent enough; even if France or China were stable, they were not within striking distance in terms of economic or military strength. In addition, Russett and others showed that one could get at abstract factors through proxies. Presumably, a state would have to enjoy a decent amount of political stability in order to score well on human development. Similarly, a state's measurable scientific production and its diplomatic standing should provide at least a circumstantial case for its competence in wielding power when it came to foreign affairs. One could include stability and competence in the index for power and still remain quite physical; this may have led a future generation of realist critics against Waltz's structural theory, in their insistence on unipolarity, to hew just as closely to numerical size and level variables.[8]

At the same time, Russett clearly distinguished between power resources and effective power. Building community meant reallocating resources away from more costly brute force coercion and creating a we-feeling, if not common values, to lower resistance against leading state claims to international authority. If we accept power as something employable—capability for making actors do what they otherwise would not—this is still consistent with Waltz measuring it as the means different states possess to perform similar tasks, particularly when the tasks such as self-defense involve altering the course of other actors.[9]

Again, Russett seemed to say that the ability of a state to lead others depended not just on countable resources but on how it invested those resources, and this jives with Waltz including stability and competence in his index of power. Rough empirical referents for stability and competence might exist, but it does not violate Waltz's instruction to admit that certain aspects of competence cannot simply be counted up in GDP statistics or research and development budgets ahead of time.[10]

A state's power—its capacity for making a standard opponent move, almost like a calibration weight in physics, and presumably for getting valuable things done—might decline even if its military superiority for defeating a standard conventional army was on the increase. Most obviously, the economic basis for sending expeditionary forces might fall away before military spending actually dropped; this has been noticed by some contemporary realists who always expected unipolarity after the Cold War to vanish quickly and now cast a wary eye on American sovereign debt.[11] More important, stability or competence could change without immediately affecting economic or military rank. With the passage of time, a democracy might have unexpected difficulty sustaining casualties abroad because of political instability at home.[12] Circumstances or processes of state interaction could change so that the task of defeating a conventional army in Saddam Hussein's Iraq became less valuable for applying power across the Middle East. None of these exceptional situations are excluded under Waltz's definition of power. They have nevertheless been ignored by scholars intent on discussing the implications of unprecedented unipolarity in the modern state system.

Before delving into polarity though, it is necessary to clarify how Waltz's concept of power can incorporate psychological and sociological dimensions. Since it can, polarity of the system—using Waltz's original definitions—need not follow simple arithmetic: the decline of the Soviet pole in a bipolar system need not leave us with a unipolar world.

The psychological dimension refers to the contribution of individual desires and individual perceptions on the efficient actuation of power at the state level. Keeping Waltz's levels of analysis in mind, application of his system theory ought to avoid what he called the reductionist trap of forcing outcomes to reflect unit-level characteristics. However, insofar as political stability within a leading state helped determine the distribution of power for the system, Waltz might be concerned with how well a government could mobilize state resources. The psychological dimension might not have changed power rankings in 1979, but at another time, the effect of power on men's minds within the state as well as in foreign capitals could matter quite a lot for the assessment of power at the system level.

The implosion of a pole, as occurred in 1989–91, was possible in Waltz's framework though not easy to anticipate if the psychological dimension cracked first. Nothing in Waltz undermined what Ambassador George Kennan wrote to his secretary of state after World War II: "Russian rulers have invariably sensed that their rule was relatively archaic in form . . . fragile and artificial in its psychological foundation," or subsequently in *Foreign Affairs*: "[W]ho can say with assurance that the strong light still cast by the Kremlin . . . is not the powerful afterglow of a constellation which is in actuality on the wane?"[13] Psychological power, or what Bertrand Russell called the state's power of propaganda, was easy for Waltz and others to blandly hold constant, given the challenge of trying to isolate such capacity and place its weight on some quantitative scale.[14]

At times, though, the psychological quotient has been worth the trouble. Russell and Kennan both employed it when the physical distribution of power offered no happy solution to the great international conflicts of their time. The two great totalitarian systems of the twentieth century—fascism during the 1930s and communism during the 1950s—seemed poised at one point to master the task of mobilizing resources for collective projects. They cast a strong light, indeed, perhaps sufficient to provoke desperation or surrender in Western democracies, unless the fragile psychological foundations of totalitarian power were deducted from the ledger. This currency, the motivational contribution of a democratic as opposed to authoritarian creed, put time on the side of the united nations during World War II and the Atlantic Alliance during the Cold War—even if America as a leading state in these alliances took extra time to learn the byways of Great Power competition.

Interestingly, Russell was quite specific about the power resource of science, not just as a provider of technology to the modern state but also in the profound sense of shaping individual beliefs. In the same series of essays, written in the shadow of Hitler, Mussolini, and Stalin, Russell could write: "[S]cience has made it inevitable that all must live or all must die," and the "chief cause of change in the modern world is the increased power over matter that we owe to science"; yet it is "not ultimately by violence that men are ruled, but by the wisdom of those who appeal to the common desires of mankind."[15] Science via technology changed men's beliefs, even trumped their religious convictions, by facilitating satisfaction of individual wants for nourishment, shelter, communication, power, and the rest.

Yet, the process of science, its arrangement of logic and evidence, spoke in a universal language. Its method bridged cultural barriers. Science's ambition and discipline, if not global, was at least civilizational in a way that was inclusive, so more and more nations accepted its creed. As contemporary analysts of globalization acknowledge when they discuss transnational security issues and the system-level changes wrought by advances in transportation and communication, science had sociological implications as well.

First, communication and mobilization technologies in the hands of the state raised the potential for cutting across class, ethnic, or religious divides. Totalitarian methods might resolve the problem of social cohesion for the state, at least for the short term. Russell judged, though, that unity of effort could come at the cost of suppressing individual genius and crippling society's capacity for taking up and applying new knowledge. As an alternative to the totalitarian ambition, then, the scientific ideal could also bring society together.

In the extreme, of course, a perfect marriage between the state and reason would bring unhappy consequences. Jonathan Swift's rendering of Laputa in *Gulliver's Travels* anticipated the vapid rule of a scientific sovereign. Even Plato, who granted few concessions to natural idiosyncrasies in his Republic, allowed that his philosopher kings would require excellent mythmakers to maintain their legitimacy before the mass of ordinary citizens.[16] Finally, the most successful totalitarian states on the right and the left during the twentieth century executed a political plan validated as much as it was served by science. Scientific certainty and universality helped justify violence and oppression used to shear off natural variation and force individuals to fit accepted categories for implementing the state's agenda.

Max Weber, at the close of the nineteenth century, had appreciated the political significance of rational organization and bureaucratization being adopted by the state as technologies for production, transportation, and communication rapidly advanced. He sought to shield science, to strengthen its integrity by divorcing it from political ethics.[17] However, he weakened the enterprise in the sense that it could serve whichever sovereign, regardless of political values. Science was unmoored, left free to extinguish an entire religion, ethnic group, or class in order to forge the best society.[18]

Ultimately, marriage with the state, either as an equal partner or an obedient spouse, might not be the happiest ambition for science. Science and the state are destined to interact best at a prudent distance, though this ensures that science alone will not solve all the government's challenges in holding society together. Moreover, recognition that the scientific ideal is not value-neutral, that it can generate bonds and develop commitments crossing sovereign boundaries and channeling a state's international influence, leads to another idea: the sociological dimension of power extends beyond the domestic writ of the state and into the international system.

If sociology is required in order to appreciate the contribution of scientific achievement toward international influence, this presents a problem for the Waltzian framework. It may have linked measurable quantities like power and polarity to a few very important properties of International Relations, but Waltz's conception of power as described so far left little room for a sociological dimension. In addition, Waltz defined system structure in terms of self-regarding, functionally similar units under anarchy. Not surprisingly, major works discussing the social aspects of international politics are nearly always taken as wholesale rivals rather than friendly amendments to Waltz's theory.[19]

Nevertheless, given the advantages of Waltz's framework, its parsimony and its focus on the likelihood of Great Power war, it might also illuminate a spare yet useful way to think about the sociological dimension of power. Waltz's model established a degenerate case: in the limit, what social behaviors remain when the system is composed of like units under anarchy? Despite the lack of functional specialization, states could communicate and learn from each other. If not social cohesion around norms of appropriateness, we could at least observe convergence around adaptive imitation, albeit without much role for trust. Interestingly, this nascent social behaviour paralleled interaction among units of the international scientific community: repeatable experiments produced successful theories that were then employed by competitors across cultural divides, with plenty of occasions for healthy skepticism.

In either system such communication and exchange takes place through a medium. Waltz did not spend time on this notion, but neither did his theory of international politics rule it out, certainly not in the explicit way that the theory excluded the empirical realization of *unipolarity*.[20] In fact, Waltz included competence among his factors for measuring unit power. Competence was separable from the economic or military stock that also compelled other units to choose from a rather narrow menu of responses when Great Powers acted.

Yet, competence—more so than GDP or defense spending—was in the eye of the beholder. Again, it presumed a certain amount of communication among the units. Waltz cited approvingly Canadian prime minister Pierre Trudeau's metaphor for living with the United States. The minister compared it to lying in bed with a twitching elephant.[21] There is no inconsistency with Waltz then in imagining that power itself, not just the effect of power, varies with a special set of circumstances that make up the medium for communicating power across units. Trudeau's experience of U.S. power, to follow the metaphor, would depend on the size of the elephant and the skill of the elephant, to be sure, but also on whether Trudeau found himself with the behemoth in a wooden bed or an Olympic-size swimming pool. In fact, the elephant might grow to twice the size it was relative to Trudeau, and Trudeau could still measure competence and indeed his neighbor's unit power as *less* than before, once they were both thrown out of the bed and into the pool.

System Change: From Bipolarity to Asymmetric Multipolarity

For most scholars of International Relations, especially those working along the general lines of realist theory, the medium through which power was communicated or transmitted in the system was invisible. The ether around state units did not require attention because it did not make a difference, either in the structure of the system or the effects of that structure on stability, alignments, and interdependence among states. However, the structural change occasioned by the fall of the Soviet Union was unusual. Unless the *circumstances* under which material resources converted into constraints for other states were taken into account, the simple arithmetic was inescapable: two superpowers minus one Soviet Union equalled a one-pole, or unipolar, world.

The word "unipolar," however, does not appear in Waltz's *Theory of International Politics*. Many scholars interpreted this as a theoretical error of omission due to lack of historical experience with such a lopsided distribution of power among modern states.[22] Waltz had concluded that bipolarity was the most stable structure, and from the vantage point of 1979, he presumed that neither the United States nor the Soviet Union would disappear anytime soon. There was, accordingly, no need to discuss unipolarity—a degenerate case that would not arise in practice—so he simply left it out. The omission, in this explanation, gave scholars and practitioners much to write about in coming to grips with a novel international system. Waltz himself contributed to this growth industry, adopting the term "unipolar" and discussing its fragility in prominent articles after the Cold War.[23]

This trajectory for structural realism and IR theory may have made the most common sense, but it was still a blind departure from Waltz's original statement, which had intended to clarify the concept of polarity after the growth of West Germany and Japan and the loosening of bloc politics during the 1970s.[24] Several scholars at that time wrote about the shift from bipolarity in the aftermath of World War II back toward something more akin to multipolarity of the interwar years. Waltz denied that the system structure had changed and attributed the confusion to lack of theoretical rigor among the community of scholars who were willing to adjust their definition of a pole in order to meet prior conclusions they had taken on world politics.

The phenomenon Waltz warned about occurred again in the 1990s. Scholars migrated toward the model of a unipolar world, but in doing so they changed the definition of a pole in a way that suited their conclusions about coming U.S. dominance in world politics. By Waltz's most formal statement of structural theory in 1979, the world had finally slipped back to multipolarity—with consequences that were overlooked by observers glued to high military spending ratios at the end of the twentieth century. Ironically, these same consequences might have been appreciated by those who were too eager, despite steep capability ratios, to treat Germany, Japan, or China as emerging poles in earlier decades.

In order to fashion a unipolar world after the fall of the Soviet Union, scholars focused on the physical indices of power discussed in the previous section. Back in the 1970s, Waltz's main criticism of the multipolarity camp had been that they elevated one of the resource indicators like gross national product when a state's rank—whether it made the cut as a Great Power—depended on its performance across all the indicators: military, economic, demographic, and geographic. The empiricists of the 1990s noted that by several measures across these resource categories, one state, the United States, undeniably stood alone.

In his seminal analysis from the journal *International Security* in 1999, for example, William Wohlforth included tables demonstrating the physical predominance of the United States in GDP, defense spending, research and development, and high-technology exports. The United States not only had more capacity than other states with large population and territory, it also enjoyed qualitative superiority across a range of power resources.[25] The breadth of U.S. superiority appeared to address Waltz's 1979 critique. Accordingly, two superpowers minus one Soviet Union indeed made a unipolar world for the United States.

The real strength of Waltz's 1979 contribution, though, was in the deductive rigor of his theory not the quantitative operationalization of his concepts, including power and polarity. With regard to Waltz's theory, dedicated empiricists never dealt sufficiently with the deductive results. Under Waltz's conceptual definition (in contrast to operationalization) for polarity in the international system, a single pole *could not* exist. According to Waltzian geometry, two was "the smallest number possible in a self-help system."[26] If states in such a system cast their lot with the stronger side, we would indeed observe action in which a single state provided security for all the rest, but then the original properties of the international system—the starting postulates for Waltz's deductive framework—would no longer apply: minor states would not be sufficiently independent to be self-regarding; the lead state would have a unique function in the system, and the set of all states in the system would no longer survive under anarchy. In fact, we would see "a world hegemony forged."[27]

Toward the end of his 1979 book, Waltz speculated about the alternatives to bipolarity. Since consequential states, or poles, were consequential because their actions would do most to either preserve or erode system structure, Waltz's ideas in a narrow sense connected to U.S. policy. Should the United States along with lesser units in the system aim for the disappearance of the Soviet pole?[28] Waltz saw only two logical possibilities for promoting change in a bipolar distribution, somehow assist the rise of a new unit, perhaps a unified Europe, to the higher rank or build a world hegemony. The result of the Soviet Union not keeping up and no other unit ascending consequential rank was not "unipolarity"—a term that did not enter Waltz's 1979 lexicon and indeed makes no sense in his system theory. Rather, the result was hierarchy under one security provider, one world policeman.

Like Immanuel Kant and Reinhold Niebuhr before him, Waltz warned that the "perils of weakness were matched by the temptations of power."[29] A single nation with a monopoly on the use of force in the world and a singular power to treat other groups as subjects would be tempted to use those capacities to end costly conflict. Unfortunately, great power on earth has never implied a necessary link to superior wisdom or justice. Niehbur saw this in the New Testament; Kant in humanism. Waltz simply asserted that "justice cannot be objectively defined."[30] If U.S. policy to escape bipolarity succeeded and the world transformed into something other than multipolarity, America would still have to worry about catastrophe on a historic scale. World hegemony, after all, was "an invitation to prepare for world civil war," and when it came to afflictions involving "the unnecessary and foolish employment of force," leaders of the American global hegemon would "not [be] immune."[31]

Waltz's portrayal of international politics under conditions of monopoly, when there existed just one significant state, was not missing. It loomed as large as Dante's unified kingdom on earth to mimic the image of one God. It could be overlooked about as easily as the immortal ambitions of Alexander, Caesar, Philip II, Napoleon, Hitler, and perhaps the most extreme enthusiasts for

American empire after September 11. After the Cold War many scholars could agree that the United States enjoyed the greatest concentration of power since the time of Rome. Nevertheless, Rome did not rule the world, as attested by the fluidity of its boundaries after A.D. 100.

Moreover, what stretched beyond the imperial capital, although more sophisticated than the reputation allowed by the history of Western civilization, was still far less organized than what the United States faced two thousand years later. Economic statistics and defense spending may have spoken clearly: China, Russia, India, Brazil, Germany, France, and the United Kingdom were far less powerful in terms of physical and technological resources than the United States. The weaker entities may never have formed an alliance against the United States: indeed, they cooperated with the United States on some important issues. Yet, these units never gave up their independence nor surrendered authority for defense of their societies to the U.S. imperium. Quite the opposite, on international economic issues, military interventions in fragile states, and transnational concerns regarding climate or the environment, they participated, often in institutions convened above the state, if not as equal powers, with recognized sovereign rights. Empirically, apart from economic and military accounts, post–Cold War system structure was not at all like ancient Rome, and conceptually, "unipolarity" was an unfortunate term.

It falsely implied that peoples tottering on the margins of influence confronted a stark choice: submit themselves to the interests and desires of the American metropole or consign their national life to an aimless, primitive, and foredoomed barbarity. This was no choice at all, and the theoretical judgments simply could not have emerged as a reasonable extension of Waltz's structural realism. Waltz accounted for unipolarity when he rejected world hegemony as neither likely nor desirable. If it came in any case, we would need a whole new theory of international politics built on different postulates: the units in this system would no longer be functionally equivalent or self-regarding—American hegemony would have replaced anarchy.

Anarchy, though, is what the United States got after the Cold War, more than a taste of it in Somalia, the Balkans, and the no-fly zone over Iraq, followed by a larger comeuppance after September 11 with the grinding expeditionary missions in Afghanistan and again Iraq. It was not just that the level of chaos was beyond U.S. power to control; the United States enjoyed no sort of governing authority over the national security decisions of other significant states in the system. The crisis of legitimacy—so painful after U.S. failures in

Iraq that hard power advocates inside and outside the Bush administration softened their tone—could only make sense under anarchy, as unipoles or world hegemons could suffer no such deficit, by themselves structuring the choice in world politics between civilization and barbarism.

After the global financial crisis hit in 2008, not all national economies blindly followed the so-called unipole. As important as GDP ratios were for measuring the distribution of power, it became clear that sovereign debt mattered, too, and, again, other states with economic power retained their independence. The political elites in Washington did not structure economic choices for Chinese or Brazilian growth at all as they might for Ohio or California.[32] For the concept of unipolarity to have analytic value beyond a shorthand expression for asymmetric distribution of resources, the threshold for shaping system outcomes and structuring the choices of other units needs to be high. Otherwise, Waltz already had a concept for an international system with several consequential powers. Even if they did not possess the same size, territory, population, economy, and military, the system was multipolar.

To this, the empiricists and arithmeticians could counter that Waltz also had a deductive prediction about such systems: several poles will form balances of power. With no evidence of balancing after the fall of the Soviet Union—that is, no peer competitors and no recognizable alliances against the United States—how can it make sense to speak about a multipolar system?[33] Well, as the limits of U.S. military and economic power have become ever starker, more International Relations analysts have written as if the system were in fact multipolar, even though Brooks's and Wohlforth's measures still indicate a "unipolar" distribution of relevant resources.[34]

While it makes sense to distinguish between power as resources and power as control, the community of International Relations scholars is starting to recognize that the separation for purposes of scientific hypothesis testing can be taken too far. Waltz, after all, spoke about poles as *consequential* states (my emphasis). When he developed his theoretical parallels to microeconomics, he elaborated on the differences between price makers and price takers in the system.[35] Waltz's poles of international politics, like oligopolists, duopolists, or monopolists in the theory of the firm, indeed had special roles: their "production decisions" had direct effect on the overarching price, or incentive constraints, of the whole system, while minor states no matter their course of action had no such effect.[36]

True, Waltz was careful to separate power from success in foreign adventures because, from a structural perspective, it would confuse matters to imagine that the distribution of power changed with every undertaking—American failure in Vietnam, for example, had not upset all the power indicators and created a multipolar system. Nevertheless, economic and military potentialities on Waltz's classic list were selected because they affected and could be used to affect the security of other states. Investment of those resources might not bring the expected return, but if that happened, other centers of power or unusual circumstances had gotten in the way. If, on the other hand, something was always in the way, then something might be occurring at the system level. The system dynamic was playing out as if multiple consequential states were interacting on international controversies, rather than a single state setting the economic and military price constraints for all the rest.

To insist as Wohlforth and most leading scholars did that the international structure was unipolar because the empirical referents for polarity were still concentrated in the United States was to hollow out the concept of polarity. We should not be surprised, then, that theory with respect to a world with so-called unipolar structure was dazzlingly unstructured: unipolarity could produce hard balancing, soft balancing, bandwagoning, or all three; there might be stability or not; the leading power might be highly constrained or not. All the important conclusions of the theory were not conclusions at all but tentative propositions about what raw data from international affairs might reveal.

Stephen Walt argued that "the [structural] condition of unipolarity also creates greater obstacles to the formation of an effective balancing coalition."[37] Yet, leading structural realists, including Kenneth Waltz, John Mearsheimer, and Christopher Layne argued instead that unipolarity was a fragile, fleeting condition, in line with the venerable proposition in International Relations that "great concentrations of capabilities generate countervailing tendencies toward balance."[38] The empirical question of whether any sort of balancing was taking place in reaction to asymmetric capabilities favoring the United States was interesting in its own right, but the answer had little to do with standard theory. Standard theory, in Waltz's 1979 work, made predictions about multipolarity and only vague speculations about a very different hierarchical system called world hegemony—nothing at all on "unipolarity," an unfortunate, oxymoronic term that could be used to imply just about anything consistent with one state having an advantage in GDP and defense spending.

The question remains though, if Waltz's assumptions about the anarchical international system are still good enough and we live in a multipolar age, where is the balancing? For applying standard realist theory, it may be wise not to make too much of this. China, the rising challenger, and Russia, the direct descendant of America's most recent peer competitor, have both increased their defense spending when economic conditions allowed.[39] These increases do not look like much against the budget allocations of the United States during the same time period, but without undermining the theory, this may be what internal balancing looks like under conditions of unprecedented asymmetry. Few would interpret the Chinese or Russian decisions on defense during their growth years as a kind of tributary obligation to reinforce U.S. hegemony.[40]

Moreover, precise symmetry in classic power resources may be less crucial than it was in the past for blocking leading states' capacity to set system constraints on other actors. The unipolar crowd is well aware that several of the passive powers (price takers) in their framework possess sufficient nuclear weapons to deter a conventional invasion of their territory. In his 1979 work, Waltz rejected the idea that nuclear weapons in themselves transformed a state into a system pole. China's lack of economic development and inability to project military force precluded it from playing the role of a superpower. A full suite of capabilities was necessary in order to have weight at the system level.[41]

Consistent with this approach to polarity, if several states with significant territory and population took away invasion as a viable option for the leading state, this would affect the mechanism linking capability distribution with system-level incentives and system outcomes, including stability.[42] Nuclear weapons distribution, among other changes of circumstance in the international milieu, could affect the *competence* of leading states to revise system constraints out of their reserves of material strength without going so far as to change the number of poles in the system. Standard neorealist theory, then, could accommodate stability effects apart from changes in structure.

After the fall of the Soviet Union, a number of other factors whittled away at the significance of conventional capability shares as displayed in many fine charts of the unipolarity tracts. The loosening of bipolar alignment brought back a fluidity to international politics, now accentuated by the development in Africa, Asia, and the Middle East of postcolonial state units. Samuel Huntington in *The Clash of Civilizations* likened it to the lifting of an ideological fog, a time for cultural ties to hold greater sway over state security policy. Still other elements of the international environment took on more substance—physical geography, information, and economic exchange networks. These mattered, systematically, for how mobilization of economic and military strength affected the targets of power politics. Not since the time of Westphalian diplomacy had great states—still the primary organization for arranging economy and security of settled populations—been buffeted by identity claims from levels above, across, and below.[43]

For the medium, the substrate, in which poles could flex their military and economic potential, the result was—from the wood-frame bed and into the swimming pool—looser coupling between the absolute magnitude of force in play and the reaction of other units. U.S. invasions of Afghanistan and Iraq were at first interpreted as caprice by the unipolar power.[44] It may have been easy to do that in 2003 when the U.S. juggernaut seemed unstoppable, but after the U.S.-led military adventures turned difficult, and the limits of U.S. power to set system constraints on nuclear-program states like North Korea, Iran, Pakistan, and India became painfully apparent, the United States started asking for help.

The last superpower may have rumbled like an elephant and spent like a unipole, but it turned out there was insufficient bang for the buck and the United States knew fear like a self-regarding unit in competition with other powers. In retrospect, the faux unipolar era unfolded a lot like John Mearsheimer's asymmetric multipolarity. China and other states did not have to wait twenty years in order to pull and haul against U. S. policy or exploit U.S. missteps, not just on Taiwan or the South China Sea but in resource-rich regions across the globe. Much in the early 21st century rode on fluid alignments. Despite obvious asymmetry in defense spending, the international order, such as it was, did not fully spring from politics confined to the internal gyrations of an anointed hegemon.[45]

Hegemony after Multipolarity

In an important treatment of international politics, just five years after Waltz's theory, Robert Keohane explored the potential for international order to persist or even progress once American hegemonic power declined. As Waltz had remarked, American strength for enforcing the rules to facilitate cooperation and reinforce polar alignments appeared to be on the wane after Vietnam. Keohane's argument about what would happen next was nevertheless hopeful. Trade arrangements and the kind of integration that brought Europe closer to becoming whole and free or helped a variety of states meet transnational challenges could continue with the presence of properly constructed institutions.

These special organizations could overcome common barriers to cooperation among independent units under anarchy, keep states engaged, and prevent cheating by delivering the benefits of coordinated action, only when members played by the rules. Cooperation important to the fate of the West could continue *After Hegemony.*[46]

As previously remarked, the fifteen years or so after Keohane's influential book were astonishingly favorable to American power and influence. By 2001, G. John Ikenberry argued that international peace and prosperity would be better served if the United States, as the last superpower standing *After Victory* in the Cold War, helped fashion institutions that could credibly signal restraints on American hegemony in order to reassure resentful or anxious follower states in the system.[47]

Yet, after victory in 2002 and 2003 came a decade of inconclusive war in the greater Middle East and a global financial crisis. U.S. capacity to affect the system constraints on other states' security policy was in question, again. Ikenberry recently reprised the query from the anxious days after Vietnam. Could the liberal regime of international institutions and norms function after the United States faded and new powers such as China, Brazil, and India came to the fore?[48]

Indeed, it is timely to revisit what happens after hegemony. Sure, analysts often recall how the United States has been counted down before and prematurely. Still, there is another way to approach the problem of what happens now. Rather than a tale of U.S. decline from Great Power status, the frame of reference could have others catching up.[49] More precisely in light of the theory presented here, since the end of the Cold War, the United States without entirely capturing the implications has attempted to lead a multipolar world. American statesmen may not have minded the facile perception that the world was unipolar—without a peer competitor and without a conventional balancing option available to other states.

Under conditions deemed unipolar, it may have been easier in the beginning to imagine that the United States would as a result of immutable system structure achieve its first choice when resolving the world's problems, and debate could be relegated to determining U.S. priorities.[50] Yet, within a few years, the rest of the world did start pushing back. As has been true for many centuries, at least since the time of Alcibiades seducing imperial Athens, the trouble with actually engaging economic and military might is that other states learn the limits of traditional capabilities under new world conditions. To paraphrase the

Canadian minister Trudeau, they learn just how little they need twist and turn when the elephant stirs. The unipolar jig is up, and now the most pertinent question becomes how the United States can lead when other units recognize that system structure does not grant the U.S. a special functional role. We have come full circle from Keohane's 1984 blockbuster. Can U.S. hegemony continue in some form? Is hegemony viable *After Unipolarity*?

Hegemony is still possible, but as with power and polarity not all of the influential analysts have used the term in the same way. Here, I opt for a middle of the road approach. Hegemony cannot mean simple asymmetry in economic and military resources. That would not distinguish it from the empiricists' very strict perception of unipolarity, the older notion of empire, or Waltz's use of "world hegemony" in his theory. Another common usage avoids this confusion and makes the question of hegemony after multipolarity meaningful for statesmen under today's distribution of power.

During the Cold War, the United States was said to exercise hegemony over the West.[51] It did so with the advantage of material asymmetry, to be sure, but without imperial control over secondary powers in Europe. Hegemony in the West was akin to club membership.[52] Members retained their sovereignty; each had its own reasons for joining, but there were overlapping values—and fears—as well. In order to keep the club together, despite Soviet efforts to weaken the West by dividing it, the United States as leader had to take other sovereigns into account; it had to lobby and huckster for their consent.

At times, America reminded its friends of its raw power, as when President Eisenhower parried France and Great Britain during the 1956 Suez Crisis or when the Reagan administration during the 1980s urged voluntary export restraints upon Japanese automakers. More important, though, in order to sustain leadership of independent-minded allies, the United States had to demonstrate a willingness to help solve common problems—provide aid, information, or institutional infrastructure—to keep states aligned.

The upside to U.S. hegemony helped compensate other states when they had to settle for second- or third-best solutions in deference to the first state among equals. Empire would have provided greater order in the short run but one designed around efficient extraction of resources from the periphery for purposes solely of the center. Hegemony as club leadership had to offer something beyond mere survival to attract members who retained options for voice and exit far wider than system constraints would allow in a hierarchical arrangement of states revolving about a single pole.[53]

These options for minor states only grew after the collapse of bipolarity. A declaration of unipolarity based on GDP and defense spending data seemed to imply that others had *fewer* sovereign options. With balancing being unrealistic, the rest of the world could try to hide or more ostentatiously align themselves with the unipole. By contrast, multipolarity implied that material asymmetry meant less, and club leadership skill—the special talent for herding cats on display before Gulf War I—became more important.

Some scholars who perceived a qualitatively different system structure resulting from the extraordinary imbalance of power favoring the United States counseled the United States to take care in how it flexed its muscle.[54] The warnings to cultivate legitimacy and boost the attractiveness of American power or heed the limits of American force projection in building democracies around the globe would have served as well and made more sense if the system structure had been properly identified as asymmetric multipolarity. By the same token, calls to fill with American power the vacuum left by Russia's decline and deteriorating Cold War arrangements in Europe, the Middle East, and Africa would have been received with appropriate caution.[55]

Of course, recognition of multipolarity does not clarify all the important questions. Which states were poles in 2005 or 2010? Would a Great Power war be required in order to go back to a bipolar structure? Unlike unipolarity, however, multipolarity puts system constraints on U.S. imperium. The United States will push only so far beyond its base in North America before another consequential state in Europe, Asia, or Latin America starts to push back.

Writing from a perspective largely consistent with Waltz's structuralism, John Mearsheimer judged the most likely candidate for checking U.S. power to be a rising China.[56] When the United States instead mobilized its resources for a thrust into Iraq on top of the mission in Afghanistan, Mearsheimer along with his collaborator Stephen Walt wrote that Operation Iraqi Freedom was poor statecraft.[57] The war of choice misread the threat and at cost to American lives and treasure neglected the calculus of power in the international system. Although Walt also made major contributions to theorizing unipolarity, in *The Israeli Lobby and U.S. Foreign Policy* the geopolitical opportunity costs were products of blinkered U.S. leadership under Mearsheimer's asymmetric multipolarity.

In a 2009 special issue of *World Politics* devoted to the consequences of unipolarity, William Wohlforth puzzled over whether China would scrap liberal international regimes molded by vastly superior U.S. power, especially in the

West during Cold War bipolarity and eventually worldwide during post–Cold War unipolarity. Why would China go through the trouble of dismantling rules and infrastructure that after all permitted it to rise and overtake the United States in key measures of power? Wohlforth's answer was that China might do so in order to establish primacy—to upgrade its status in the system.[58]

Perhaps unipolarity was fading faster than expected, given that it supposedly described a stable distribution with no balancing mechanism to undermine it. More plausibly, the United States created the international trade, financial, and development institutions first under asymmetric bipolarity then asymmetric *multipolarity*. Other states actually had a say in how the rules were written and enforced. In fact, alternative voices grew *stronger* after the Cold War when China and Russia increased their engagement with international organizations. Under multipolarity, the United States could not devise global constraints entirely to its liking or create enforceable standards that would tie China down, for example, by forcing its currency up.[59]

Multipolarity brings bad news for optimists like Jacek Kugler, Douglas Lemke, and Joseph Nye as well.[60] The American-sponsored order was never complete or solidified by uncontested American power. Now, the rate of erosion should increase markedly as China gains and the United States struggles on traditional indices. China rose in spite of not because of liberal institutions. It engaged them cautiously and selectively, adopting aspects of global capitalism without protecting the intellectual property of foreign concerns, loosening Communist Party control, or adopting international human rights standards. Time and again when the United States treated with China on trade and investment, U.S. wealth was not enough to hide U.S. weakness. Despite the large U.S. influence on system-level constraints, China came away each time with important concessions to its national interest. As Mearsheimer warned in the *Tragedy of Great Power Politics*, and the younger Waltz might have seen, politics among oligarchs reflects the balance of power more faithfully than a bible of shared norms. When U.S. presidents went to China after 1990, they were face to face with another oligarch—another consequential unit in the system for state survival—not some dynamic foreign subsidiary of an American-run monopoly.

Yet, all this may bring further credit to Wohlforth, who sounded the alarm against complacency: "While diplomatic efforts to manage status competition seem easy under unipolarity, theory and evidence suggest that it could present much greater challenges as the system moves back to bipolarity or multipolarity."[61] How much more feasible, then, to deal with a structural shift that really is no shift at all but an artifact of conceptual misinterpretation. The system cannot lurch back to multipolarity because it is already there. Competition for power and status has been ongoing since the unraveling of the first President Bush's New World Order in Somalia, the Balkans, the Middle East, and finally Afghanistan. The jockeying will likely become more acute as China rises or the United States declines, but this will merely be power shifting. The gap between the United States and the rest is shrinking, but no quantum leap to a new system structure is in the offing: we are going from asymmetric multipolarity to somewhat less asymmetric multipolarity in a loosely coupled system that in any case dampens these sorts of changes.

Managing multipolarity has historically been difficult, but many of the most important actors will have had experience. For more than a decade, multipolarity, though rarely labeled, has been challenging statesmen, and stakes for the foreseeable future will remain the same as before: (1) revealing the limits of American power, which is to say employing it, without inviting catastrophic violence and (2) renegotiating international ways and means to reflect more lasting power shifts among the poles.

Under the original Waltzian interpretation and consistent with Robert Gilpin's *War and Change*, hegemony as international leadership in a multipolar world is possible but not guaranteed. As the distribution of economic and military resources becomes more symmetric (and system coupling becomes looser), skill and competence, the least discussed elements of power in Waltz (1979), come to the fore.

If American hegemony is to survive economic and military decline, the United States will need to find new levers of influence. It cannot bank on the stickiness of international institutions or the attractiveness of its civilization. Rather it needs to organize its assets to suit the temper of the times. For one, the United States can sell hegemony by accentuating the benefits, lending its formidable remaining strength toward new forms of cooperation and reallocating power resources toward problems highlighted by the international community, including the chorus of nongovernmental organizations: global financial instability, nuclear proliferation, illicit trafficking of goods and people, climate change, sustainable development, and the rest. If this global management strategy is a good one for underwriting hegemony after multipolarity, then the national contribution to Science as a cosmopolitan enterprise merits more attention. The by-products of scientific achievement—those civilizational effects rolling out amid novel technologies—track closely with the requirements for hegemony in the twenty-first century.

A national commitment to science provides a golden opportunity for the state to come to terms with the challenge of speaking truth to power. A hegemon determined to meet at least some important needs of other consequential units in the international system must become intimately acquainted with the revolutionary potential of new discoveries. Science, of course, pushes the pace and depth of discovery. The enterprise encourages both self-examination and expert specialization, which makes it essentially philosophical and political, a relentless meditation on how to live well together.[62] The following chapter in this book evaluates how well U.S. democracy during the first American Century has met this high standard for self-awareness, and why the ailing superpower insists on worshipping technology at the expense of national scientific achievement. Once charted toward Science, the modern state will not escape dilemmas dealing with autonomous, undemocratic professions, but national enthusiasm for Science, if embedded among the citizenry, would help democracy avoid the domestic shoals of technocracy. Moreover, a true Scientific State would enjoy new navigational advantages for twenty-first century geopolitics.

As a cosmopolitan enterprise, Science addresses international cooperation and transnational coordination, reinforcing hegemony under conditions of multipolarity. Our international case study in Chapter Five on U.S. scientific diplomacy with Brazil illustrates how, even among competing powers, basic research provides incentives for working together. Science is close enough to technology to serve as a credible reminder of the state's hard power and as a promise of future practical benefits, yet far enough away to inspire talented individuals across national boundaries in a common quest for knowledge without betraying military secrets or violating intellectual property rights.

Finally, statesmen from other poles in the system perceive that many issues on the transnational list have scientific content. Agreed solutions among independent sovereign states would be more effective with a better common understanding of how Nature responds to human activity, hence headlines in the global media verifying whether scientists commissioned on behalf of a UN panel politicized their results on climate change. Chapter Six's transnational case study on global governance of outer space reports how the United States struggles to balance concern for maintaining its strategic position in the ranking of Great Powers against the challenge of openly informing negotiations and engaging stakeholders, conceived as an inclusive, diverse international community, toward shared vision and construction of solutions for the common good—global solutions worthy of a twenty-first-century hegemon. Under conditions of asymmetric, loosely coupled multipolarity, the international structure prevailing after the Cold War, and one that promises to continue for some time, scientific achievement is good medicine for extending American hegemony at all levels of analysis—domestic, international, and transnational—even when other powers rise.

4   Science and the American State: Mobilizing Democracy

In an era when the United States must craft grand strategy while overcoming relative decline in its hard power resources, investment in science and technology (S&T) has a certain appeal. In economic terms, there may be smaller corporate contributions and no public budget surpluses to pour into research and development, but among its customary benefits, science and technology investment often leads to innovative products and more productive ways of doing business. If a Great Power like the United States finds itself suffering economic crises and waning influence in a multipolar world, it could hope to innovate its way back to robust economic growth through stimulus spending, accepting greater debt now in order to conquer new markets in the future.[1]

The problem with countercyclical science and technology spending is that it runs against the conventional logic of corporate executives. When businesses are losing money, short-term threats loom larger than long-term returns; companies first need to endure in order to enjoy the benefits of R&D. Cutting investment in science and technology staunches the bleeding without causing immediate harm. With respect to public sector stimulus for driving macroeconomic growth, the policy forces the government into the awkward position of picking winners, plucking high-return projects from the mass of supplicants. The opportunities that somehow eluded private venture capital typically involve an inordinate amount of risk, and given the demand for accountability of public officials, particularly in democracies, incumbents have precious little margin for spectacular failures—the most likely outcome of a technically ambitious, high-risk grant.[2]

Considering science distinct from technology creates some happy distance from return-on-investment logic. Scientific advancement, revealing the patterns of Nature, is not itself a marketable service or a secret weapon. The retail price of a peer-reviewed article clearly does not signal its broader contribution to society. Taken as a whole, a nation's scientific effort has civilizational effects beyond new technologies for wielding economic or military power over other states. We have discussed these civilizational effects in terms of three categories: the modernization of state institutions; the enrichment of international diplomacy; and the management of transnational collective action problems.

State-to-state scientific cooperation and global governance will be addressed in subsequent chapters. This section focuses on the hegemonic state's need for national unity through highly developed political institutions and how successful scientific enterprise supports this requirement. For democratic powers, especially, a national commitment to scientific achievement brings with it a salutary discipline, moderating popular opinion and refining political culture so that officials inside state institutions and the general electorate may cultivate a keen appreciation for the long shadow of the future. Secondly, because state-of-the-art scientific work involves specialization and professionalization, democratic institutions must flex in order to accommodate a national commitment to science, resolving a classic principal-agent dilemma in favor of greater autonomy for scientists even as they utilize larger shares of taxpayer contributions. Finally, under democracy, optimized institutions will not come to pass without concurrent developments in societal ethos. A successful move toward science as distinct from technology influences public values toward education and moderation, which in turn preserves free-market regimes and liberty under the rule of law.

National Unity and the Strategic State

From the time of the Founding, American political leaders understood national unity, or union, as a prerequisite for the growth of an important state in world affairs.[3] The authors of the U.S. Constitution looked to Britain, the mother country, to be sure, but also to negative lessons from ancient Western civilization—the decline of Rome and the fall of Athens. Thucydides, the participant in and greatest historian of the Peloponnesian War, attributed Athens' ultimate defeat not to the military disaster in Sicily or the machinations of Sparta but to internecine conflict and the destruction of democracy at home.[4] The eighteenth-century historian Edward Gibbon, with an eye toward the destiny of Britain, saw the seeds of decline in Rome's internal changes; Rome's general trajectory was set in the transformation from republic to empire and the consequent erosion of virtue among her leaders and citizenry.[5]

Examples from modern international relations, when the initiative in creating international order belonged to the Great Powers of Europe, demonstrate both the importance and the difficulty of maintaining national unity for surviving interstate competition. Through the end of the Thirty Years' War, Habsburg Spain relied on state Catholicism. Wielding more power than the pope, King Philip II held together a vast empire, in part by assuming the role of the church's chief defender on earth.[6] Two centuries later, France expanded its global influence under the command of Napoleon, yes, but buttressed by the rallying call of *la mission civilisatrice*.[7] In its perverse way, Germany's bid for hegemony in the twentieth century was made possible by extreme unity under Hitler and the cause of national socialism.[8]

In each of the cases, modern Great Powers managed to avoid the fate of Athens; they were defeated in war before they disintegrated at home. Russia and Britain were different, of course. The Soviet Union indeed gave up the international game in order to reconstitute its state for greater economic and eventually political freedom. Britain held on to its constitutional monarchy, preserved its national unity, and avoided defeat in war, though of all the leading powers from the European Age, it had the most democratic institutions, the greatest interest in promoting a global market, and the political will to concede international security responsibilities to the rising United States. For the other European cases, national unity, or rather sources of unity, had nonlinear effects on hegemony. Without unity, the modern Great Powers would not have competed well enough to attain positions of influence in the international system. Yet, as time went on, counter-reformation Catholicism, *la gloire* of France, and Nazism blinded statesmen to real vulnerabilities as well as opportunities for accommodation, distorted their strategic calculations, and accelerated the collapse of empire.

For the United States, the most recent candidate vying for world leadership, seeking to extend its hegemony even as economic activity shifts toward new power centers in Asia, the classical and European examples should give pause. Americans rally around a creed that prizes individual freedom under self-government. This ideal has the potential to unify a people across ethnic, racial, sectarian, and class divides, laying a foundation for national resolve even stronger than last century's National Socialism, which withstood Allied attacks to the last bunker. However, government by the people and democratic accountability notwithstanding, the American creed does not inoculate the United States from the hubris of power or strategic near-sightedness in pursuit of its ideals.[9]

The American national purpose suffers at least two vulnerabilities. Americans disagree on how far the government should restrict individual liberty in order to meet communal objectives such as equal dignity and opportunity across classes. The formation of organized opposition to government programs—partisan politics—means that American statesmen, in order to survive in their office, may compromise strategic criteria, so foreign policies will play better politically at home. The second vulnerability is that American statesmen who lack strategic justification for their actions can shore up political support by appealing to American universalism, the idea that liberal values, limited government, and free-market capitalism will work abroad in places like Iraq and Afghanistan as they have at home.[10] Messianic rhetoric of U.S. democracy promotion, particularly as it is perceived by typical targets of Great Power intervention, echoes the Catholic and civilizational formulas of empires past.[11] Like the European powers of old, the United States might imperil its international influence—claiming exceptionalism and blindly imposing its liberal democratic creed without taking accurate stock of its own limitations. In short, traditional sources of U.S. exceptionalism are probably not sufficient to prop up American hegemony as the international structure shifts toward a more symmetric, multipolar distribution of power. The United States, despite its unique Founding, is prone to some of the same debilitating errors as past aspiring hegemons.

Fortunately, *la mission scientifique* of the Scientific State brings certain advantages over *la mission civilisatrice* of the traditional hegemon. While it is difficult to do modern science without the educational, communications, and production infrastructure that governments provide, it is also difficult for a nation to become a world scientific leader without tuning its political culture in ways that happen to reinforce national unity under the stress of strategic competition. The scientific mission reorients popular energies toward progressive enlightenment and improved understanding of Nature, moderating the corrosive demand for immediate gratification from the political system. In addition, building the intricate circuitry for advancing scientific theory as a national project generates a kind of cohesion that permits religious liberty, at the same time balancing against centrifugal forces unleashed by deeply held, divergent faiths. Finally, science combines theoretical ideals with pragmatic skepticism; it gets citizens in the right mindset to succeed under the American Constitution, conditioning them for the constant tension between pristine Founding values and the untidy reality of American political institutions.[12]

Under rule by the people, a scientific ethos rewards individual excellence without indulging individual consumerism. Not that private demand is bad. It drives private production, after all, and innovation, which overwhelmed the Soviet's state-controlled economy and brought a happy, peaceful end to the Cold War.[13] If consumerism runs rampant, though, it leads to pathologies that distress a liberal political-economic system. Consumption as the determinant of status in society exacerbates inequality. Even during periods of economic growth, the lower classes may be made to feel even lower as they fall further behind in consumption; recession under this political culture places still greater strain on national solidarity.[14]

Since representatives of the poorer sectors of society always outnumber the rich, increasing inequality under consumerism prompts increasingly shrill demands for democratic politicians to regulate the economy and intervene against the mounting concentration of wealth by redistributing benefits: health care, wage security, unemployment compensation, and the rest. This political groundswell breaks along the national fault line mentioned earlier, the painful trade-off between freedom and equality, resulting in an increasingly polarized and destructive political process.

Burgeoning partisan division within a premier world power broadcasts the leader's vulnerability with high fidelity in a globalized age, and it makes it harder for a country like the United States, in spite of its unparalleled material resources and human capital, to address sure companions of unbalanced consumerism: financial overextension and spiraling debt. In order to sway the voters, parties can always wrangle over just who shall bear the burden of recovery, thereby extending the economic vulnerability of the Great Power and striking further blows at national unity.

Science can help bind these wounds if it can appeal to some of the values across parties. Elevating scientific achievement promotes equality of opportunity by establishing standards for progress apart from profits. Certainly, funding is necessary to sustain research; at the same time, the most expensive experiment often is not the most clever or important one for revealing Nature. In order to raise this kind of funding, democracies will likely tax the rich—no party can expect to win on a platform to perform basic science by taking necessities from the lower classes. In this way commitment to science within a democratic political culture works against conspicuous consumption, putting a healthy distance between consumption and status. For their part, the rich favor this sort of tax over additional transfers to the social safety net. As long as the science is excellent, all classes of the nation benefit from this redistribution of wealth; neither does it set a precedent for societal blackmail, or never-ending bailouts for the poor.

Acceptance of science as a national mission reaches beyond economic divisions to address a potentially debilitating social conflict over religious pluralism. Modern democracies, including those wielding substantial influence in international affairs, confront the seemingly intractable problem of how to permit authentic religious liberty and at the same time persuade free citizens holding diametrically opposed beliefs to live peacefully among one another. In the immensely powerful United States, the contradiction manifests with bitter debates over health and reproduction such as appropriate government involvement in decisions on health care, sexuality, birth control, and abortion. In secular France, Turkey, or Egypt, some of the most violent internal disputes swirl around the place of Islamic beliefs in domestic policy and law.

Science can help with the religious tolerance question in two ways. As previously discussed, during the development of Great Powers in modern Europe, science and religion served as rival handmaidens at the side of Athena, matriarch of state power. Through the Age of Enlightenment and the Industrial Revolution, clerics and men of science competed for Athena's favor. The excesses of the secular French Revolution against the positive example of religious freedom in the American Constitution set the tone for a modus vivendi between Athena's confidants such that scientists could be persons of faith, and prestigious institutions for higher education could sponsor scientific learning literally alongside influential schools of divinity.[15] The same pattern of diplomacy that eventually allowed an amicable relationship between science and faith can light the way for constructive dialogue among different religions or between believers and secular humanists.

Secondly, although science cannot resolve clashes over religious doctrine, it can mitigate conflict over social issues by presenting a parallel space, a kind of safe zone, for achievement and service to the community. The scientific enterprise accommodates a broad spectrum of beliefs, encompassing the vast majority of humanity. Modern democracies like the United States, presuming a reasonable immigration policy, can hope to attract scientific talent from the complete list of Huntington's world civilizations and all the hearth lands making up the globe's cultural geography.[16] If diverse communities within the United States can succeed in setting the world standard for national science, this registers as an Olympic achievement that cannot be easily misinterpreted or faked. Setting these sorts of records powerfully demonstrates to domestic and world audiences the truth behind the slogan "Strength in Diversity." For society, cosmopolitan science magnifies incentives toward unity and greater co-operation across ascriptive differences, counterbalancing centrifugal forces that inevitably follow genuine freedom of religion.

Scientific triumphs, the demonstrable advances in our understanding of Nature, validate the scientific method for framing and resolving problems. Theories are generalizations about how the world works under specified initial conditions. Because no one can be sure of the limits as to when and where these conditions—the postulates, or laws, of Nature—obtain, scientific activity is infused with skepticism: the more apparent success for a theory, the greater the glory of tearing it down in favor of superior logic that resolves some of Nature's outstanding anomalies. Democratic political culture can benefit from scientific skepticism. With regard to the nation hanging together against the machinations of foreign rivals, the community as a whole benefits when each of the domestic parties holds back from final solutions. Policy preferences may derive from class or religious identification—implacable bulwarks—but patience, tolerance, and compromise are more likely in a free society if the theory undergirding ideological proposals is open to testing and subsequent revision in practice. National science may breed a certain humility and adaptability among the citizenry, which can shelter the polity and keep it from turning on itself during turbulent times when economic or military threats are running high.

Science as the Revered Servant

In response to special pleading for reinvigorated national science, critics could legitimately point out that the United States, by traditional measures of funding, productivity, and recognition, is *already* Number One. Besides, with all the famous discoveries and Nobel Prizes, to some, American political culture and institutions are still in decline.[17] American citizens disparage their own free institutions, expressing little confidence in any of the three federal branches of government, the privately owned media, or the leaders of business and banking, especially after the financial crisis and subsequent economic recession of 2008.[18] The military, according to the public surveys, might be the only exception, which is problematic for democratic control, and even this relationship has been complicated by the ravages of war: veterans, especially among the enlisted ranks, who fought and sacrificed for their country in Afghanistan and Iraq are not necessarily welcomed with open arms and a decent wage upon their return and discharge from the armed services.[19]

Moreover, the bridging and healing functions of scientific accomplishment discussed in the previous section have been conspicuous in their absence. Party politics in the United States have become more polarized since Republicans triumphed in the House of Representatives in 1994 after forty years in opposition. Social scientists report that further back, since the Watergate class of 1974, both parties have become more ideologically homogeneous, with fewer moderates from either side of the aisle able to hold on to their seats.[20] Interestingly, as part of the context for toxic party wrangling, both sides accuse the other of abusing science to hoodwink the electorate, subordinating authentic democratic representation to airy ideals, which themselves are subject to hijacking by politicians aflame with the banal desire to win election and rule.

If science has failed in the country where science is best, what can be done? If science is to step into the breach as an "honest broker" among factions, refining political culture without stifling America's democracy, it needs to earn and maintain the public's confidence.[21] To do that, though, it is not enough for American science to be Number One, today. American science must not decline; the lead over other national establishments must not diminish.[22] Furthermore, ordinary citizens must be secure in their belief that greater society will ultimately hold scientists accountable. For this type of confidence, there has to be competence in math and science among the sovereign people, which is unfortunately absent, right now. Without this last secret ingredient among the mass of citizens, it will be exceedingly difficult to reform U.S. institutions in a way that will properly distinguish scientific activity from common technology development. Scientists doing cutting-edge work for revealing the mysteries of Nature require a generous measure of autonomy in order to maximize achievement and elevate science in the public mind to where it can mend political culture.

Science, however, must bring about American union, sturdy enough for the rigors of international leadership without usurping Athena's throne and assuming state power for itself. The following sections discuss science's role as both master and servant to the state and how ambiguity in this relationship leads to a principal-agent dilemma that has gone underappreciated by those responsible for institutional design. American democracy, in fact, has overlooked significant benefits from scientific excellence, constructing within its executive branch a mission-oriented science and technology establishment. In order to be responsive to the people's representatives in Congress, these bureaucratic sponsors have tended to emphasize practical applications and technology over basic research. Loyal adherence to principles of democracy and the rising demands of alliance leadership combine to lock in a suboptimal pattern of public disinvestment in pure science, a profile less pernicious under the international circumstances immediately following World War II than the globalized, multi-polar world of today.

Science and Democracy's Principal-agent Dilemma

The great International Relations realist Hans Morgenthau, surveying the situation during the Cold War, in particular the role of physics in bringing about a delicate balance of terror between the superpowers, wrote an extended essay for the New American Library called *Science: Servant or Master?*[23] In this slim volume, he wrestled with a monumental question that had seemingly been dispatched by the German sociologist Max Weber in the aftermath of World War I.[24] For Weber, modernity required that men of extraordinary scientific ability see it as part of their calling to maintain self-restraint. They should not seek to dominate political questions that in actuality lay outside their field of expertise. Weber warned that if researchers abused their scientific credentials in order to receive a special hearing in the public square, the admixture would corrupt politics and damage science. Societal values, the guiding stars for prioritizing investigations of Nature, would have to be forged somewhere else; Weber suggested that a kind of gut instinct, or public spirit, might be nurtured in order to properly place science in society's harness.

Morgenthau, on the other hand, witnessed the horrific results when the spirit of National Socialism, fanned and exploited by Adolf Hitler, filled the vacuum left by Weber and set the course for German science. If science were purely the servant of society and the state, what would prevent another industrial magnitude Holocaust? Indeed, what would stand in the way of a charismatic fanatic appropriating nuclear weapons—the venomous fruits of science—to attack Nature herself if he were denied his utopia on earth? The ease and rapidity with which nuclear destruction could be wrought made the absolute subjugation of science to the state exceedingly dangerous, affording the decision-makers of a nuclear superpower inhumanly slender windows of time to think before they acted.[25]

Contrary to Weber, then, science itself championed a certain set of values that could inform positions in the public square. Articles of faith in human reason, for example, and in the simple beauty of Nature awaiting our discovery were embedded in the postulates that defined the scientific method. Evidence was cumulative; theories were progressive without being definitive. Unless cosmopolitan Science existed in order to destroy Nature and Man—an increasingly plausible fear in the nuclear age—values that could properly be called scientific should point, like other kinds of values, toward the preservation of certain elemental things, among them life, Man's capacity to reason, and Nature, the subject of Man's inquiry. During a time when ideological conflict decided the fate of leading states, perhaps the entire world, Morgenthau concluded that national science could not just stand aside, entirely neutral, waiting indifferently to serve the winner: national science was somehow both master and servant.

This realization, the toppling of Weber's wall of separation between science and political philosophy, is the germ of a fundamental problem for democracy. In science, as in philosophy, art, commerce, sport, or religion, all men are not created equal. Unwavering adherence to the democratic principle in all aspects of life would in fact ruin human endeavors widely recognized as markers of civilization. Alexis de Tocqueville, the nineteenth-century French statesman and sociological observer of American democracy, understood that the starting conditions of social equality in the New World along with Americans' love of equality, shaped political principles and U.S. decentralized institutions; they also posed an obstacle to national greatness. Building a world civilization and ascending to international leadership would at some point require great undertakings—specialization, coordination of talents, central organization, and hierarchy as opposed to democratic monotony. How, for example, could a nation of half-educated, fiercely independent merchants compete with European science sponsored by the royal houses and noble families, the very symbols of an unequal society?

During the late nineteenth and early twentieth centuries, of course, America did manage to grow in power and influence, accepting extraordinary concentrations of capital and minimal compensation for wage labor before expanding the central government in Progressive and New Deal administrations, not to reinstitute social equality but to regulate inequalities born of the free market. As the scale of industry and the scope of government expanded, Tocqueville's contradiction between democratic principles of equal voice and the urgent demand for professional competence became more acute. In growing powerful, the United States managed national projects—none greater than winning World War II—without resort to Tocqueville's noble aristocracy—by creating a raft of professional agents, indeed a highly educated professional class that penetrated most industrial sectors as well as the halls of government.[26]

For both industry and government, the professionals were organized according to the Weberian separation principle: in the workplace they were to observe unfailingly the bureaucratic hierarchy, molding their specialized skills to suit the preferences of their masters; at the end of the day, upon returning to their private lives, including perhaps civic interests, they were expected to blend with the *demos* in the shopping districts and public squares, re-embracing the old ideal of "one person, one vote."

In theory and practice, modern democracies encountered a major challenge with the rise of the professions.[27] There could be no modernity, and no ascent to international influence, without skilled experts in positions of responsibility but no real democracy without political control by nonexperts, accountable not so much to a professional standard as much as public opinion. In a powerful democratic state, it seems, the inmates—that is, the benighted beneficiaries—were tasked with running the asylum. With respect to industrial-age production or information-age services, the conundrum for principal-agent relations was how to direct the energies of skilled labor without either fouling the works or granting so much autonomy that managers, the ones putatively in charge, were practically marginalized on key decisions.

In government, principal-agent problems intensified with the rise of the professions. Policy principals in Congress or higher reaches of the executive pushed the limits of time and personal knowledge as government portfolios and bureaucratic specialization expanded. Commercial success is hard enough to measure with the interplay of near-term and long-term strategies. Public policy success, and therefore agent work, is more difficult for bosses to monitor without a standard currency to tally "the profits," or benefits, from public expenditure. Moreover, agents implementing policy for the politicians in charge, unlike most laborers, take a keen interest in product features. In the context of a government by and for the people, bureaucrats are voters and consumers of the programs they are working. Agent preferences, then, run far beyond their personal compensation for professional services rendered; public agents often have their own highly informed ideas about what economic or social policy would be good for the country.

Not surprisingly, students of decentralized American government, with its separation of the law-making and executive powers, checks and balances across the branches, and cross-cutting mechanisms of electoral accountability, have discovered multiple applications of the principal-agent framework. To what degree do members of Congress represent the interests of their district versus the good of the nation as a whole?[28] To what extent do presidents employ their authority for executing the law to divert government programs from the will of Congress? Continuing along the delegation chain, how much control do modern chief executives have over their own sprawling bureaucracy—and how much for commanders-in-chief over a million-man military?[29]

Few practicing scientists are ensconced inside the government bureaucracy. However, the federal government funds an estimated 60 percent of basic research in the United States, and resources from the private sector dedicated to pure science have been declining for decades. Policy-makers and scientists alike acknowledge that state and private universities will not sustain the national pace of scientific discovery to meet even the old Kaysen objectives for international economic competitiveness and national military strength without federal support. Of course, taxpayer money must be appropriated by the people's representatives in Congress and administered by agency bureaucrats accountable to the president. None of those responsible officials, or principals, are likely to know as much about the details of theory or experimentation as the nation's scientists themselves. Once again, democracy has a problem with professions. Under conditions of starkly asymmetric information—the necessarily large gaps in scientific expertise between principal and agent, including between links in the long delegation chain between the sovereign masses and investigators at the heart of the matter determining the truth about Nature—how can the people or their politicians retain control of the national scientific enterprise without interfering, distorting, and ultimately hamstringing the precious labors of their expert agents?

U.S. Science and the Case of the Office of Naval Research

Deborah Avant, a leading political scientist on the application of principal-agent theory to the problems of civil-military relations in a democracy, encapsulated this last question in what she called the accountability-efficiency dilemma.[30] If the professional military spends more of their time reporting to civilian authorities on their activities or genuflecting toward civilian taskers in order to demonstrate subordination to democratic control, then there is less time to actually practice their profession—improve their specialized skills and realize their vocation. Efficiency for the military profession comes close to an important criterion for international influence, military effectiveness.[31] The remnant of any distinction links right back to the principal-agent dilemma. An army could efficiently equip itself to fight a different enemy or complete a different mission than what its political masters had in mind. No democratic military can be truly effective until it steps out of the principal's role, which means leaving, at the end of debates, ultimate decisions on the use of force to civilian, nonprofessional preferences.[32]

With respect to scientists as professional agents of the state, there emerges yet again an accountability-efficiency trade-off. The parameters of the "service contract" are not the same as in democratic civil-military relations. These differences, it turns out, push the optimal balance toward greater autonomy—that is, less formal accountability—for the professionals in order to reap scientific rewards for the nation.

As previously mentioned, scientists are not inside the government in the same way military departments are part of the executive branch. Scientists have no experience, no administrative organs to implement their preferences if the incumbent government disintegrated. Even if some were able to manage public infrastructure to provide services and promulgate policy, among the professions enlisted by democratic government, only the military has the guns and the know-how to organize force on behalf of the state. The scientists, speaking hypothetically, have no chance of displacing the government unless they were to co-opt the military, an unlikely development.

Part of the reason is that the scientific mission is less political than, say, the military one. Scientists ought to be less inclined than certain other professions to undermine democratic control. When prioritizing national security threats in order to defend the nation, those discussions can fall along ideological fault lines; political analysts can build a case for the military favoring one party over another, as apparently occurred in the United States during the Reagan era, with partisan fires flaring again during the Democratic administration of the late 1990s.[33] Admittedly, during the early Obama administration, pundits criticized the president's Republican predecessor for putting conservative ideology over climate change science, and there was political wrangling over the validity of predictions on global temperature change and its likely consequences. Yet, this controversy centered on the link between scientific findings and science *advice* to politicians. Persuasive communication to political elites, not the salience of sea temperatures in climate research, ignited the partisan rancor.

Greater autonomy in the accountability-efficiency balance would break the connection between politically charged science advice versus apolitical decisions on the merits and methodology of alternative research projects. Samuel Huntington hoped for a similar dynamic when advocating greater autonomy for the powerful standing military in the United States after World War II. The separation of political from professional questions should be easier to effect in the case of science, especially if the main mission of sponsored science is not to draw implications for specific policy debates but to further scientific achievement, to unlock the secrets of Nature.

The record of American democracy on the accountability-efficiency trade-off shows a steady bias toward greater accountability—at the cost of scientific excellence. No example better illustrates this trend than the evolution of the Office of Naval Research (ONR). ONR was the first permanent science and technology office in the United States after World War II, preceding even the National Science Foundation. While there is no archetypal science office in the U.S. establishment, the story of ONR nevertheless demonstrates how the ubiquitous demand for democratic accountability pushes public resources away from basic research toward technology development. Whatever is left for pure discovery, science managers for the government view the project proposal differently from the scientist—basic science like other activities supported by the taxpayer must have a return on investment, and that payoff is easier to bank when experiments are designed as incremental rather than groundbreaking. Despite the massive lead built by the United States in research and development spending, America's international leadership in science is vulnerable because her domestic institutions are hardwired to channel rivers of mostly public money toward the Kaysen objectives: pursuing technology at the expense of discovery and privileging low-risk, marginal knowledge gains over prospects for a theoretical revolution.[34]

Congress authorized the creation of the Office of Naval Research in 1946, some four years before the National Science Foundation, as in so many other instances, in order to compromise between contentious stakeholders while still administering to the national interest.[35] Some prominent scientists who had advised President Roosevelt and executive agencies during the war interpreted the widely perceived contribution of new technologies to the Allied victory as an opportunity to access a sizable chunk of national resources, a true national program budget, and direct it, free from political influence, toward the most worthy research projects. That proposal for a national science agency would have swung the balance far toward scientific efficiency after the war, but neither President Truman nor key committee members in Congress were comfortable with the absence of accountability implied by an independent board allocating significant public monies.

The defining compromise, then, for the U.S. postwar science establishment was to tuck the first national science office inside a mission agency. Among the government organizations for economic planning and defense that expanded dramatically during the war, the U.S. Navy—more precisely a faction within the navy—was the most progressive, the most forward thinking, about how to bring scientists on board. Harvey Sapolsky, author of an authoritative history of the Office of Naval Research, noted that the navy by virtue of its tradition as the technical service with an inherent interest in research areas like global navigation and nautical engineering and an acquired desire for tropical medicines that might emerge from advances in medical biology, among plausible mission agencies at least, was a natural fit for a science office that would press for a novel degree of autonomy.

Besides, the navy had already worked out many of the kinks of a modern research office before the U.S. entry into the war; part of the function of the naval liaison office in London was sponsoring cooperative projects with the Royal Navy in order to hedge against technological surprise from potential adversaries, in particular the rapidly arming German Navy. Finally, taking into account incentives from internal competition among government bureaucracies, some naval officers worried that if their service did not step forward soon, it could fall hopelessly behind the army in science leadership. The army, after all, had managed the now famous physicists, chemists, and engineers for the Manhattan Project; the Army Air Corps had delivered the city-busting bombs from that prodigious research effort, dramatically curtailing the war against Japan's empire; and the army then led the way to incorporate knowledge from the defeated German scientists to beat the Soviets on rocket propulsion.

The U.S. Navy's reaction to postwar circumstances mirrored the response of the United States in general. Since scientific advances rapidly fueled economic and military triumphs, the order of the day for a decentralized, pluralist government was for each economic and military mission agency—with their various patrons in Congress—to figure out how to put science in the harness. This, of course, swung the balance toward the opposite pole from what many of the scientists wading into public affairs preferred, away from efficient, independent science toward maximum accountability under pre-existing, mission agency goals.

Over half a century later, the first impression from a panoramic view of the U.S. science establishment calls to mind an image of a ramshackle mansion ensconced in a fertile valley.[36] The grounds of this estate, containing the rich soil for producing scientific discoveries, represent the nation's universities, which today as a group perform the largest share of basic research.[37] Other science performing entities mixed in with the university population include nonprofit research institutes, industry research and development centers, and federal labs. Each budget year, with the blessing of Congress and the president, servants rush out from tiny closets adjoining the massive rooms scattered throughout the government establishment to plant seeds and offer a little water to the fecund earth. The seeds (basic research grants) come from the largest science and technology fund in the world, but the government servants—and basic research—are nevertheless in a precarious situation, for at each harvest they must report to their masters how well the seed has grown. The separate rooms in the mansion—that is, our government department and agency heads—have little reason to coordinate their plantings, their investments in science, unless it pleases the president—the mansion's chief executive—or Congress, who owns the building.

The sprawling mansion metaphor illustrates three consequential characteristics of the U.S. science establishment: fragmentation (closets scattered throughout the government); deep reserves (massive adjoining rooms for each closet); and intense mission orientation within but not necessarily coordinated among the fragments. During the Cold War, encompassing the birth and evolution of our science office exemplar, the ONR, these overarching qualities were considered strengths compared with the centralized, hierarchical state-science relationship in the Soviet Union.[38]

Fragmentation across different executive departments prevented any single U.S. cabinet secretary from concentrating the federal budget for massive spending on a narrow slice of science. Because of the uncertainty in basic research, no funding authority could know whether a proposed experiment would succeed as designed, produce a surprise discovery, or lead to revolutionary technology; it was self-defeating for the government to imitate as close as it could a unitary actor and try to pick winners. The best a state could do was set the conditions for talented scientific minds to indulge their intuition and follow where the method took them.[39] The decentralized structure, culminating from several federal sponsors following upon ONR and pursuing a variety of mission-oriented interests in science, would produce something akin to a random search algorithm, that would, it was hoped, outperform Soviet program management for cracking Nature's hidden codes.

In the case of a national emergency, when the science was sufficiently mature and the urgent need of the republic rather specific, the executive and Congress could act together to properly fund science and technology megaprojects. This indeed happened with the Ransdell Act and the creation of the National Cancer Institute in the 1930s; during the war in order to beat Nazi Germany to the atomic bomb; and after the *Sputnik* launch to beat the Soviets to the moon. In fact, the most prominent federal agency whose mission was not to provide a specific government service but to promote American scientific achievement emerged from an extraordinary concert of wills across the branches of government. Even then the National Science Foundation, like so many other mission-subordinate science and technology offices, would not escape unrelenting democratic pressure to put science in the harness and accelerate those efforts considered relevant for a traditional government objective on defense or the economy.

ONR, then, was not only the first after the war; it became representative of U.S. science in important ways. The office was created to promote scientific discovery, but it always belonged to a larger department, in this case the navy, and a more powerful department head, say, the chief of naval operations, whose mission was paramount. That mission, securing superiority on the seas, contributed directly to U.S. hegemony and international influence. The defense and economic concerns of deputy national security advisor Carl Kaysen, via the larger navy mission, would shape ONR's evolution toward technology development as they did for other U.S. science and technology offices. At an annual budget of around $2 billion, ONR is a significant government actor in the science and technology arena with resources to seek out and launch the careers of promising scientists around the world—but again, as with other U.S. science agencies, a small portion of the budget, less than the reported 20 percent, actually goes toward basic research.

The fact that ONR is a research arm within the Department of Defense does exacerbate certain S&T challenges. Compared with civilian agencies such as the National Institutes of Health (NIH) or the National Institute of Standards and Technology (NIST), ONR's relations with universities, corporations, and private research institutes are complicated by certain information security concerns. On the other hand, if principal-agent problems hampering cooperation among the state-science-society trinity can be addressed by ONR—shifting the balance toward science efficiency and less burdensome mechanisms of formal accountability—this should lay the template for similar approaches—that is, improved governance—at other military as well as civilian agencies.

An important part of the heritage at ONR is setting new standards for how the state relates to science. On commemorating ONR's fortieth anniversary, scientist Charles Townes celebrated the science office's steadfast faith in supporting his research on microwaves, and its willingness to extend funding as well as facilitate the dissemination of knowledge when the light emissions of stimulated gas atoms (LASERs) took on novel applications for targeting, telecommunications, and precision cutting across a range of military and industrial activities. Although the path between Townes's original scientific research proposal and naval capability advances in the field was long and serendipitous, the navy's wager paid off for the nation, indeed far more than what would appear on a traditional return-on-investment calculation. This was so not because the navy could foresee the development of laser technology in the proliferation of waveguides after World War II but because it recognized Townes's potential as a researcher and his framing of problems as good science.[40]

The knack for sensing and nurturing good science was itself cultivated by extraordinary and surprisingly free thinking naval leadership of the research office after the war. MIT political scientist and ONR historian Harvey Sapolsky reckoned, "[T]here was hardly an aspect of the scientific enterprise in America in which ONR was not centrally and constructively involved during the period between the Second World War and the Korean War."[41] The Research Office sprang from at least two proud ancestors, not just the Assistant Naval Attaché office for research in London, the one responsible for Anglo-American technological and tactical cooperation from before the war, but also President Roosevelt's Office of Scientific Research and Development.[42] Captain Robert Conrad, the first planning director and contracts officer for ONR, had built his career in the naval technology development tradition but once in charge accepted the science mandate, in the absence of any national foundation, with equal seriousness:

> Our powers of self-destruction appear like a baited trap which mankind is powerless to evade. Where is the new hope? Where is the new security? . . .
> In a more limited sense, the study of our research results will reveal the evil possibilities against which we must guard ourselves, and this is a natural

responsibility of the Navy. But in the broad sense, the common enemy of mankind is man's ignorance . . . . Research to create knowledge, and education to spread it to all people, are the basic safeguards of civilization, and the only weapons which will succeed against ignorance, our ultimate enemy.[43]

During the crucial postwar reconstruction years in Europe, ONR through its office in London organized research reconnaissance trips to the smoldering ruins of Germany. Among the rapporteurs was Hans Bethe, a senior theoretical physicist on the Manhattan Project who would go on to win the 1967 Nobel Prize.[44] Chief of Naval Research Thorwald Solberg endorsed the thrust of the London Office reports, which advocated more aid for basic research in prostrate Germany. In the cover letter to London's August 1948 report on the "Rehabilitation of Science in Europe," the U.S. Navy engineer wrote: "[D]ue regard should be given to the fact that a healthy industrial recovery and recovery of adequate standards of education, health and general welfare may not be secured and maintained without sound and stable conditions with respect to science, both in research and education."[45]

Over time, however, the science branch of ONR faded, beaten back by competing organizations in the U.S. science establishment and democratic demands for better technology. Today, in ONR parlance, the *discovery* of so-called 6.1 research often merges with the *invention* of projects in category 6.2, as in the oft-quoted statistic that 40 percent of the navy's nearly $2 billion S&T portfolio addresses long-term capability issues under the rubric of Discovery & Invention.[46] The presence of the National Science Foundation and putative 6.1 funding in other mission agencies pushes the balance at ONR toward 6.2, with emphasis not on probing Nature but on harvesting new devices from the general pool of scientific knowledge. The mounting call in congressional hearings is not so much to deepen the scientific pool as it is to traverse more efficiently and more rapidly between the laboratory bench and the field. This pressure, perfectly understandable in a democratic, representative body, gets the recipe for national science leadership exactly backward. S&T managers scramble to justify 6.1 money by tying futuristic capabilities back to fundamental discoveries.[47]

During a period of growing insurgency in Iraq, Chief of Naval Research Jay Cohen explained the value of basic research as the first step in a highly integrated science and technology enterprise. In the postinvasion hothouse environment, he promoted Navy Secretary Gordon England's vision for a modern-day Manhattan Project to "detect, defeat, and destroy explosives at range."[48]

Defeating improvised explosive devices (IEDs) would mean getting the phenomenology right through advances in pure science, including chemistry and physics with contributions from outside ONR 6.1, say, from the National Academy of Sciences and the National Science Foundation.[49]

Meanwhile, smaller investments in research and development from the shipbuilding industry created an added burden for ONR 6.1. A shift toward industrial priorities in naval architecture and marine engineering prompted a reaction from ONR, from 6.1 to 6.2 concerns within the Discovery & Invention block. The practical benefits of pure science are usually difficult to specify up front, which, again, makes the 6.1 category easy pickings in the democratically accountable budget process. Rear Admiral Cohen also discussed recapitalization of the University Naval Oceanographic Lab Ship fleet in cooperation with contributions from the National Science Foundation. Framing the shipbuilding as infrastructure for basic research—in order to tap 6.1 funds—made the ships affordable. Admiral Cohen, though, recognized that this was "not the preferred solution," for it put ONR in the business of ship contracting and left fewer resources for evaluating and sponsoring science to discover new patterns in Nature, the latter activity being the key to scientific leadership for the nation.[50]

With the unremitting clamor for democratic accountability, it is puzzling how ONR in the beginning, in the immediate aftermath of the war, could have been so daring in reaching out to the universities and sponsoring pure science not necessarily bound to a strategic technology plan. Later, when external money, especially DOD money, reached a larger share of science funding, scientists and university administrators fretted over the future of scientific autonomy. University of California president Clark Kerr argued that research was "rooted in the logic of history"; powerful democracy in the age of modernization would naturally generate a ravenous public appetite for technology. Pure science's "reasoned choice among elegant alternatives" would whither secularly, before market imperatives of the "knowledge industry."[51] Relentless consumerism from a free society notwithstanding, a more precise answer may be that ONR and other science agencies instead confronted a series of political storms, each time surrendering more of their research arm to urgent mission capabilities and never quite making up for lost momentum in pure science.

An unclassified summary of greatest hits from ONR's European Office after the first thirty years (1946–76), if it can be taken as representative of ONR's total effort, points toward discreet shifts in the sponsor's relationship with pure science.[52] By decade, the report listed eighteen projects, twenty projects, and finally twenty-five for the last period, 1967–76. During the first two decades, roughly one-third of projects tied directly to development of new devices for the navy. After 1967, more than two-thirds aimed toward new technology rather than scientific investigation of natural phenomena. Intriguingly, though, the middle decade, 1957–66, saw only seven technology projects, six of them clustered, in the report, between May 1960 and July 1963. The spikes of interest apparent in this admittedly unscientific sample are consistent with the surge—and contemporaneous second thoughts—with respect to Kerr's knowledge industry bursting onto the university scene in the 1960s. The high tide of technology projects in ONR's third decade coincides with the crisis in U.S. policy toward Vietnam and prefigures the broad embrace by science and engineering departments of external funding during the 1980s.

Once the bargain between universities and the federal mission agencies—as well as some private R&D laboratories—was made, it seems there was no shortage of urgent national needs—more storms—to pull scientists away from fundamental research. Again and again, the nation called upon the knowledge industry, sacrificing scientific efficiency for consumer-oriented productivity and chipping away at the margin for maintaining America's postwar science leadership. As Harvard physicist and science policy advisor Harvey Brooks warned during the gush of federal funding toward nominally basic research for President Reagan's Strategic Defense Initiative after 1983, the much larger increases in applied monies and technological development for missile defense would condition—and ultimately limit—SDI as science policy.[53] The 1990s saw government and industry demand that science labs assist in maintaining U.S. economic competitiveness after the Cold War, and as mentioned, the Iraq and Afghanistan wars of the 2000s shaped not just applied but basic research priorities for ONR and other mission agencies.

The National Science Foundation (NSF), the one semi-independent government agency whose mission is science rather than more immediate public welfare or security, cannot escape the storms of national crises. As part of the Obama administration's $800 billion plan to stimulate economic growth and arrest spiraling national debt in 2009, the NSF received $9 billion, a dramatic 50 percent increase over its normal budget. Yet, how the agency allocated those extra funds appropriated by Congress to stimulate science depended on factors tangential to the needs of pure scientific research. The money, as part of a controversial package approved mainly by Democratic majorities, was not guaranteed, in fact not likely, to be renewed, so there would be no steady stream to fund that creative, randomlike algorithm so vital to major progress in basic research; projects would get cut off before they had a chance to blossom in terms of theoretically significant findings. Moreover, the stimulus billions had to be spent quickly, so quickly that the NSF director would not have time to attract fresh proposals. Rejected proposals still on the rolls from fiscal year 2008 were the only ones available to receive the funding upon which the hopes of the nation rode.[54] In the present climate, even when policy-makers respond to a crisis by voting more public money for basic research—at the most prominent agency dedicated to scientific leadership—democratic accountability weighs in and a compromised standard of efficiency for scientific advancement obtains.

Escaping Democracy's Trap: Rebalancing the Accountability-efficiency Trade-off

Describing the U.S. science establishment, including a special look at the history of the first modern science agency under the Office of Naval Research, it becomes clearer that despite the impressive record of U.S. scientific leadership after World War II, science as a national enterprise poses several of the same problems as other vital professions for democracy. In science, as in finance, medicine, professional sport, and the military, egalitarianism and public accountability—deference to the *demos*—at some point becomes the enemy of excellence, which again is critical for status and influence in the competition among nations. Science like the other professions falls into democracy's principal-agent trap: the sovereign people—meaning the principal—are not in a position to trust their agents, to grant their experts the autonomy necessary for them to pursue professional excellence, even for national greatness.

This was a core insight of Alexis de Tocqueville before the development of modern social science and the point of departure as well for Samuel Huntington's *Soldier and the State* (1957), a seminal study that bridged contemporary subfields of American politics and International Relations. As previously remarked, Peter Feaver in *Armed Servants* (2003) formalized these ideas, fitting them into the principal-agent framework. His solution prefigures our answer for rebalancing the accountability-efficiency trade-off.[55] The nation's best scientists, assuming a role of social responsibility similar to that of the best investment bankers or the best military officers, are unlikely to receive adequate license without improved education all around: for citizen-politicians who represent and sometimes refine the will of the people, for the professional body of scientists who might win greater trust if they appreciate political dilemmas of the lay persons who govern and fund their research, and finally for the mass of citizens who elect the governors and are the ultimate beneficiaries from excellence of the professions.

Among these educational imperatives, improved elementary and secondary education for all is probably most important for strengthening U.S. scientific leadership. Student performance in STEM (science, technology, engineering, and mathematics) in terms of both the number and quality of graduates pursuing careers in these areas has already been recognized as a problem in the United States, most prominently by the National Academy of Science's call to action, *Rising above the Gathering Storm: Energizing and Employing America for a Brighter Economic Future* (2007).[56] The Committee on Prospering in the Global Economy of the 21st Century, which authored the report, was chaired by Norman Augustine, a retired chairman and CEO of Lockheed-Martin Corporation. As the committee chair's background and the report title imply, the old Kaysen trinity, harnessing science for technology, engineering manpower, and knowledge capital for the nation, drove ultimate policy recommendations. For the *Gathering Storm* initiative, educational solutions were scattershot: do everything at all levels to produce more and better scientists and especially engineers who could minimize the damage—that is, slow the erosion of U.S. market share in the changing global economy.[57] *Gathering Storm* presumed that government can lead everywhere at once—industrial R&D partnerships, higher education for sciences and engineering, skilled worker training, K–12 education, and sponsorship of basic research. For a number of reasons—the national custom of science and technology policy administered by mission-oriented government agencies, the lack of a *Sputnik* moment to galvanize public opinion, and spending constraints brought on by a weak U.S. economy plus the global financial crisis, one or more pillars in the committee's multifaceted approach is bound to suffer.

Greater attention to the principal-agent trap at the core of democratic governance and the civilizational (non-Kaysen) benefits of scientific progress as distinct from advanced technology pushes policy-makers toward the K–12 set of educational goals—better appreciation of math and science for everyone to build a more vibrant democracy and more legitimacy for the leader among sovereign nations in a multipolar world. The Carnegie Corporation of New York and the Institute for Advanced Study get the priority correct in *The Op-*

portunity Equation: Transforming Mathematics and Science Education for Citizenship in the Global Economy (2009) but not for all the right reasons—and without all the justifications on the table, a transformative effort to rejuvenate American science leadership is unlikely to succeed.[58]

In democratic politics, competing demands will pull public resources from broad science education. For example, under current conditions of high unemployment, job openings for skilled labor go unfulfilled for lack of qualified applicants. Under the open exchange of the global economy, it appears that the skill advantage of the American worker will have to be great indeed to compensate for wage and benefits packages several times more costly than those of his foreign counterparts.[59] Augustine's committee itself pointed out that only 4 percent of the U.S. workforce engages in STEM-intensive jobs.[60] Taking into account the faster rate of STEM job growth, estimated at a factor of three over the past decade, worker training and STEM education are unlikely to solve America's massive employment problem directly.[61] *Gathering Storm* concluded that the most important consequence of government education initiatives would be to generate more STEM entrepreneurs, tech savvy patriots who could create more good jobs here at home.

This line of reasoning moves the focus toward higher education, maintaining the nation's flagship research universities that will graduate many of those job creators, even as Asian institutions and more European champions come on the scene.[62] Yet, what might be called the Yale plan for science and technology leadership has its own problems. For certain scientific quests—splitting the atom, sequencing the human genome, bending the limit of computer processing speed, or measuring the Higgs-Boson particle at the boundary between energy and matter—bigger is frequently better: greater concentration of financial capital and incorporation of human genius enables advancement in science.[63] In other cases, however, revolutionary theory or earth-shattering discovery emerges from the lonely, underfunded periphery, from the serendipitous random walk that managed to draw early grants from the upstart Office of Naval Research after World War II. Yale president Richard Levin may have been correct that winners are easier to pick among science versus commercial technology endeavors. Nevertheless, being at the "top of the class" when it comes to world science also requires a certain percentage of long-shot investments in order to stay ahead of other science sponsors.[64]

Furthermore, making the richly endowed, flagship universities even richer works up to a point, but if potential competing institutions are starved as a result, the U.S. science establishment can ossify. The principles expounded by science adviser Vannevar Bush in his 1945 report *Science—The Endless Frontier* and cited by Levin are not unassailable.[65] For example, government experts selecting proposals for public funding on the basis of scientific merit alone may remain more or less independent of party pressures, but as we have seen, nonpartisan mission agencies and NSF cannot ignore popular demand for return on taxpayer investment in the form of published test results and new technology. Academic disciplines and prominent journals are hierarchical, not simply administered as marketplaces of ideas but manicured in part as elite gardens for the preservation of valuable scientific reputation. Scientific merit is in practice not evaluated independently from dynamics of the university science network, which must become more closed, more risk averse, as public money flows only to the richest, long established, flagship universities. Levin (2010) criticized Japan and China for underfunding basic research relative to applied and then releasing grants almost exclusively to the most senior scientists, but his flagship strategy for maintaining world-class science could exacerbate these same trends, already apparent in the United States.

All this said, the most significant limitation on the Yale approach grows out of democracy's principal-agent trap. Leading voices on strategies for how to stave off decline and extend American hegemony mistakenly discount the weakening education statistics for the United States compared with nations on the rise. Fareed Zakaria noted that the low math and science scores were averages and told more about inequality in American education than the capacity to produce enough science and engineering students for what remains the strongest and highest-rated university system in the world.[66] Adam Segal of the Council on Foreign Relations argued that the United States could overcome higher labor costs to compete with China in world markets by outinnovating them, the key policy shift being concentration of talent from government, business, and academia to accelerate new technology flows from the idea or laboratory stage to market.[67]

Zakaria, Segal, and like-minded analyses brush past the challenge of professions at the core of democratic governance. Just who will be among the expert agents who take public money with the promise to win economic competitions abroad for the United States? Will elected representatives in charge understand how scientific patriots get the job done? Even if some officials do, will they be able to justify the government's largess to an unsophisticated electorate without smothering the pure scientists in democratic accountability—overly burdensome reporting requirements and short-term demands for welfare and security gains?

The answer to the latter question is likely to be no, unless some thought goes toward the Carnegie Corporation concern for general, K–12 math and science education. Broad literacy in math and science is not primarily about building productive citizens who can find jobs in the global economy and understand contemporary policy debates.[68] A large portion of the STEM jobs and technical policy decisions will require more than general education. Improved math and science literacy will instead "fuel vibrant democracy" by ameliorating the principal-agent trap, allowing the government to play some favorites, to sustain movement along the lines suggested by Levin, Zakaria, and Segal, so the nation's best scientists can soar. As Tocqueville pointed out long ago, Americans love freedom but fear inequality. Without *trust* from the people and duty from the professions, concentrations of wealth or power—even those necessary to achieve excellence—threaten democracy.

The great vocations for national capability and international influence—professions of arms, finance, law, medicine, engineering, business, and now science—face similar regulatory challenges in democracy. The rising benefits of science, as distinct from technology, under changing world conditions make it imperative for the faltering U.S. hegemon to shift the accountability-efficiency trade-off toward greater efficiency and thereby higher excellence in scientific achievement. In a consolidated democracy this cannot be accomplished unless the sovereign people will it so, unless citizens as a body preserve the distinction between knowledge of Nature and development of technology. To do this, society as a whole must raise its levels of education and self-confidence, so it can monitor scientific progress without micromanaging it. Society must cultivate the patience for balancing Kaysen's economic and defense objectives, which of course are still relevant, with the civilizational rewards of scientific leadership.

As deputy national security advisor in the early 1960s, Carl Kaysen identified products, manpower, and knowledge stock as economic benefits from scientific activity that provided the postwar United States practical advantages for international competition.[69] In today's globalized economy and multipolar international order, scientific achievement also provides a second trinity of civilizational advantages for the American hegemon seeking opportunities in cooperation with other powers: a more vibrant democracy at home; forthcoming diplomatic exchanges abroad; and greater influence over multilateral arrangements that tackle transnational issues of global development and human security.

Regarding the first, domestic category of civilizational rewards, real gains are in the journey rather than the destination. Knowing more about the structure of the universe or the origins of life is unlikely to perfect democratic institutions directly. Although during the Age of Enlightenment there may have occurred significant transfers of this sort between natural science and politics, the mechanism now coheres in all the work democracy must accomplish to establish commitment in the most profound sense toward basic research. American democracy, in particular, must dig deep within itself to solve the principal-agent dilemma actually posed by several of the modern professions. By educating itself and instilling a sense of duty in its professionals, including university-trained and publicly funded scientists, America prepares for its next great experiment in self-government: granting a historically aloof cadre the freedom to explore an *Endless Frontier*, somehow trusting this elite to take important decisions without becoming, like the fictional Laputa, ruled by them.

Harvesting the civilizational benefits of excellence in science will not be easy for the United States, whose people recoil at any hint of technocracy and conflate world leadership with prerogatives to consume not simply discover. Nevertheless, it is still possible for democratic statesmen to lead public opinion, to educate and mobilize the popular sovereign. Differentiating science from technological innovation in the national mindset would begin the journey and compel Americans to address lingering friction between equality and excellence, indeed, an oft-neglected vulnerability in their own Constitution.

Should the quest for scientific excellence and global science leadership find some success, other rewards will accrue at the international level. A fit democracy flourishing on the *Endless Frontier* will attract many suitors: weaker powers in search of development associated with scientific progress and strategic partners who can increase regional security for the hegemon in a fluid, multipolar world.

5   Science and Diplomacy:
U.S. Hegemony and the Rise of the Rest[1]

The classic threat to an incumbent hegemon, which holds the first position among Great Powers in a system of states, comes not from domestic infighting or transnational disappointments but the international arena: it is the rise of a rival power.[2] When this development occurs, the metropole often senses challenges to its global interests in several regions simultaneously, at the very moment when economic constraints begin to tighten. Extending hegemony, then, has historically been a question of accommodating rising states in a manner that buys time, years or decades, for either a soft landing or for economic trends to again switch course.

We have seen that national commitment to scientific achievement approaching the ideal of a Scientific State, which rewards pure understanding as distinct from pursuit of specific technologies, inculcates a moderating influence on powerful democracy. Investment in science may refine transactional, consumer-oriented political culture and strengthen institutions to properly navigate principal-agent dilemmas, which have grown more acute for democracies with the rise of professions. As science soothes the relationship between the state and higher Truth, it also sends a clear signal to other actors in the system that the leading state is not tyrannical or lusting for greater power in order to enslave other communities. Science, unlike technology, helps others distinguish hegemony from imperialism, the hegemon leaving behind old exploitive systems of zero-sum competition for a society of states with at least some important goals in common and certain interactions aimed at mutual benefit rather than raw accumulation of power.

The civilizing side-effects of science, formative influence on political culture, governing institutions, and foreign perceptions—apart from spurring advanced technologies, create a reservoir of what Joseph Nye termed soft power. Scientific leadership attracts the admiration of other states, and in spite of an international environment rife with conflicts of interest, rival powers recognize certain problems such as freedom of navigation, ethnic or religious conflict, and environmental degradation as transnational, ones that cannot be managed without goodwill from the Scientific State. With an admixture of admiration and indirect interest, then, other states observe the scientific hegemon—the Scientific State—holding a certain respect and predisposition toward long-term cooperation that is absent for Great Powers that try to coerce inferior governments as efficiently as possible.[3]

Unfortunately, the temptation for a democratic power is to muddle science with technology and use practical machinery promising military or economic advantage to purchase allies. Diplomacy by technology, though, tends to falter over the long run because ordinary states cannot distinguish this from muscle-flexing under anarchy, as when a tyrannical empire employs its hard power to get its way by undermining independence of other actors in the system. In the perceptions of small states dealing with a gross power imbalance, the sale of arms or high-tech manufactures by the lead state, rather than a sign of generosity or service to stabilize the system, merely reflects a less violent version of the ancient Melian dialogue: the weak suffering what they must without pretense of right behavior.[4] Although science and technology (S&T) are lumped together as a matter of S&T policy, technology as a slippery currency of hard power facilitates the Thucydides cycle—the rise and fall of leading states; science by comparison is highly viscous. It attracts favor while sticking with the host, an enduring asset for enduring diplomatic relationships.

When the United States is compared against this model, its protestations of exceptionalism notwithstanding, the superpower stumbles into the same technology trap. Toward rising powers and potential rivals it reacts first to preserve American technological superiority. It tries to prevent advanced weapons or products designed in the United States from falling into the wrong hands using export controls, information classification, visa restrictions, and counterespionage. Only then may scientists step forward to foster cooperation with potential diplomatic partners, but even these scientific activities are highly circumscribed. Ordinarily, sponsored research projects must compete to align with downstream technology vectors aimed at surmounting specific security or commercial problems.

Mission-oriented research blends easily with long-range development plans, and it can attract funding in the competitive atmosphere imposed by decentralized government agencies. However, zooming out from domestic R&D to bilateral relations, there are drawbacks from reflexively and blatantly hijacking scientific initiatives in order to score diplomatic points in the short run. Trojan horse projects fool no one, and rising scientific communities these days can look elsewhere—within their region, in Europe, or Japan—for genuine partners. In addition, with mission-oriented science tied so closely to technological advantage, recipients of U.S. attention may infer that the United States will demand a steep price for whatever amount of technology transfer. In any case, for state actors, common scientific progress and American scientific leadership must take a back seat to preserving their own independence. Ultimately, pride and insecurity with respect to innovation fuel suspicion and make developing countries, especially rising powers, prickly partners for U.S. science and technology diplomacy; they pose a problematic match for U.S. strategy that elides distinctions between basic research and technological development.

In the Western Hemisphere, given Brazil's size and international profile, the results of bilateral scientific cooperation with the world-class research establishment of the United States remain disappointingly meager. A relatively fallow relationship on scientific matters has implications for the relationship as a whole, not just for joint research on alternative fuels, deep-sea drilling, or space satellites but also on broader dimensions such as global trade negotiations, international peacekeeping missions, and assistance in the battle against international terror networks.

Because other actors on the world stage perceive Brazil as a rising star, the twists and turns of Brazil's interaction with the hegemon do not go unnoticed. Missteps or lost opportunities for the United States with regard to Brazil, for example, may create openings for China, cultivating new markets in South America or seeking investments for the extraction of raw materials.[5] In other words, correct apprehension of science's civilizational role—that is, beyond its utility for generating future technology—should improve a powerful and inherently threatening state's diplomatic performance. A Scientific State can build cooperation with more partners on a wider range of issues by smoothing rough edges inevitable in asymmetric power relationships, the very conflicts of interest and suspicions that historically curtail the lifespan of hegemons.

The United States and Brazil: The Unconsummated Partnership

Since Brazil's independence from the Portuguese Empire, a transformation in which far-flung boundaries remained intact along with grinding inequalities inside the new monarchy, Brazil assumed the role of Great Power in waiting. A continental, populous, richly endowed blend of cultures, Brazil always appeared poised to leap onto the stage of balance of power politics and become its first South American champion. In this vision of *grandeza*, a Brazilian sphere of influence stopped short of eclipsing the United States. Sober limitations meant that once Brazil resolved its economic sclerosis and built consent-based political institutions to mobilize its full potential, it could enter Great Power competition involving Europe or Asia without sacrificing peaceful partnership with the United States that would comanage the Americas.

These historical circumstances make Brazil an intriguing case study for exploring shortcomings of the U.S. hegemon's bilateral diplomacy. Brazil's rise does not pose the existential threat of some Great Power shifts in previous state systems. Thucydides fingered the deep cause of the Peloponnesian War, which eventually consumed the independence of Hellenic civilization, as the growth of Athenian power relative to Sparta. The success of Napoleon's armies in the nineteenth century, the expansion of German, then Soviet power in the twentieth, and now, perhaps, China's growth at the dawn of the twenty-first, have occasioned crises of this extreme category.[6]

Clearly Brazil's movement does not present the same danger—neither its capability profile, which does not include an oceangoing navy or nuclear weapons, nor its strategic intentions follow the script for a hegemonic rival. Yet, Brazil is growing, in several recent years much faster than the United States, even before the financial crisis of fall 2008 crippled U.S. output. Brazil has what George Kennan and postwar realists might have called a legitimate interest for inserting itself into global trade negotiations, energy agreements, and world forums tackling transnational issues—the G20, for example, or should it open permanently to Brazil, the UN Security Council. For the United States as global hegemon, increasing bilateral attention toward Brazil now makes common sense. In fact, several powers are currently coming into their own, so astute accommodation with Brazil may set a valuable precedent for the maturing U.S. superpower close to home in the Americas. Lessons learned in faraway Europe, before the United States mobilized for the Cold War, may be revisited and reapplied under twenty-first-century conditions.

Now, if bilateral diplomacy does not succeed in this instance, it will not spell the end of U.S. international leadership: Brazil will not take over the world, and its economy, either in terms of size or productivity, will not approach that of the United States for the foreseeable future. Nevertheless, Brazil is a visible player in the so-called BRIC (Brazil, Russia, India, China) and IBSA (India, Brazil, South Africa) groupings, loose organizations of rising regional powers that, as U.S. relative power declines, are likely to have more frequent influence on cooperation at the global level. If the United States cannot properly manage the relationship with Brazil, under favorable conditions, similar difficulties will likely attend attempts at accommodation with other rising states. In addition, crisis outcomes with a future peer competitor like China, for example, might hinge on which way important swing countries such as Brazil align their policies. Thus, efforts to adopt diplomatic best practices like the one treated here—distinguishing and consistently nurturing scientific achievement so as to avoid crowding out by official technology promotion—should not be underestimated. Faltering American national commitment to science hampers diplomatic outreach, and the illustration of Brazil showcases both direct and indirect consequences for U.S. hegemony.

Economic Factors

Direct consequences for global leadership flow from the major issues animating U.S.-Brazil interactions.[7] Currently, most of these concerns fall under the subject of economics though included on the list are conflicts of interest that could, at some crisis point in the future, leapfrog trade or investment in diplomatic priority. In economic terms the highest, and probably most enduring, global stakes hinge on the outcome of negotiations to shift worldwide rules toward freer trade for the exchange of goods and services.

During the recent Doha round of global trade talks, the United States supported multilateral protection of foreign investment and pressed for greater access to growing markets, especially expanding populations of middle-class consumers in the developing world. While China could certainly claim many of those potential buyers, at Cancun in 2003, the IV Summit of the Americas (2005) in Rio del Plata, Argentina, and the 2008 G8 Summit in St. Petersburg, Russia, Brazil raised its profile, leading various groupings of developing countries to demand "reciprocity" through special differential treatment. There could be no grand bargain on world trade, nor progress on the old vision of a Pan American free trade area, unless the United States along with the European Union in the global case, reduced subsidies and lowered tariff barriers to agricultural imports.[8] The United States refused and abruptly encountered the limits of its twenty-first-century influence, securing neither freer exchange in the World Trade Organization nor a Free Trade Area of the Americas (FTAA).

Frustrated trade talks also represented a lost opportunity to engage and help modernize Brazil's export profile. Continued over-reliance on mining and agriculture commodities such as iron ore, coffee, and soy has left Brazilian growth vulnerable to frequent global price fluctuations.[9] Despite this handicap, responsible financial policies and fiscal discipline over the past fifteen years, including during the presidential terms of Lula da Silva from the Workers' Party (PT), helped boost Brazil's GDP. Today, Brazil vies with the United Kingdom for the Number Six spot in the world: $2.5 trillion in GDP, compared with $7.3 trillion for China and $15.1 trillion for the United States.[10] China, of course, recently surpassed the United States as top manufacturer to the world, and the United States remains strong in exports of high-technology goods and services. Brazil, intriguingly, has demonstrated world-class sophistication and know-how in areas such as agribusiness, hydropower, nuclear energy, and aircraft design. This would seem to indicate staggering potential for Brazilian export-led growth—to match the consumption potential of its burgeoning middle class. What is more, the keys to unlocking latent export value lie with Brazilian science, its ability to inspire Brazilian workers in labor and management as well as its role in fueling commercial innovation.

The rise of a sophisticated exporter in the Western Hemisphere would be sufficient to draw sustained diplomatic attention from the U.S. hegemon, but beyond this remarkable trajectory, Brazil has labored until it presently finds itself on the cusp of an energy revolution. Admittedly, recent months have not been kind to Brazilian dreams: first, expanding production and productivity until the country can provide good jobs and clean energy for most of its citizens, and second, expanding Brazilian presence in international markets for sugar-based bio-fuels, civilian nuclear technology, and now petroleum, given discoveries in the so-called *pré-sal* layer off the coast of Sao Paulo and Rio de Janeiro.[11] Part of the challenge emerged out of the downturn in the global economy affecting risk calculations of petroleum companies and potential investors in the presalt layer from Europe and the United States. On the Brazilian side, a dip in economic growth—from a robust 5 percent in 2011 to below 1 percent in 2012—complicated the work of the Brazilian Congress and the state oil company, Petrobras, budgeting domestic resources and regulating foreign stakes in the new reserves.

Yet, Brazil also faces challenges on the level of science and technology policy. In every major facet of its energy matrix—hydropower, bio-fuels, petroleum, and nuclear—foreign contracting and technology transfer have played critical roles. Brazil's profile as a new-style world power for the twenty-first century will depend on its contribution to the transnational demand for affordable, clean, and reliable energy.[12] The sophistication and ultimate success of Brazil's energy matrix, in turn, rides on S&T diplomacy. Because Brazil is blessed with raw materials and natural assets—its rivers, sugar cane, petroleum reserves, and uranium deposits—technology as a critical, *foreign* ingredient for Brazil's futuristic energy plans arouses special sensitivity.[13] Moreover, vulnerability associated with the Brazil case highlights the need for an oft-neglected distinction within S&T diplomacy: support for international science versus technology transfer.

Brazil's commodity-weighted export profile and its potential as a world-class energy supplier raise the stakes for S&T policy. Brazilian growth could set in motion a positive feedback cycle with greater responsibility in global governance. Rising shares of major export-import markets, though, can hardly be achieved without threatening the revenues of other economic powers. Not surprisingly, during 2011 Brazil involved itself in multilateral discussions on currency manipulation.[14] That spring, the U.S. and Eurozone economies were struggling in the aftermath of a financial crisis and mounting debt concerns. China had weathered the global storm, but there were few constraints on its government's desire to intervene in currency markets and suppress the yuan. This left Brazil, which had pledged to fulfill its financial responsibilities so as to retain confidence of foreign investors, bearing the brunt of higher prices on its exports for many of its major customers.

The currency trap of 2011 reinforced the notion that Brazil should parley its growing significance for the global economy into more prominent positions in international institutions. By virtue of its recent success, Brazil merited inclusion in the so-called G8 summits, gathering together the world's largest economies. Rather than running the world like a classic developed economy in the Bretton Woods tradition, Brazil led coalitions of midsize countries to advocate reapportionment of benefits from the rich core to developing states struggling to climb into more sophisticated, and more lucrative, transactions of the global economy. Accordingly, Brazil contributed a leading voice to G20 and other global forums deliberating on the financial crisis; its style has been to balance global concern for environmental protection against national targets for economic growth and to propose mechanisms for technology sharing while retaining some incentive for innovation.[15]

Political Cooperation and Security Factors

Being that Brazil does not possess raw market power compared with that of the United States or even the United Kingdom in strategic sectors such as financial services, it must manage multilateral institutions, or fashion new ones, to reform established patterns of the global economy. Over the past couple decades, Brazil accomplished some of both.[16] Shifting the locus of discussion on the financial crisis to the G20 was a method of reforming the G8. Settling its own debt and helping others, including its regional partner and sometime rival, Argentina, repay loans early sent a strong reform message to the U.S.- and European-dominated International Monetary Fund. On the political dimension, Brazil's leadership in MINUSTAH, the international peacekeeping mission to Haiti, strengthened Brazil's case for change to the anachronistic permanent membership at the UN Security Council.[17] Brazil cooperates as a nonweapon state signatory to the Nuclear Nonproliferation Treaty and a member of the rather exclusive Nuclear Suppliers Group, but it did bristle at additional transparency protocols aimed at its civilian nuclear power plants, pressing the United States to retreat from its Bush-era, post-9/11 pretense as self-appointed enforcer for nonproliferation agreements. Instead, the United States pragmatically endorsed political assurances from Brazil, no more a mere target regime of U.S.-dominated counterproliferation institutions but now an independent strategic partner.[18]

Growing independence meant more opportunity for Brazil to shift international alignments. Perhaps the most dramatic example unfolded when Brazil authored an initiative with NATO member Turkey to clear an alternative pathway for Iran out from beneath Western sanctions imposed against its nuclear activities.[19] The plan failed to gain traction, but it sent a clear message to the UN Security Council (plus Germany) that the West had room for flexibility in order to reach a nuclear settlement with Iran. U.S. irritation with Lula da Silva's improvisational diplomacy did not impede Brazil's several projects, including regional economic integration through the Southern Market (MERCOSUR) and the preliminaries for political cooperation that might enhance Brazil's voice in global affairs through the Southern Union (UNASUR) and the India/Brazil/South Africa group (IBSA). For many years, the BRIC acronym simply announced that certain large countries with untapped reserves of labor were preparing to overturn the status quo in the global economy. More recently, however, Brazil, Russia, India, China—and South Africa—have met to discuss creating a new institutional development bank, an alternative source of capital that would further shake the old Bretton Woods system by competing against the World Bank.[20]

Within its own region, Brazil has managed to sustain a semihard balancing strategy in order to check securitization of U.S. policy in Latin America.[21] While Lula's center-left administration dedicated additional resources toward poverty reduction, it hardly ignored defense, maintaining active peacekeeping capability, supporting the company Embraer's global position in the market for military aircraft, and investing in the Brazilian Navy, including plans for a nuclear submarine and modernization of the *São Paulo* aircraft carrier.[22] These defense measures did not balance the United States in the traditional sense of being able to challenge the hegemon militarily, but when UNASUR defense ministers, without the United States, met to discuss cooperative security in the region, Brazil's voice, buttressed by clearly superior defense budgets, carried extra weight. When U.S. planning documents offended several Latin American countries by describing a 2009 basing rights agreement with Colombia as providing new platforms for exerting American influence against hostile governments in South America, Brazil was in position to reinforce Venezuela's efforts to reverse the accord without tarring itself in Hugo Chavez's radicalism. In fact, when the Colombian Constitutional Court rejected the treaty, the new Colombian president and former defense minister, Juan Manuel Santos, declined to restart the political process, which would have required passage through the Colombian Congress in order to save the expansive basing agreement with the United States.[23]

Even with its recent economic growth and political development, Brazil cannot defeat the United States on the battlefield. It will not likely surpass China as the obvious Number Two, which would attempt to clip the hegemon and carve its own sphere of influence, reprising the role of classical Athens—and many subsequent challengers to world order across the centuries. Nevertheless, Brazil's growing independence matters for U.S. international leadership. Brazil's foreign policy already affects the costs for the United States of maintaining hegemony, in key areas such as promoting freer trade, discouraging proliferation of nuclear weapons, and stabilizing fragile states that drag on the American-sponsored international order. While science and technology are neither necessary nor sufficient for U.S.-Brazil democratic cooperation, a positive S&T relationship facilitates productive bilateral interaction in general. Many of the strategic concerns drawing together the United States and Brazil involve significant S&T content. Moreover, success in the realm of science and technology can spill over into economic and political discussions of the relationship.

Unfortunately, as in other cases of S&T diplomacy, the United States with Brazil has zeroed in on the technology implications of joint research and product transfer, fixing narrowly on direct links between scientific advance and reified commercial or military capabilities. This tunnel vision yet constricts the opportunity for pure science—the joint exploration of Nature—to leaven the threat and diffuse suspicions inherent in asymmetric power relations. Rhetorical niceties notwithstanding, U.S. scientific diplomacy cuts too quickly to the chase, the technological payout (or payoff), before trust can be established.

This pernicious tendency creates at least two problems for the United States in its quest for international influence. For any pole in the international system, state-to-state trust, especially when a diplomatic partner may soon cross the threshold to Great Power status, is crucial as an ingredient for conserving authority and extending international leadership.[24] Secondly, without trust, it will be exceedingly difficult for a lead state, including the liberal-democratic United States, to gain full appreciation for its interlocutor's scientific and therefore technological potential. Crudely lumping science with technology brusquely swipes away the choicest fruits available over time from S&T cooperation; this can only retard informal networks across national boundaries and stunt the growth of bilateral relationships that ought to be undergirding liberal hegemony. Should the United States place more emphasis on pure science diplomacy rather than S&T innovation, it will find a capable partner awaiting the shift toward joint science in Brazil.

Brazil's Worthy Scientific Portfolio

Brazil boasts a large land area, temperate climate, and rich natural resources. On the basis of these fundamentals, it might be expected that the country would fare well in a globalized economy. The record shows, in fact, that Brazil has experienced periods of great success, and except for one midcentury span, stretching from Depression-era suppression of U.S. manufacturing to the post–World War II peak in Latin American import-substitution industrialization (ISI) policies, Brazilian economic miracles may be attributed to surging export revenues driven by high commodity prices. Notably, Brazilian science—the Complexo Público de Ensino Superior e de Pesquisa (CPESP), or the "triple helix" of government-university-business—has not, apparently, boosted Brazil to the rank of twenty-first-century emerging powers nor accelerated the country's internal development.[25]

The tiny share of high value-added goods and services among Brazil's exports, however, does not imply a vacuum or hapless ignorance for Brazilian science. In fact, with respect to fields of study such as physics and medicine, Brazil can point to a proud tradition of accomplishment and a research establishment that came into its own, negotiating a complicated relationship with the state—balancing subordination and professional autonomy—around the same time that public policy debates broached these issues in the United States.[26] Now, a century later, Brazil supports a robust network of state universities, federal universities, and research institutes capable of producing scientific contributions to high international standards. The problem is not a lack of scientific potential in Brazil. Rather, the difficulty is diplomatic: Brazilian scientists must surmount a number of hurdles before they engage their U.S. counterparts in joint research. As will become apparent, several of the most important of these obstacles lie within the ambit of U.S. science and technology policy and, specifically, with neglect of the science component in scientific diplomacy.

The Scientific Tradition in Brazil

Historical conditions of inequality differentiate Brazil's scientific trajectory from those of other powerful states in Europe and the United States. Yet, centuries as a possession of Portugal, decades as a pawn of global finance centered in London, and another century struggling against the bonds of underdevelopment and widespread poverty have not precluded the establishment and replication of a thin but wealthy and sophisticated elite atop Brazilian society. As we have seen through the surprisingly productive record of science in authoritarian states, it does not take much, only a tiny cadre of talented investigators, to found science for the nation, and this small community may survive, even flourish, under general conditions of severe political and economic inequality. Across advanced liberal-democratic, authoritarian, and developing countries, similar pressures jeopardize scientific autonomy though these forces, it turns out, may be weaker within the lesser developed world. Certainly, less capital is available, in private coffers or the public treasury, for massive investment in big science. At the same time, Brazilian scientists, particularly those sheltered by the state and dedicated to basic research, will be reluctant to surrender their hard-earned freedom of inquiry without dramatic benefits in additional labor or superior equipment that could come from closer collaboration with a scientific powerhouse. These scientists may prove surprisingly independent, driving hard bargains in S&T cooperation with reputable organizations in Europe or the United States.

Back in the age of empire, from the founding of Rio de Janeiro in 1565 to Dom Pedro I's declaration of an independent monarchy in 1822, Europe's main interest in Brazil was mercantilist rather than scientific, extracting raw materials or producing commodities—gold, sugar, and wood—for export back to the motherland. Of the three elemental motivations attributed for the conquest of Iberoamérica—Gold, Glory, and God—gold or profit were attained most of all. Even after independence shattered imperial ambitions of the new constitutional monarchy in Lisbon, and Catholicism's traditional hold over souls in Brazil receded under waves of indigenous custom and the steady pull of modern secular preferences, the exclusive elite—landowners, *coronéis* (colonels), and eventually a select few industrialists—remained in charge and well compensated from Brazil's natural bounty. Science, then, during this early period, in line with the modernist model of George Basalla, consisted of explorers, surveyors, and collectors sampling the alien environment and sending specimens back to laboratories in Europe.[27]

Dom Pedro I's assertion of sovereignty for Brazil favored a budding faction of the elite that believed the country's destiny lay in its capacity to centralize power in Rio de Janeiro, in tightening the sinews of order across Brazil's diverse expanse. This plan cried out for scientific activity that could flourish apart from the centers of learning in Europe, but, the nationalist ambitions of Dom Pedro I and his son, Dom Pedro II, notwithstanding, science at the highest standards was still a cosmopolitan enterprise. To achieve progress in Brazil, just as capital was required from Britain, transmission of new knowledge and scientific feedback were vital from London, Berlin, and Paris.

The advent of republicanism at the end of the nineteenth century adjusted the balance of influence within Brazil once again between national power brokers and regional masters of the economic engines in areas such as Minas Gerais and São Paulo. The reapportionment of political power along with the rise of new constituencies, especially labor and a small but vibrant professional class in urban centers, opened the way for broader cultural communication with Europe. Marked by newly widened avenues and fin de siècle architecture in Rio, Brazil latched onto the notion, also prevalent among North American elites, to import best practices from the Old World and adapt them for their own nation's modernization. It was this dynamic era—of dramatic export growth and liberal optimism—that attracted young historian Nancy Stepan's attention when she challenged Basalla's diffusion hypothesis and placed the beginnings of genuine Brazilian science, "as an organized, institutional endeavor," early, around 1900, with the birth and subsequent achievements of the Oswaldo Cruz Institute at Manguinhos (Rio).[28]

By the time the Rockefeller Foundation of New York initiated cooperative projects with the institute in the 1920s, Brazil had founded scientific centers in Rio and São Paulo, and the best of these had already contributed to the country's reputation for scientific work in tropical medicine.[29] Professor Stepan's later work on the history of international efforts to eradicate killer diseases like yellow fever, malaria, and eventually AIDS—epidemics that could cripple a developing nation's productivity and damage its international standing—revealed a daunting landscape. The field for joint research that might inspire life-saving advances in public health programs was strewn with seemingly permanent obstacles that might hamper progress today as much as they did for Rockefeller at the beginnings of Brazilian science.[30]

Throughout twentieth-century history of S&T diplomacy, field scientists and program directors from the United States *did not know* what they did not know as they encountered Brazil; they alternately underestimated and overestimated Brazilian capacity at different moments. Stepan recounted how Rockefeller Foundation scientists during the 1920s deprecated important findings of Oswaldo Cruz's successor, Carlos Chagas, as director of the Cruz Institute on the evolution of the trypanosome infection from acute to chronic stages in its human hosts. The Americans disagreed, without actually being more advanced, on sanitation methods for eliminating parasites from village water supplies and on the significance of large nonimmune populations for disease transmission. At the same time, the American foundation overestimated Chagas's ability to unify "tropical science" in Brazil, despite the several distinguished posts he held. Like Chagas, Rockefeller scientists were caught on their heels when yellow fever returned to ravage Rio de Janeiro—a modern, Europeanized capital city—the antithesis of remote backwaters in the late 1920s where potential sources of infection had escaped the attention of joint public health efforts.[31] Laying an unfortunate precedent for future bilateral relations, the ambition and nationalist sensitivities of Brazilian elites meshed uneasily with the arrogance and persistent stereotyping of well-financed North Americans.

By raising the stakes with outside money, scientific expertise, and political influence, U.S. advisers and patrons exacerbated divisions within republican

Brazil. Resistance from poor, uneducated inhabitants of Rio against mandatory vaccination and eradication programs imposed by seemingly unaccountable authorities had occurred a generation before, threatening the reputation of Oswaldo Cruz himself. In the 1920s, public health experts also challenged a local clinical tradition in Brazil that had grown treating influential individuals in Rio and other cities who could afford the care. The new-style Brazilian scientists not only brushed aside social norms of medical practice, they appeared to do so with backing from a foreign power.

When a 1930 coup inspired by Getúlio Vargas ended the Old Republic, the Brazilian state became more centralized. On the one hand, tighter control over the Paulista coffee producers and nascent industrialists of the southeast made it easier for foreign agencies to insert themselves in the capital where they could leverage federal bureaucracy in order to establish novel programs in departments across the country. At the same time Vargas's nationalism erected barriers of mistrust that complicated sharing of results and transfer of new ideas—in both directions—with respect to the United States. As the 1930s wore on, the Rockefeller Foundation, still a lead player in US scientific outreach, shifted toward basic research—and away from Brazil. With the advent of Vargas's *Estado Novo*, scientific relations with the national government turned even more programmatic. Rather than exploring together, U.S. doctors in Rio lent their margin of expertise to help administrate health services for the populist national government.[32]

Nevertheless, as in other cases of centralizing state institutions and increasing authoritarianism—in Nazi Germany and Stalinist Russia, for example—science continued; indeed, it flourished as a kind of refuge. In the decades before World War II, science departments at the state university of São Paulo improved their capacity for teaching and research, laying the foundation for a fateful transition from a coffee economy to one that would attract scientific and engineering talent.[33] Within half a century, São Paulo would become the largest city in South America and one of the largest industrialized population concentrations in the world. Getúlio Vargas asserted strict control over the state's major constituencies, the military, landowners, business elites, and the burgeoning labor force, but for sciences like biology and physics he permitted relatively high levels of autonomy. After 1929 the Academia Brasileira de Ciências (Brazil's National Academy of Sciences) in Rio actually consolidated its network and regularized its journal output under Vargas, and it would continue to thrive under the *Estado Novo*.[34] The parallel development of state-sponsored institutions exemplified in São Paulo and a nationally oriented scientific community in Rio established a pattern of dual systems for S&T achievement in Brazil. By the beginning of the twenty-first century, both state and federal universities in several Brazilian cities (USP, São Paulo [state]; UNICAMP, Campinas, outside of São Paulo [state]; UFRJ, Rio [federal]; UFMG, Minas Gerais [federal]; UFRGS, Rio Grande do Sul [federal]; UFSP, São Paulo [federal]) had cemented their scientific reputations.[35]

Considering the polarized political movements of 1930s Brazil and the authoritarian turn taken by the state—in part to control inter-regional and class conflicts—the blossoming of a decentralized scientific establishment, fostering perhaps the very best faculty and research teams in rival São Paulo, set a remarkable contrast.[36] It was as if scientific activity was sufficiently neutral and yet so important for the prestige, and perhaps the political-economy, of the *Estado Novo* that departments of scientific research, despite their relative independence, enjoyed a certain amount of protection from political interference. Unlike many endeavors organic to the Brazilian state under Vargas, science engendered moderate and ultimately productive competition between federal and local identities. Even without close diplomatic alignment toward the United States and admiration, albeit temporary, for fascism in Italy and prewar Germany, authoritarian Brazil managed to grow both a dual-university system and a politically heterodox scientific community that helped lay the foundation for modernization, industrial growth, and eventual democratization, largely on Brazil's own terms.

Modern Brazil and Eternal Diplomatic Courtship

In thinking about Brazil's development, two seismic shifts help explain the polite distance enduring between the United States, the hemisphere's sole Great Power, and Brazil, Latin America's most viable candidate for subregional hegemon. The awkward courtship already described for scientific cooperation and associated S&T policy both reflected and contributed to disappointments in the broader bilateral relationship. Brazil's leaders understood that modernization would be far more difficult, perhaps impossible, without guidance from the North Americans. At the same time, Brazil's historical trajectory was too independent and its national potential too strong to simply float in the wake of the United States.

In general, the dramatic arc of Latin American states after independence traced a tragic sequence—portentous attempts at inclusive economic growth and greater human freedom followed by collapse of foreign demand, widespread impoverishment, rising inequality, and violent authoritarianism.[37] On those occasions when Brazil gathered its considerable resources and fortified its political will to break this cycle, U.S. advice and foreign assistance received due consideration. The United States, however, never managed to inspire sufficient trust to forge the grand alliance with Brazil that might yet achieve those best hopes for the hemisphere customarily articulated at Pan American summits. Economic modernization under President Juscelino Kubitschek in the late 1950s built a new glittering capital on the remote plains of Brasilia, a developing giant's bold architectural claim to mastery in the aerospace age, but modernization instead descended into bureaucratic authoritarianism and in relatively short order under military rule a Lost Decade of anemic growth and hyperinflation. A generation later, with the United States preoccupied by the "war on terror" and consequent military operations in Afghanistan and Iraq, Brazil challenged liberal orthodoxy. While fulfilling the country's international financial commitments, Workers' Party (PT) president Luiz Inácio Lula da Silva increased state involvement in other areas of national policy, including environmental protection, social spending, and management of industry champions like the oil giant Petrobras. During both Brazilian springs in the late 1950s and again in the late 2000s, the country blossomed on the world scene by mixing attractive policies inviting international engagement with prickly nationalism. At the level of science diplomacy, both eras offered opportunities for breakthrough collaboration with U.S. science and technology that were never quite consummated. Like their bilateral relationship in general, science enterprises within Brazil and the United States seemed caught somehow in an eternally frustrated courtship.

Kubitschek's meteoric presidency enthralled post-Vargas Brazil during the heyday of import-substitution industrialization and the emergence of a military-industrial complex for space exploration in the world's most advanced economies. Brazil's vigorous response was to prop up its own complex without accepting dependence on any international partner. U.S. assistance would be called upon in the nuclear field, particularly in the immediate aftermath of President Vargas's 1954 suicide, and in space technology, the precursor to Brazil's premier space research institute (INEP) worked with the U.S. National Aeronautics and Space Agency (NASA) as soon as the 1960s.[38] Yet, within twenty years Brazil would have its own Nuclear Energy Research Institute (IPEN), its own National Nuclear Energy Commission (CNEN), and diplomatic agreements with West Germany in order to score technology transfer and advances against its regional rival, Argentina, on programs related to producing nuclear weapons; with respect to space, the strongly anticommunist military government would permit the technologists to select Red China as the primary partner for satellite programs connected to environmental remote sensing.[39]

Late in the period of the Second Republic, two major science and technology institutions organized in the industrial region surrounding São Paulo. The Brazilian Air Force established Comando-Geral de Tecnologia Aerospacial (CTA, High Command for Aerospace Technology) in 1953 and Brazil's "MIT," the State University of Campinas (UNICAMP) opened in 1962. Even before Labor Party president João Goulart's call for revolutionary change in the economy and the consequent military coup of 1964, the Brazilian state tipped its hand on postwar science and technology policy: the lion's share of investment would be directed toward applied research in order to attain focused and perforce narrow technological competencies; moreover, those technological achievements would primarily serve the aims of national defense or national industry champions friendly to the military.

The aging populist president, Getúlio Vargas, had signed Petrobras into existence in 1953, and the state oil company would continue to flourish under military rule, constructing in Rio its CENPES (Centro de Pesquisas), the "largest research and development center in Latin America," by 1968.[40] Embratel, the state communications company after 1965, at first purchased the right to operate foreign-built satellites in geostationary orbit. As Embratel began to develop its own technology, it benefited indirectly from space infrastructure produced through activities rooted in the São Paulo military industrial complex and coordinated by INEP, the Brazilian civil space agency at nearby São Jose dos Campos.[41] The linkage between Embraer, the state aircraft company, and the Brazilian Air Force's CTA was even closer, with Embraer's first operational buildings in 1970 situated next to the CTA campus, again at São Jose dos Campos.[42]

In the years since democratization, *civil* organization and sponsorship of scientific research have expanded through the Brazilian Research Council (CNPq) and Brazil's agency for financing innovation (FINEP), both of which operate under the Ministry of Science and Technology (MCT) in Brasilia. MCT is aware that while the quantity of peer-reviewed scientific papers produced in Brazil has climbed skyward, high-technology exports remain frustratingly earthbound.[43] Part of the explanation for the chasm between pure science and commercial development in Brazil may be path dependency in Brazil's S&T

profile: at midcentury and through the early economic growth years of military rule, massive state-directed investments set the course for technological innovation in a way that limited spillover benefits for small-scale entrepreneurs who might have followed an independent creative impulse and facilitated access for private-sector scientists and engineers. Freelance commercial innovation might have perturbed the tense protocol holding together military, state, and society in Brazil under bureaucratic authoritarianism.

Brazil's second spectacular run at modernization in the twentieth century was different, in that it took place as part of democratic consolidation—democracy's dawn rather than its twilight phase. Despite additional opportunities provided by globalization, including rising international demand for commodities and increased foreign investment to fuel domestic industrialization, Brazil as late as 2010 still had not overcome some of the same challenges that have plagued it since the beginnings of Brazilian science.[44] Even after constructing a reputable university system and inventing a third way—a political economy that took account of global norms promoting financial responsibility while it combated grinding inequality at home—Brazil neither sought nor received a firm embrace from the United States, in the realm of science or across the bilateral relationship. In general, U.S.-Brazil diplomacy remained cast as it was in 1900 and 1950: replete with unrealized potential.

This latest opening for a more productive arrangement between Brazilian science and the state came with the taming of inflation during the mid-1990s. Fernando Henrique Cardoso, a famed social scientist and dependency theorist of the late-1970s, led the implementation of the *Real* Plan as finance minister for Brazil's struggling young democracy. Using a multistage process that bewildered Cardoso's old allies on the left, the plan introduced a new currency that, among other things, mounted a psychological attack on inertial inflation by challenging public pessimism regarding future price increases. The plan was aided by improving economic fundamentals and a willingness on the part of Brazilians to accept cheap imports, relatively high interest rates, and, relatedly, new waves of privatization and foreign investment.

So successful was Brazil's genuflection before international markets that despite the understandable resistance from state governors desiring greater federal spending and protests from the left at the government's weak support for wages and social programs, even Lula, Cardoso's chief opponent from the Workers' Party (PT), as president continued many of Cardoso's financial measures, actually embellishing them in remarkable instances such as the early repayment of IMF loans in 2005. Moreover, Brazil weathered two global financial crises, the so-called Asian Flu of 1997 and the U.S. housing collapse followed by the credit crunch of 2008, without suffering deep recession or the return of hyperinflation.

Despite positive economic trends and nearly a quarter-century of demo-cratic stability, there were surprisingly modest implications for Brazilian sci-ence. With inflation under control since the *Real* Plan, relative openness to foreign investment, and spurts of economic growth that created the potential at least for nurturing new globally competitive industries as well as tackling age-old inequalities of Brazilian society, it was reasonable to entertain hopes for a breakout of Brazilian science. The scientific enterprise, for example, might have followed the path of Brazil's regime to become more democratic, reaching out to train talented individuals from more sectors of society and helping to expand the professional class, in geographic terms and as a percentage of the labor force. Consistent with this expansion and the incubation of new indus-tries, S&T activities in Brazil might have spread beyond the military-industrial complex led by the cluster of aerospace institutions around São Paulo. Scien-tific innovation might have become more civilianized, so that observers during the information age could detect, as in the United States, "spin-on" from com-mercial advances to military practice.[45] Brazilian science, in other words, might have finally broken free of its postcolonial shell, cutting its dependence on Eu-ropean standards or North American grants and increasing its responsiveness to modern Brazil's economic and social challenges.

In fact, maturation of Brazilian science and technology has remained quite limited. Knowledge transfer in economics and agronomy *does* appear to have taken root in Brazil, generating large-scale success stories under Brazilian con-trol: the Lula administration's leadership of Pink Tide policies in Latin America that combined aspects of global capitalism with democratic socialism; explo-sive growth of the soybean industry at the same time Brazil addressed, under critical glare of the global spotlight, protection of its Amazon rain forest; and, again on international development's center stage, policy formulation for a ris-ing middle-income country with a clean energy profile. Nevertheless, the prin-cipal-agent relationship between science and the Brazilian state is yet mired in suspicion and mutual recrimination.

Recent troubles in GDP growth left analysts scratching their heads, won-dering whether Brazil might be switching places with benighted Mexico.[46] Key leaders of the Workers' Party (though Lula himself was not charged) were convicted, including Lula's first chief of staff, on continuation of patron-client corruption in the form of *mensalão*, sequential payments to literally buy votes in the legislature.[47] These legal cases demonstrated rising governmental accountability and transparency to the public, but they resurrected the specter of cross-party technocratic elites cynically buying off elected representatives of the people, *excluding* the public in order to carry out centralized modernization plans parallel to constitutional checks-and-balances. The traditional *jeito*, the system of favors that plagued both the Vargas era and bureaucratic authoritarianism of the 1970s, may live on to infect the present democracy.[48] If so, there remains a daunting obstacle to healthy relations between scientific experts and the Brazilian state.

While the dual university structure is still in place to educate the children of provincial and national elites, secondary education for the population at large scores far below developed country standards, especially in math and the basic sciences. This means that Brazilian science in important respects is frozen in its Old World guise; despite successive waves of democracy, it cannot yet serve effectively as a channel for social mobility. If much of the middle class and almost none of the lower classes in Brazil can partake of quality science education, much of the nation's human potential, its seed corn for germinating truly novel ideas in theory, experimentation, and engineering, is, generation after generation, needlessly wasted.

The very soil for small-scale entrepreneurship—an important source of new jobs and economic growth in developing countries—does not exist without successful secondary education. In the case of Brazil's state-directed development, widespread ignorance of science along with suffocating bureaucratic red tape prevents agile small firms from springing up to break new commercial ground and keep the industrial giants alert.[49] Brazil's national champions drove modernization and urbanization within the country under military rule but failed to revise Brazil's export profile.[50] In the Lost Decade of the 1980s, this disappointment could be chalked up to long-run limitations of import-substitution industrialization; after a while state protection for home industries that prevented them from having to compete with foreign companies turned into a handicap that kept them from entering global markets.[51]

Even today, when the model of export-led growth followed in the Asia-Pacific is widely admired, Brazil's champions still struggle to avoid humiliating missteps. In spite of its enormous research and development center (CNEP) in Rio, Petrobras, the nation's largest oil company and symbol of the state's pledge to reserve the land's abundance for the benefit of Brazilians, faltered in tapping billions of barrels deposited in the presalt layer offshore. The discoveries of the mid-2000s were supposed to make Brazil, once bedeviled by spiking oil imports, a global energy powerhouse, but technical difficulties were exacerbated when the Brazilian government insisted that Petrobras retain control of the fields at the same time the government redistributed company profits— that is, potential R&D funds, for social purposes. Petrobras, after fifty years of state-directed operations, still needed foreign companies with deep-water experience to transfer technology but had little to offer in return for fear that outside oil corporations, if permitted to buy a normal concession, for example, would protect their monopoly on scientific know-how and once again collect the value-added premium on Brazilian raw materials.[52] Unable to extract the oil on its own, Brazil essentially blocked everyone else from the presalt layer, thereby demolishing the resource's present value, allowing time for discovery of other options such as North American shale, and clouding Brazil's future as a global leader in the politics of energy.

Petrobras's difficulties in meeting the presalt challenge illustrate the strong connections between competence, trust, and productive cooperation. The mechanism holds domestically as well as at the level of international diplomacy. For the United States during World War II and the Soviet Union after the atomic bomb, it was possible for the state to sponsor a talented scientific elite in order to make rapid progress on weapons development. Yet, national development and global economic leadership are long-term ventures. Without effective secondary education in science and engineering, a trust gap eventually developed between the knowledge experts and the people; this was problematic for any powerful state but particularly acute for a democratic one. Brazil's new democracy is not immune from the principal-agent problem posed by a national science establishment.

While elite public opinion urges the state to keep a close rein on national champions like Petrobras in order to ensure the company fulfills its social responsibilities, similar concerns migrate toward pure scientists researching at universities and directing grants from the state, earmarked funds usually tied to the Ministry of Science and Technology in Brasilia. Given the international prestige and publication record of Brazilian science, there can be little complaint that scientific excellence is for some reason impossible to cultivate in developing Brazil. The critics, however, do impugn the relevance of Brazilian scientists.[53] How, indeed, can the heavily centralized Brazilian state harness knowledge for economic and social purposes by setting aside sinecures for academic nobility? Elite scientists, it appears, justify their independence by invoking developed country standards that lionize unfettered inquiry, which relieves certain Brazilian professors, according to the critics, of having to answer key questions put to other publicly funded programs—namely, how their investigations result in net benefit for the country as a whole.

Into this inhospitable climate enter U.S. S&T diplomats. The United States as hegemon may take genuine interest in promoting global science, conceiving it as a public good. Yet, outstanding features of the U.S. diplomatic approach seem designed to cause friction and raise suspicions within rising powers like Brazil. At one level, Brazil, with accomplished scientific institutions of its own, has grown beyond the need or desire for tutelage. On another level, though, the Brazilian state is conflicted and insecure about how well its expert scientific agents are serving society. The United States, despite all it has to offer in the realm of science, comes on quite strong, insistent on apolitical scientific objectivity for distinguishing quality research at the same time it trumpets technological productivity—the direct economic payoff—from S&T/R&D investment. Given the ambivalent status of science in Brazilian society, democratically accountable officials in Brazil can hardly formulate an appropriate response to U.S. proposals at once ham-fisted and garishly clothed in amour propre.

U.S. Scientific Diplomacy toward Brazil

Given the range of issues animating the U.S.-Brazil relationship, there is significant overlap with S&T concerns as well as the opportunity for spillover to matters of high politics. On item after item in the science and technology category, the U.S. team engages their Brazilian counterparts true to form, and given Brazil's potential—military, economic, political, cultural, and scientific—the results somehow fall short of expectations.

The U.S. style of scientific diplomacy reflects its leadership position in world politics. The United States speaks more than it observes or listens. In addition, because of its decentralized governmental structure, the United States actually talks with many voices. These voices represent different, sometimes competing, missions of the U.S. government. Yet, they all overwhelm potential interlocutors with promises of technological—not necessarily scientific—progress and future diplomatic favor from the United States. At the highest political level, this hash of confusing offers, of course, only amounts to much if the United States maintains the Number One world ranking adorning its science diplomacy, and it maximizes the chances of hoisting those honors once again if it manages to profit more than its partners from whatever technological advances emerge out of joint investigation.

In the example of U.S. scientific diplomacy toward Brazil, a governmental agency previously mentioned as a prototype for executing mission-oriented S&T policy at home also serves as an important marker, a bellwether, for S&T outreach abroad.[54] The Office of Naval Research (ONR) was the first U.S. government agency after the transformative experience of World War II to scout abroad for scientific talent. ONR-Global began in London, where there had been in-house collaboration on naval technological development with the British before America's entry into the war. Amid the smoldering destruction of the Allied offensive, ONR-Global helped sustain the postwar effort to rescue German science—particularly physics and chemistry.[55] As years passed and U.S. competition against the Soviet Union metastasized into a global rivalry, ONR's foreign interests expanded, especially toward Japan and East Asia.[56] The end of the Cold War did not curtail the navy's S&T outreach: new offices opened, including a Singapore "detachment" in 2000 and the Prague Office in 2010. In addition, ONR-Global dedicated some of its scouting resources to the Americas, but despite Brazil's long-term investment and impressive scientific footprint relative to the rest of Latin America, ONR-Global situated its South American outpost with a reliable *diplomatic* partner in Santiago, Chile, in 2002, around the time Lula was finally winning election to his first term as president of Brazil.[57]

Lula and U.S. president George W. Bush approached problems of economic development from opposite ends of the ideological spectrum, but this clash of world views, as has been mentioned, did not prevent them from agreeing on a host of issues. When Bush's vision of a free trade area for all the Americas was finally crushed at the unruly summit in 2005, it was Hugo Chavez of Venezuela and Nestor Kirchner of Argentina who accepted credit from the Latin American left and then took the blame from the United States. Lula, meanwhile, invited Bush to his private residence in Brasilia, and although the two presidents failed to reconcile trade priorities, Lula assured the press that "bilateral relations were going through 'one of their best moments ever.'"[58] If serious policy differences could not poison U.S.-Brazil cooperation in general, it is puzzling why ONR-Global, publicly committed to science and technology advancement, could not reside in Brasilia or São Paulo—in other words, a major hub for the best science and engineering in the region.

The real reasons for this missed opportunity are not ones that either side would care to advertise, but political difficulties likely played a role. In addition to being an expression of the U.S. approach to S&T policy, ONR-Global offices reward the host country. Professional scientists embody the U.S. Navy's technological sophistication, and without the expense or pomp of a battle fleet at a port of call they remind allies that U.S. superiority at sea is dedicated in part to their protection. Siting an ONR office sends a signal of importance that the host country matters to U.S. strategic calculations, and confidence that the host can maintain discretion and positively contribute in the rarefied company where scientific discovery meets technological innovation. Although ONR recruits specialized personnel and has developed a reputation for unique problem-solving skills, the agency cannot buck the evolutionary trend toward greater democratic accountability; ONR cannot easily divorce itself from its mission sponsor.

Brazil may have the most impressive science portfolio in Latin America, but it did not align well with what ONR-Global could offer. In the 2000s, Brazil wanted to establish its military competency and a global reputation for excellence in regional peacekeeping; it pursued uranium enrichment without desiring to share data according to the most stringent nonproliferation protocol; it wanted to build its own rockets for launching payloads into orbit; it hoped to extend operations of its refurbished aircraft carrier and develop a nuclear-powered submarine. Modern, democratic Brazil angled toward an independent military presence on the global stage—it would concede policy disputes in order to promote cooperation, but it was not willing to submit its national military, economic, or scientific efforts to U.S. influence, since, as a rising regional power, it harbored strong suspicions about the long-term benefits of U.S. protection. ONR-Global negotiated using the idiom of science and technology/research and development, but it *acted* on behalf of U.S. interests through the development of better systems for performing U.S. military missions.[59] In the end, ONR's S&T outreach—its best foot forward in terms of committing a regional headquarters—confronted Brazil with daunting prospects for international security competition that were inseparable from, conjoined institutionally with, the hegemon's offer of deeper cooperation.

The pattern of seemingly irresistible opportunity for joint scientific progress and a robust technological harvest, then soul-searching about what might have been and solemn resolutions to do better in the future, has endured since the time of the Rockefeller Foundation's forays into tropical medicine and to-day extends beyond S&T agencies associated with the U.S. military. It is true that the Department of Defense's S&T rangers must constantly justify their own bureaucratic survival by demonstrating a military payoff from cooperative science projects, and for the case of Brazilian research and development in par-ticular, this modus operandi exacerbates sensitivities along the host country's own civil-military fault line. Yet, the first grand initiative for U.S. scientific di-plomacy toward Brazil preceded World War II; it featured not the U.S. Defense Department but Rockefeller's foundation from U.S. civil society; it focused not on weapons development but eradication of tropical disease in the Brazilian hinterland. The bittersweet legacy in *civilian* science from a hundred years ago lives on today through projects related to energy and the environment. As in the Rockefeller precedent, some good has been accomplished, but much re-mains to be done.

During the latter stages of the military regime when the balance of influ-ence gradually shifted from the *duros* of the ruling junta in favor of soft-lin-ers, U.S. agronomy did help modernize Brazilian agriculture. Soon after the democratic transition and once inflation was brought under control, Brazilian soybean production climbed steadily, from roughly 1 million bushels in 1994 to 2.6 billion bushels in 2010.[60] In other aspects, however, this scientific diplomacy was not a complete success. It did not lead to a flowering of "tropical science" in Brazil. Economically, it benefited mainly a few well-connected companies; plus, increased productivity—as in cases of other industries—raised incentives to clear more land, aggravating tensions with the landless rural population and jeopardizing Brazil's unique environmental resources, especially its shrinking Amazon rain forest.[61]

Improved productivity spilled over to Brazil's traditional crops such as sugar cane. Because of this grass's high heating value, Brazil's dominant position in world sugar production—over twice the weight of India, its nearest compet-itor in 2010—had major implications for the international politics of energy. Appropriately enough, Brazil and the United States concluded a biofuels agree-ment in 2007 with a touted provision on joint research.[62] Indeed, the United States, by far the largest oil consumer, and Brazil, the second largest ethanol producer with potential to greatly expand its exports, held complementary in-terests. Yet, just behind the glowing surface of publicized scientific cooperation festered the old nemesis of trade competition. Less efficient corn producers in the midwestern United States did not relish the specter of cheap sugar-based imports flooding in from Brazil.[63] A refined Brazilian brand could undercut demand for homegrown ethanol before U.S. R&D investments in, for example, a novel transportation infrastructure that would open sufficient business for all suppliers could possibly pay off. Rather than scientific collaboration on biofuels deepening U.S.-Brazil diplomacy as hoped, atavistic trade jealousies would likely dampen advancement of joint science and spoil the U.S. image as a benevolent hegemon.

Within the sprawling U.S. science establishment, the National Institute of Standards and Technology (NIST) boasts one of the strongest records of accomplishment in the basic sciences.[64] The agency's Nobel-caliber scientists enjoy unusual autonomy as they pursue the physics of measurement to the extremes of precision—extending the theory of atomic decay, if necessary, in order to reliably mark the passage of time.[65] Again, motivated by growing U.S. interest in Brazil rising, NIST increased collaboration with its natural partner in Brasilia, the Instituto Nacional de Metrologia, Qualidade, e Tecnologia (IN-METRO), opening the door for intensified joint work at the level of pure science. Not surprisingly, however, public accounts of NIST-INMETRO activity fixate on economically significant negotiations related to future product standards that could in effect lower nontariff or technical barriers to trade (TBTs, in the argot of the World Trade Organization).[66] This layer of trade obstacles might indeed become quite salient, at such time when Brazil's export profile finally transforms toward a higher percentage of value-added technologies or the United States removes its own agricultural protections that have stood for more than a decade as explicit barriers to freer trade in the Americas. In any event, there is little outward indication that NIST, as one of few U.S. government agencies besides the Department of Defense with capacity for groundbreaking science, has aggressively pursued the scientific enterprise in its contact with Brazil despite conducting this very specialized diplomacy under the auspices of S&T policy.

In the field of education, where so many choices shaping service to constituents are taken by the public sector, ostensibly on behalf of citizens, one might expect to find autonomy and adequate flexibility to stave off usual democratic demand for immediate return on investment. After all, the university system—that is, linked institutions of higher education—is where most basic research in the United States and Brazil gets done. In line with its ambition to become a First World power, the Brazilian Congress passed an educational initiative seemingly consistent with the ideal of a Scientific State. Brazil's Science without Borders program (2011) set a target for sending 100,000 exchange students abroad, many of them to the United States, in order to study science, technology, engineering, and mathematics (STEM).[67] On its face and in light of the Obama administration's reciprocal 100,000 strong initiative for sponsoring U.S. students in Latin America, this constituted a massive government effort to boost scientific cooperation, mainly with the United States and leaders of the European science establishment. Moreover, this interaction would take place in university environments conducive to study of the universe and joint investigation for unlocking Nature's secrets rather than development of new commercial techniques for product manufacturing.

Upon closer inspection, however, the sort of educational exchange organized under Science without Borders accomplished less lofty ends. Sending thousands of students abroad required funding, and in order to implement the legislation, it was, despite indications of the government press release, written to require a substantial share of private sector grants—one outside Brazilian *Real* for every three *Reais* allocated by the Brazilian government.[68] The robust private support—and in the Brazilian program's first year the private call was oversubscribed—confirmed the logic of the Augustine Report back in the United States on the crisis in STEM education. Even under conditions of high U.S. unemployment, the corporate demand for skilled workers in STEM-related fields has remained intense. Such workers do not need to adopt the philosophy of the professional scientist or join the Republic of Science. They simply need adequate background and training in order to continue learning and acquiring new skills once they are inserted into the production chain. In fact, the Brazilian "science" scholarship typically funded just one undergraduate year of coursework at a foreign university, enough perhaps to cement a future engineer's commitment to complete training back home and contribute to profits for a national champion like Petrobras or Vale mining company.[69]

In other words, while Brazilian educational initiatives and the positive U.S. response espouse worthy goals, in practice these programs fall short of being transformational. In fact, they may reinforce the existing state-directed production profile in Brazil. Certainly, 100,000 subsidized STEM workers could make a difference in seeding a new corridor for small business innovation outside of São Paulo or Rio. Such a cadre might even be large and influential enough to organize Brazilian civil society in ways that improve understanding between the mass of ordinary citizens and the internationally oriented elite scientists at

Brazil's universities and research institutes. Unfortunately, the initial numbers quoted in the news are suspiciously small: six hundred students the first year, fewer than two thousand the next, and funding committed only through 2015. If the program doubled every year for five years, it will have reached just thirty thousand students. The budget years after 2015, then, are key, but program supporters will be asking a newly minted, democratically elected administration to make unprecedented investments for enrichment of STEM education.

Chances are that Brazilian politicians will make calculations similar to those of their American counterparts. During a national academic conference call, former U.S. State Department director of policy planning and current president of the Council on Foreign Relations Richard Haass was asked about the importance of government-sponsored cultural exchange programs.[70] The question came in the context of Haass's new book, *Foreign Policy Begins at Home*, which argued that in order to avoid squandering its hegemonic advantage in resources and losing influence abroad, America should repair its dysfunctional domestic politics, especially with respect to Washington debates on education, infrastructure refurbishment, and skilled immigration. Despite being personally disposed toward the philosophy and ideals behind scientific and cultural exchange programs, Haass reluctantly answered that in practice such initiatives are consequential only "at the margins." It is difficult to fathom how officials in Brazil's democracy will conclude differently or how millions of *Reais* spent on Science without Borders will not in reality pay for a select group of well-trained "Engineers within Brazil's Heavy Industries."

Balanced against this sort of cold pragmatism, nevertheless, is an instinctive idealism, also running through U.S. foreign policy, all the more poignant when expressed by the U.S. State Department's first director of policy planning and one of the founding fathers of American postwar realism.[71] Late in life, George Kennan, in line with many realists, believed that the United States had indeed squandered hegemonic resources by chasing democratic ideals. In remote corners of the global chessboard, Democratic and Republican presidents had wasted U.S. lives and treasure attempting to purify regimes whose unlikely redemption would in any case matter little to the strategic balance of power vis-à-vis the Soviet Union. Yet, despite his misgivings about imposing American morality on the internal affairs of other nations, Kennan insisted that U.S. policy ought to follow a moral code—that American hegemony should not and could not endure without high purpose to guide American power.

This purpose centered on preservation of the world in which the United

States was competing with other Great Powers. Echoing another great postwar realist, Hans Morgenthau, especially in Morgenthau's essay on prioritizing science over politics, Kennan reasoned that national interest was beside the point when states' single-minded pursuit of it led to nuclear war or ecological disaster.[72] Part of Brazil's potential as a Great Power yet lies in its environmental resources—its offshore petroleum reserves, precious minerals, fertile soil, and teeming rain forest. As the Brazilian state becomes more competent, as it finds ways to more efficiently mobilize the talents of its people to solve problems of national development, there is growing risk that Brazil could damage its own environment on such a scale that this disaster would constitute a grievous loss for the world.

Both the U.S. government and American scientists shared the concern voiced in Kennan's and Morgenthau's warnings. U.S. officials and epistemic communities outside the government, including environmental scientists, attempted to address ecological threats in Brazil. Brazil, in turn, responded positively to international efforts such as the Pilot Program to Conserve the Brazilian Rainforest (PPG7 to recognize the donations of rich G7 countries), offering compensation to Brazil after the UN's Rio Earth Summit in 1992 for preservation and sustainable development practices.[73] At first blush, this appears to be a case in which scientific concerns, including some interaction on environmental sciences, progressed from the margins toward the core of policy priorities. In another positive wrinkle, the U.S. hegemon gave financial support while allowing the United Nations and specialized nongovernmental organizations to take the lead in persuading Brazil to participate. Soft-pedaling implementation and ceding direct control over global environmental management undercut potential resistance based on the nationalist argument that Brazil, in accepting payments, was somehow submitting itself to U.S. imperial designs. The United Nations and NGOs, banking on their international scientific credibility, helped the United States hegemon avoid some of the usual liabilities attached to its bilateral scientific diplomacy.

Unfortunately, global environmental policy—in general and with respect to Brazil in particular—has not entirely succeeded. Despite the foundation of scientific data for enlightening sovereign actors in the international system as they balance risks to the environment in their policy agendas, neither the United States nor rising powers have reached consensus. While ecological catastrophe ought to be avoided, the United States and Brazil, for example, disagree on the marginal benefit of preserving the next hectare of rain forest and, even more important, on who should pay the opportunity cost of leaving it pristine. Brazilian politicians observe U.S. refusal to ratify the Kyoto Protocol under the UN Framework Convention on Climate Change, and global influence embracing the Amazon rain forest devolves from social construction of a cosmopolitan moral obligation to manufacture of a negotiable asset for Brazilian diplomacy. Heeding science and protecting the environment today are still on trial. In spite of their cosmopolitan moral purpose, they must somehow deliver prosaic benefits. Otherwise, in Brazilian democratic politics, conservation programs cannot compete with land use policies that promise accelerated national development.[74]

Scientific Autonomy and Hegemonic Diplomacy

Across the board, for military, economic, health, and environmental issues, items on the U.S.-Brazil bilateral agenda link to the state of science, not just application of the scientific method to engineering problems but improved theoretical understanding of how Nature works. This interrelation is both a blessing and a curse. On the one hand, it thrusts Gilpin's concept of the Scientific State into mainstream international politics, which historically have generated cycles of increasingly destructive Great Power war. When science as distinct from technology becomes the most reliable route to earthly power and influence, states are forced to reconsider the place of science in their own society *and* the role of scientists in diplomacy toward other powers. On the other hand, whatever moderating influence science might bring, it is largely counteracted by now familiar principal-agent dynamics—who or what guards the guardians in practice?

Brazil, especially when compared with other states in Latin America, possesses enviable scientific capacity in its dual university system, prestigious research institutes, and venerable professional societies. Yet, when the United States approaches Brazil, the North Americans cannot effectively separate their scientific leadership from perceptions of the United States as a traditional international hegemon. When science becomes an instrument of U.S. diplomacy, it loses its appeal for Brazil, as it does for other rising powers, which fear that pure scientific goals sooner or later must succumb to ulterior motives in the U.S. national interest. Small and temporary benefit of external funding for Brazilian science does not compensate the costs, from Brazil's perspective, of sliding further into the political maw of the American behemoth.

The Faustian bargain presented by the hegemon is made more hazardous by incompatibility between science establishments. When President Obama and President Rousseff meet, the U.S. head of state may offer closer scientific cooperation as part of an invigorated strategic partnership with Brazil. Yet, there is a limit to how strategic U.S. scientific diplomacy can be, given that the several agencies sponsoring scientific research are each accountable to a different government mission. Usually the main purpose of the parent department is some sort of constituency service, created by Congress as a body but in practice overseen by a specialized committee that is not in strategic synchronization with the whole of government.

Brazilian officials may observe, for example, that a branch of the U.S. Office of Naval Research-Global assigned to the Americas planted stakes in Santiago, Chile, rather than Brazil, Latin America's most advanced scientific state. Meanwhile, ONR-Global for Eastern Europe selected Prague, just a couple of years after the Pentagon's Missile Defense Agency (MDA) promised $600,000 in support of Czech science.[75] Wary candidates for partnership with U.S. science could be forgiven for suspecting that mission-related preferences of the navy or OSD in the case of missile defense heavily skewed U.S. investments nominally directed at international progress. The greatest exception to the incessantly competitive U.S. approach may be the semi-independent National Science Foundation (NSF), which has for its mission the promotion of basic research without the constant pressure of a specified technological application. Of course, the NSF budget is relatively tiny, a few billion dollars out of tens of billions spent annually by the U.S. government on science and technology, and NSF, unlike mission departments such as ONR or MDA, cannot sponsor foreign scientists. If Brazil or some other partner wishes to accept U.S. funds for science, in essence they must also sign on to a U.S. government mission.

For a couple of reasons, Brazil resists the U.S. amalgam of science-diplomacy. As a rising power with foreign policy ambitions of its own, Brazil has to examine U.S. proposals like a new technical standard from the NIST-IN-METRO collaboration very carefully because the scientific basis for new rules will be interweaved with U.S. trade interests. Secondly, as a developing country, Brazil built a more centralized science establishment than in the United States, with important network connections flowing toward a single hub—the MCT in Brasília. Furthermore, the federal science granting agencies in Brasília are separated from the technology hub in São Paulo, which remains embedded in the political culture of military aerospace. The thrust of U.S. diplomacy manages to land in the gulf between both scientific establishments without addressing Brazilian development. Brazil's pure scientists of international caliber are not as encumbered by government missions as their U.S. counterparts, especially those U.S. researchers already participating in scientific diplomacy. U.S. technologists, on the other hand, are not tied into military systems as frequently as their Brazilian opposite numbers in São Paulo. American-sponsored S&T projects, then, struggle to find a sweet spot between irrelevance in the Brazilian context and preoccupation there with any relative gains contra Brazil.

Faithful commitment to global scientific progress could possibly soften the image of the American hegemon, within its own hemisphere and among rising powers, as a leading state with the capability and political will to provide public goods for the international system. Counterproductively, the current mode of U.S. scientific diplomacy perpetuates an imbalance placing short-term interest oriented toward expanding the relative capabilities of the United States ahead of enlightened hegemony—that is, sustainable influence fostering a cosmopolitan vision, credible to arch-realists like Morgenthau and Kennan, and delivering basic needs for the international community of states.

Previously, in discussing science's influence on alternative democratic forms, it was suggested that a solemn national commitment to pure research—revealing the workings of Nature without necessarily having a technological application in train—would help resolve a classic principal-agent dilemma within democracies. In order for expert professions to assist a powerful state governed by and for masses of lay people, professionals needed to enjoy significant autonomy for taking decisions within their sphere of specialized knowledge. This, again, was the central insight animating Huntington's classic, *Soldier and the State*, focused on the military profession. It holds true for other professions such as law, medicine, engineering, and, in spite of contemporary crisis conditions, banking and finance. In Robert Gilpin's modernity—that is, the age of the Scientific State—each of these professions so relevant to the survival and prosperity of the hegemon is infused with the scientific ethos, none, of course, more than the state-sponsored, systematic inquiry into Nature, or, science itself.

Would autonomy of a similar sort to that which balances the Scientific State's domestic regime also work to improve effectiveness of its diplomacy? Indications from the United States/Brazil example, one in which the rising power has strong reasons to be wary of U.S. science as a potential Trojan horse, point to opportunity for revised scientific diplomacy. By credibly insulating basic research for scientific achievement from applied military and commercial technological development programs, it might lead the way toward mutually beneficial overall relationships supportive of international order. Implemented as part of bilateral diplomacy with other "strategic partners," a fresh embrace of pure science could help sustain hegemony for a Second American Century.

6   Science and Global Governance at the Final Frontier

Even with productive bilateral relations connecting the U.S. hegemon to emerging powers in a hub-and-spoke web of efficient cooperation, the United States might still find it difficult to maintain its leadership position for another generation, much less a century.[1] Hegemony rests not only on raw power advantage but on legitimacy; more now than in Thucydides' time, technological advances in communication, production, and transportation have created global challenges. Opportunities for profitable trade and investment, obligations to protect innocents from natural disaster or human rights violations in lesser developed countries, and demands to address environmental damage—these politics affect states at all ranks. While no state can address such issues on its own, the United States in particular has an interest in leading cooperation to meet global challenges. It may require taxpayer dollars to fund public goods that benefit peoples outside U.S. borders, but if the United States fosters a sense of international community such that other states can recognize American good works, then more parties in the system will accept, perhaps even come to endorse, asymmetric economic and military power concentrated in the hands of the U.S. hegemon.

Cheerful acceptance on the part of other states allows them to continue receiving aid for resolving common problems and to forgo the costs—all the more pressing with the spread of democracy—of balancing U.S. power or resisting U.S. intentions. If U.S. leadership will endure, it will survive along the lines of what Immanuel Kant recommended on the eve of Napoleon's disastrous bid for mastery in Europe, at three mutually reinforcing levels.[2] As argued in the previous chapter, solving problems at the global or cosmopolitan level earns a Great Power credit, or at least some margin of maneuver when negotiating with other states under conditions of uncertainty. State-to-state diplomacy—at Kant's international level—becomes more efficient as fewer costs are incurred in staving off rival alliances or accommodating rising powers. This inevitable and exhausting labor of the power to retain its status as *prima inter pares* becomes manageable.

Moreover, as costs for provision of services and implementation of policy at the external levels of interaction decline, this places less stress on domestic governance. Kant's civic constitution is strengthened because democracies flourish under reduced external pressure.[3] Political leaders enjoy greater room for maneuver in Harold Laswell's allocation of societal resources since they need demand fewer sacrifices of their constituents in the absence of external crises. Under such favorable conditions, democracies more easily navigate principal-agent dilemmas associated with the rise of professions. In particular, there is more breathing room for emergence of trust between the democratic state and the republic of Science, which in turn allows greater grants of autonomy for the professionals without giving up on accountability to society. Alongside technological advances, then, opportunities are created to reap long-term, civilizational benefits from a national commitment to science: democracy becomes less obsessed with consumption, less transactional, and more cosmopolitan.

In summary, scientific achievement, or pure science, plays a role in all three Kantian arenas where twenty-first-century hegemony is likely to be won—civic, international, and transnational. More important, the long overlooked civilizational mechanisms linking science to power at each level of politics reinforce one another. As President Obama and Council on Foreign Relations president Richard Haass have commented, foreign policy for a powerful democracy begins with nation-building at home.[4] When the United States is strong at its core, militarily confident, growing economically, and progressing on questions of social justice, its people and therefore its government can afford greater patience, greater generosity, and more enlightened perspectives when engaging the rest of the world. Science, then, is one ingredient, an elixir or a catalyst, for prudent policy and successful cooperation at home and abroad, even before it bears the fruits of technology. It operates at all levels of international leadership simultaneously and links them together so that success on one plane breeds success on the others.

Now, more than during Thucydides' or Kant's time, the multilevel chessboard of world politics includes the transnational level of analysis. In his classic essay on "Perpetual Peace" (1795), Kant discussed a cosmopolitan *constitution*. The term "constitution" did not imply that nation-states would surrender sovereignty to some world government.[5] Rather, sovereign states would come to see the advantages—in terms of their prosperity and survival—of accepting certain obligations in order to access benefits from an ever expanding, ever deepening world federation. Members of the federation in good standing guaranteed a political voice for their citizens in a republican civic constitution; they pledged protections in dealings with fellow states in the federation; and at the final, transnational level, they recognized rights of noncitizens, members of a global civil society, within their territories.

Kant illustrated the unwritten cosmopolitan constitution at work using the classical tradition of hospitality in the Hellenic world. In the case of ancient Greece, according to Thucydides' history, Athens put the principle in practice more extensively than its rival Sparta. Especially in early passages of his reporting, Thucydides emphasized conventional benefits of cosmopolitanism for Great Power competition.[6] The soil in Attica may have been poor for building a strong economy based on Sparta's traditional model of slave agriculture, but Athens' relatively open society facilitated new trade relationships. Not only could Athenians benefit economically from diverse produce of many lands, the profits of trade poured into *technē*—modern shipbuilding and novel tactics—for achieving naval superiority.[7] Welcoming citizens of other city-states to transact business brought further trade and travel opportunities for Athenians. Not only foreign currencies but also foreign ideas flowed into Athens, allowing more sophisticated diplomacy to increase the benefits of interstate cooperation, to be sure, and nurturing cultural achievements, so Athenian arts and sciences might earn the envy of all Hellas.[8] At the transnational level, then, Athenian grace expanded what Joseph Nye would call the state's soft power, or attractive influence abroad. Athenian success at the transnational, more than at the civic or international levels, permitted Athens to rise without simultaneous Spartan decline and without having to endure Spartan containment until a lowly democracy of former refugees finally arrived as the most powerful state and a hegemon for the Hellenic system.[9]

Kant's essay on "Perpetual Peace" is usually read as a founding document of international liberalism, a vigorous reaction to Thucydides' realism.[10] While these divergent categorizations illuminate key points from both classic works, they neglect important similarities: in a sense, Kant and Thucydides both reacted to a defect in state systems. Both appreciated tragedy in the unraveling of hegemony and the wanton destruction of Great Power war; both speculated as to the existence of a happier alternative for mankind; and both wondered if they might have located it in the interaction of politics at domestic, interstate, and cosmopolitan levels.

For Thucydides, the Peloponnesian War was total because it penetrated so many layers of political intercourse, severing human bonds that, it turned out, were crucial for preserving families, polities, alliances, and Western civilization. Thucydides' most parsimonious articulation of a cause for catastrophe—the rise of Athens *and* the fear this caused in Sparta—cried out for a rejoinder. Could power shift among sovereign states without producing such dark emotions? Kant in "Perpetual Peace" and Thucydides both seemed to believe so. Although states were immortal monsters, they might yet be bound in their own self-interest. Hegemony, or international influence, might not spawn reactionary violence if "the system" provided sufficient benefits to member states and individual human beings alike. *Transnational* success, cultivating appeal for noncitizens who were accorded status in a global civil society, just might create conditions under which a hegemon could continually win interstate competitions without inviting Great Power war. For classical Athens, Napoleonic France in Kant's time, and perhaps the United States now, losing sight of the transnational is what sets the trap of international relations.[11]

Purposeful global leadership—for the prosperity of the Delian League; for egalitarian principles of the revolution against monarchy; or for the spread of free enterprise and constitutional democracy—at some point devolves into imperialism, which is when *hatred* is "incurred in its exercise."[12] Without the transnational pillar, American hegemony is no longer exceptional, as the unlikely pair of Thucydides and Kant might both admonish, and Americans are thus condemned to follow Pericles into disaster. "Your empire is now like a tyranny: it may have been wrong to take it; it is certainly dangerous to let it go."[13]

Space and the Twenty-first-century Global Commons

To the extent that transnational politics—the arena featuring supranational institutions, nongovernmental organizations, and substate actors—is important for establishing a sustainable form of international leadership, the United States, if it wishes to retain its hegemonic role, ought to master the exercise of power, here, as well as in domestic and international diplomatic realms. Robert Keohane and Joseph Nye, in their classic work *Power and Interdependence* (1977), reconnoitered the transnational arena as sojourners in an alternative universe. They asked us to imagine a global politics in which everything significant was inverted from ordinary perception: states in the transnational operated in the background, their vaunted sovereignty bound up in ever-thickening webs of communication so that economic, environmental, and nuclear fates tightly intertwined. In such a world, conventional military strength was less instrumental—a threat or a successful attack in technical military terms often did not lead to accomplishment of political goals; indeed the classic priorities of powerful states seemed to collapse and reverse themselves.[14]

Intriguingly, despite the fundamental distortions of international "reality" in the transnational, neither Keohane nor Nye embraced the radical notion that states had lost all importance, particularly in terms of states' capacity to mobilize resources, or that states would somehow lose the wherewithal to compete against one another.[15] Especially for Nye, serving in the Defense Department under President Clinton, states mattered, but patterns of state reasoning and behavior in the newly appreciated transnational world pointed toward advantages of soft power.[16] Not surprisingly, several critics in the policy and scholarly communities countered that a mere makeover of the American Way would not cause competitors to fold in any region—Europe, Asia, or the Middle East— that featured conflicts of interest which threatened the hegemon's position. Combining hard power and soft power to make *smart* power or *common sense* power left American officials cold, not just because it left strategy pathetically vulnerable to partisan disputes in Washington.[17] The unresolved scholarly debate seemed to suggest simultaneously that a consensus formula for balancing muscular coercion and attraction was required, and that no doctrinal solution was even possible—every quarry required its own mix of policy arrows.

Yet, one aspect in which the rise of the transnational made its mark on America's approach to the world was the keen interest acquired for the global commons.[18] Rome ruled the Ancient World in part by cultivating legitimacy, providing infrastructure that benefited multiple classes of subjects. The United States recognized early the contributions of the British Royal Navy, policing the high seas during the relatively peaceful nineteenth century, and the Americans shouldered some of these burdens for the world trading system themselves after 1945, supplying emergency capital and the dollar reserve currency.[19] With rising interdependence among states—encouraged by less expensive transport and communications—general conceptualization of the commons expanded. The global commons transformed into a machine for American energies: it became an object for U.S. policy initiatives in the short term and a valued resource for both hard and soft power in the long run.[20] In protecting the seas, the environment, cyberspace, and outer space, the United States discovered a practical—and from the standpoint of sustainable hegemony—a potentially profitable way of blending hard and soft power.

Still, various incarnations of the global commons pose multiple problems of stewardship for the hegemon. In spite of the fact that interstate competition for scarce natural resources continues apace, the lead state, the chief advocate for the system status quo, now faces additional burdens: protecting common space is expensive and time consuming; yet, benefits of these efforts accrue to all states, including rivals, who use the commons. The logic of cooperation under conditions of interdependence differs from competitive strategy under classic conceptions of anarchy. Under anarchy, of course, the key parameter is the balance of power. When there is need for collective action, however, conventional measures of power resources may work against the hegemon.

For example, gross domestic product (GDP) is often considered an index of strength in the economic balance of power. A large GDP though, often correlates with extensive use of the global commons. All actors recognize the hegemon cannot govern events outside its territory by itself. At the same time, especially if the common space requires advanced technology to fully exploit, the hegemon may need a regulatory regime more than secondary states. Political scientist Stephen Krasner wrote a famous article, "Global Communications and National Power: Life on the Pareto Frontier," showing how realist-style jockeying should still occur over the distributive consequences of a good bargain, even in a world where states prioritized absolute rather than relative gains.[21] Against his theory stand the notions of asymmetric interdependence and Mancur Olson's k-group: in a situation requiring collective action, large, well-endowed states, even the largest state on its own, may benefit enough from the system to pay for its infrastructure. Under such conditions, collective action is possible, even expected, without universal participation. As other states size up the U.S. hegemon bidding for a second American Century, the Americans must pull off a balancing act in the transnational arena: adjust global standards and governance mechanisms so as to extend U.S. national power yet supply enough *collective* benefits to keep smaller players from exiting—or resisting—the system. In the global commons, the hegemon by virtue of it resource advantage toils at least in part to benefit everyone else.

Regarding sustainable leadership for the twenty-first century, a remarkable trend compared with previous eras is how rapidly physical features of the global commons have been evolving. To traditional domains of land, sea, air, and international finance, recent decades added nuclear, space, and cyber. While these latter fields opened in the mid-twentieth century, economic and security consequences of common action on nuclear energy, space governance, and cyber security in the last twenty years have mushroomed. In order to illustrate how science as distinct from technology produces currency for international influence, this chapter examines stewardship of the global commons by focusing on the example of transnational politics in outer space.

For preserving widespread international access and cultivating mutually profitable activity in space, of course, scientific skill matters, just as in the nuclear and cyber fields. Less obvious, though, is how scientific leadership may shape the bargaining behind multilateral solutions. Problems involving stewardship of the global commons combine coordination gains with distributive consequences. Space, like other dimensions of the contemporary commons, invites high quotients of technical uncertainty, which erect barriers to trust between state parties and further complicate common action. Efficiencies from state coordination in common space, including outer space, may be delayed or forgone without capacity and willingness of partners to accept scientific information from authoritative sources, and suspicion often runs high if the scientific leader is also the leader in economic and military power. Compared with nuclear and cyber, the United States, day-to-day, probably enjoys a more dominant power position in space; it is also uniquely vulnerable there, should multilateral rules and norms of cooperation break down.

In space, asymmetric economic and security stakes thrust the United States into the forefront of Mancur Olson's k-group—as the one state that needs transnational comity most of all; at the same time, obvious power resources in this field make it difficult to hide or even qualify the threat potential inherent in U.S. hegemony. Space is an appropriate place to begin the inquiry of whether and how the scientific ethos—the civilizational effect of advancement in science—facilitates stewardship of the global commons. The example of space politics may illustrate how science reduces costs to the hegemon of providing crucial "public goods" for the system. If so, science, as distinct from superior technology, indeed, through a civilizational mechanism countervailing that of technology, enables an authentic transnational politics, which resolves the paradox of sustainable hegemony: unrivaled concentration of power realizing beneficial collective action among independent, self-seeking states, without springing Thucydides' trap of imperial temptation and world war.[22]

The remainder of this chapter identifies key questions facing the international community on the stewardship of space. For each of the issues it describes the scientific content but also where uncertainty and mistrust have hampered international progress toward mutually beneficial cooperation regarding the commons. In these instances when opportunities for improved stewardship appear lost, U.S. science and technology (S&T) policy related to the space issue has suffered a now familiar imbalance between the collaborative impulse toward progress in Science as a cosmopolitan enterprise versus national concern for pursuing greater security and world influence through technological advantage. The section concludes by reviewing the implication of lost opportunities at the transnational level for sustainable American hegemony and analyzing how recent changes to National Space Policy authored by the Obama administration dilute the national commitment to Science, overlooking its value as a universal quest with sufficient appeal to nurture civilization among states.

Practical Limits of Outer Space

Surveying space for the potential of international conflict is like surveying the Arctic; the overwhelming impression is one of vastness, remoteness, and desolation. Authorities warn outer space is more forbidding than the North Pole or the high seas, so we must take care when extending Mahanian analogies from the influence of sea power upon history.[23] Yet, in the beginning, the oceans, too, were vast, remote, and inhospitable. As technology improved, it was possible to collect and convey information then increasing quantities of mass—spices, gold, and manufactures—relevant to politics at home. Embedded in the technology required to accomplish these conveyances and exploit an unfamiliar domain lay practical limitations, which aroused preoccupations over scarcity and kindled political competition.

Similar logic applies to the domain of space. Of course, technology is not to the point where we can profitably launch massive container ships into orbit and deftly land them at the port of our choice anywhere in the world. Reaching farther to capture and excavate asteroids in order to haul tons of precious minerals through the atmosphere presents its own daunting challenges. Nevertheless, the capacity to launch adequate mass—say, a thousand kilograms—for collecting and transporting information in fractions of a second across the globe confers economic and military advantages in the competition among states. The technology of exploiting space as a global commons, then, sets the stage for a mixed-motive game: the hegemon, in particular, has incentives to cooperate so as to secure absolute gains for itself and provide system benefits from activities in space; at the same time, it will want to exclude or control the access of other states in order to secure relative gains and buttress its lead role.

Because leadership in a competitive system is likely to incorporate coercion and unilateral moves—for example, to enforce systemwide rules against pro-liferating debris in space—constructing cooperative regimes for much of the global commons, including space, involves trust. The hegemon would like to make a credible commitment to provide for system members, not just for itself, while actively protecting its exclusive power position. Without trust and under conditions of incomplete information, autonomous states face a large disin-centive—what theorists sometimes reference as a prisoner's dilemma—when signing onto the hegemon's plan for regulating the global commons. Agreeing to rules sponsored by the hegemon may make it easier for the power player to exploit them so that the hegemon ultimately withholds on its part of the bar-gain, taking its multilateral partners for suckers.

Technology, in this case space technology, often sets the parameters for pris-oner's dilemma in the global commons, so science influences the transnational game in at least two ways. National science of the United States lays the founda-tion for superior satellites and launch capabilities—along the same lines cited in previous discussions of national innovation policy and Great Power compe-tition. Science's direct effects on technology development help ensure that the U.S. government goes into the transnational arena, like domestic and interna-tional political arenas, well equipped for negotiations, with much to offer in terms of both carrots and sticks in order to drive a hard bargain.

The less obvious connection between scientific greatness and hegemonic success, however, is more important for resolving prisoner's dilemma games. The civilizational effects of science help ensure that the United States enters negotiations over the international community's architecture for space with a certain amount of social capital—admiration for what U.S. discoveries have meant for mankind and confidence that U.S. commitment to the global scien-tific enterprise limits the likelihood that U.S. leadership in transnational affairs will degenerate into raw materialism. In the domestic context, Harvard po-litical scientist Robert Putnam famously measured social capital in terms of engagement and trust.[24] In a world of increasingly dense and heterogeneous networks, to include semiofficial, nongovernmental organizations (NGOs) providing widely acknowledged technical expertise on the global commons, science encourages both engagement and trust, facilitating the sort of mutually beneficial cooperation that would allow American hegemony to survive a second century.

With respect to space, the contributions of scientific achievement in the technological and civilizational modes are observable in three dimensions where international cooperation must take place in order to protect the commons: collision avoidance in low earth orbit (LEO); allocation of frequency spectrum for communications; and technology sharing, to include actual hardware, capacity on multiuse satellite platforms, or specially prepared packages of collected information. For each of these items, technological innovation based on scientific principles creates a problem set for transnational politics, and science education produces the cadre of experts who will advise governments on solutions. Subsequent technological developments may increase the size of the pie—that is, raise absolute gains to be harvested from the commons—but the catch of how to distribute those benefits on the Pareto frontier remains. For sustainable development and progress under hegemony, rather than falling out over how to use the commons, the indirect, civilizational impetus of scientific excellence offers critical support to successful negotiations over space.

Bargaining at LEO

Low earth orbit looks something like a giant ping pong ball with the spinning earth filling most of its core. The ball's shell is thick, ranging 100 to 600 miles above the earth's surface.[25] This volume represents a lot of space to fit six hundred satellites or so, even when their panels for collecting solar energy extend for 100 feet in either direction. However, at 200 miles above the earth, speed kills.[26]

Several space-faring nations and private companies find the risk at LEO worth taking because the orbit offers the ultimate high ground for earth observation. Since certain sectors of the earth—major trade routes and centers of population or wealth—attract disproportionate interest, manmade objects are not evenly distributed throughout but instead concentrated at desirable great circle routes crisscrossing above the globe. Moreover, for dynamic observation, satellite maneuverability matters, and this makes tracks in LEO harder to predict—collisions more difficult to avoid.

Because of the high velocity required to maintain low earth orbit, on the order of 17,000 miles per hour, objects as small as a centimeter across present threats to sophisticated space systems. Publicly reported figures suggest some twenty thousand near-earth objects greater than 10 centimeters.[27] This is to say that many natural objects, microasteroids or space dust, cross into this commons, but collisions involving man-made satellites still matter, as they create debris in high-traffic locations. Despite the amount of space in LEO—roughly 30 billion cubic miles—at least ten collisions of note occurred over the last three decades, the real number likely being greater since LEO is also the operational habitat for intelligence satellites, mainly from the United States and Russia.[28] For reasons of national security these operators would not ordinarily report when a secret platform went offline.

The United States, in particular, might expect to fool the international community because it makes the lion's share of investment and possesses by far the greatest capacity for monitoring objects in LEO, a circumstance that will likely persist for years.[29] The global commons of low earth orbit, then, presents the incumbent hegemon with the type of mixed-motive strategic situation discussed earlier. The United States would like to collect data and provide information in order to facilitate utilization of increasingly congested low earth orbits. Such a service would provide significant systemwide benefits related to weather and management of natural resources as well as secure multibillion dollar investments by the United States itself and several important partner countries in Europe and Asia. At the same time, the United States derives advantages from its technological superiority in LEO. It has an interest in defending the profit margin of U.S. companies producing billions of dollars in space products and services, and the hegemon wants to preserve secrets regarding the precise location and true capabilities of its intelligence satellites.

Scientific virtuosity enters this policy challenge for the United States in two ways. Most obviously, scientific achievement as the precursor to technological innovation can ease trade-offs between providing system benefits and controlling the exploitation of space. If the United States, for example, is the only government possessing the wherewithal to build and operate a "space fence"—a network of powerful, ground-based radars with the capability of tracking continuously tens of thousands of tiny, high velocity objects in LEO—then the United States is unique among space-faring nations in being able to perform system monitoring for strengthening the 1974 Convention on Registration of Launched Objects into Outer Space and verifying whether all other states are fulfilling their obligations to provide location information, without the United States itself having to reveal national security related secrets about its own assets in low earth orbit.[30] With technology flowing from superior science and a more capable cadre of scientists and engineers, the hegemon gets to square the circle, receiving credit for the public goods it provides while securing its military power advantage.

The problem with leveraging science exclusively as a form of capital for producing technology—the form in which democratic policy-makers and their constituents most easily perceive it—comes when advantages consolidated and secrets preserved eventually run dry. Technology diffuses after a while, or capabilities spread based on different physical principles, so it becomes possible, for example, for private companies to monitor sectors of low earth orbit using new sensors on their satellite platforms rather than less profitable radars attempting to scan the heavens from dispersed facilities on the ground. Accidents and unauthorized leaks occur, generating fodder for the global media and revealing a clear picture of how the U.S. hegemon exploits its technological advantage in order to exercise a measure of control, even over negotiating partners and allies.[31] Forcing science into the harness not only hinders efforts toward new discoveries that could spur technological innovation on novel physical principles; enslaving science in this way erodes trust until others look askance at the hegemon's willingness to provide a public good, lest it turn out to be a Trojan horse, a cynical, deceptive gift that undermines rather than enables civilized behavior among states. For the hegemon attempting to influence norms of military and economic competition in LEO, trust is a valuable commodity, more precious over the long term than technological advantage. The global market for remote sensing satellites, providing inputs for commercial geographic information systems (GIS) is set to expand rapidly through the year 2020.[32] Neither supply nor demand for this market will be exclusively U.S. based, which means American companies are likely to win greater market share through international cooperation, contributing much of the system integration for small foreign satellite companies and purchasing certain subsystems or launch services from abroad. These sorts of economic activities cannot happen inexpensively or efficiently without *trust* and a widely accepted set of *rules* for utilizing this dimension of the global commons.

Historically, attempts at joint system development—linking payload design, launch, and satellite operations—have been fraught with problems. We saw in the previous chapter how Brazil's frustration with U.S. space assistance led it to turn toward China, quite early, for joint development of remote sensing satellites (CBERS), even before Brazil's anticommunist junta ceded power to more progressive and independent-minded civilian presidents.[33] During the course of the 1990s, U.S. launch companies consolidated production but still struggled to provide the U.S. government rockets at a cost competitive with what the Russians were offering.[34] Back in the arena of payload design, specifically for the semisynchronous orbits of timing and navigation satellites, Western European countries and the United States fought bitterly over mere coordination, much less joint production, of Galileo and GPS Block III deigns that crowded similar frequencies for overlapping footprints at certain latitudes on earth.[35]

Several commentators on national defense have predicted that a new space race is likely to develop between the United States and rising China. Rapidly emerging systems for landing *taikonauts* on the moon with no obvious military aim are nevertheless symbolic of China's broader ambition to challenge the U.S. technological lead in space.[36] Rather than searching creatively for joint scientific projects that could be well insulated from military postures, the U.S. Congress has taken the opposite tack, placing restrictions on American space companies that could possibly facilitate *technology* transfer to foreign powers.[37] Since China has an interest in collaborating with other space powers, not just the United States, American export restrictions in the long run can have the opposite of their intended effect: American companies end up isolated from natural partners in Europe or the developing world for fear that a foreign corporation could compromise American producers' obligations to the U.S. government for protecting state-of-the-art technology. Leaving initiative in the global space technology market to China or Russia all but guarantees that, sooner or later, U.S. space will fall victim to a familiar trap from import-substitution industrialization policy, in which disengagement from global competition, attempting to wall it off, makes it more difficult for now parochial American technology to remain on the global cutting edge. What is more, the U.S. Congress, through its democratic lawmaking and oversight roles, can communicate pathological technology restrictions back to the international scientific community.[38] Statutory provisions designed to prevent China from stealing American secrets were implemented by the NASA bureaucracy, at least initially, in such a way so as to deny scientific cooperation on fundamental questions of astronomy, including, for example, the Kepler Spacecraft's search for habitable planets orbiting distant stars.[39] Banning top Chinese astronomers from unclassified data presentations because they occur at NASA facilities amounts to superfluous provocation that ultimately damages U.S. science—thereby jeopardizing U.S. future capacity both to shape transnational enterprises and to retain its coveted technological advantage.[40]

Stealth at GEO

If the real threat to American hegemony at crowded low earth orbit is that widely shared trust in American beneficence could be squandered in a technological rat race and U.S. decline hastened by fear of secular diffusion, well, at geosynchronous earth orbit, 23,000 miles above the equator, the pall of American fear is still present, but the mechanism of U.S. descent generates far less commotion. For high earth orbit, satellite operators seek to park their unblinking instruments in, roughly, a single ring around the equator such that geosynchronous satellite positions, when registered, are reported succinctly in degrees longitude. The image of a staid, celestial parking lot contrasts sharply with the high-speed, peripatetic Roman traffic circle at LEO. Yet, underneath the icy veneer at GEO burn familiar geopolitical ambitions.

For the American hegemon, perhaps the most important objective at high earth orbit is to preserve the function of innocuous sounding Defense Support Program (DSP) satellites. Their infrared detectors keep watch at every moment for the telltale energy burst of an unannounced missile launch or nuclear explosion.[41] The DSP constellation, therefore, constitutes the first line of defense, and at the same time, a critical element of deterrence against nuclear war. In the same ring orbit around the equator, several militaries now station communication satellites, but to make the security situation more complicated, an even greater number of commercial companies have lofted communication payloads into GEO that permit dual, civil-military use.

The prevalent fear is not that geostationary satellites will collide but that their electromagnetic footprints will overlap on earth in ways that make urgent information signals unintelligible. For sophisticated, low-energy relays at GEO, spectrum rather than physical space comes at the highest premium. Because frequency interference is harder to investigate or diagnose than kinetic attack on GEO platforms, the central question for space stewardship at high earth orbit is how to allocate rights—among sovereigns as well as private satellite operators—for use of limited channels within the available electromagnetic spectrum.[42] So far, the default solution has been to treat the geostationary orbital ring as free range: no fenced off parcels, just voluntary commitments to register location and spectral footprint with the International Telecommunications Union.[43] As straightforward economics anticipates, international political considerations and concomitant lack of trust plunged the rudimentary legal regime at GEO to the lowest common denominator. While a precise inventory of objects at GEO remains unverifiable to all nations except, perhaps, the United States, the hegemon in particular retains a large incentive to bypass the ITU registry for those geostationary platforms providing purely military communications or infrared warning for national security.[44] Another secret that military powers would like to keep relates to signal processing programs, which allow for encrypted messages. Signal manipulation also expands the amount of information throughput that may be squeezed into ever narrowing frequency bands. Of course, the software exploiting established physical principles can only buy time—as geostationary orbit becomes more crowded with electromagnetic transmitters, the communications satellites, like flagged merchant vessels of an earlier epoch, will find themselves drawn into increasingly intense competition for right of way.

The obvious method for staking one's claim in a crowded spectrum is to blast everyone else out. Ensuring that one state's signals over a certain patch of earth drown the others, though, would likely involve a greater government role in satellite operations, just the opposite of what has been happening for private companies based in the United States and Europe in the race for efficiency. More powerful emissions toward earth would likely mean more powerful signal amplifiers in space and more mass at launch, which would significantly raise the costs of providing service from what they could be were governments to eliminate this form of competition. The problem is not that competition fails to squeeze rents or wipe out monopoly profits. Rather, corporate energies that might be dedicated toward improving productivity are instead diverted to battling over property rights.

Now, the hegemon could impose those rights on other space-faring states in GEO by reason of obtaining efficiency for all. The next problem, though, is that initial allocations of longitudinal slots and frequency bandwidth have enormous distributional consequences. If the United States insisted on unilaterally assigning property rights in GEO, there would be no alternative to resisting everyone at once. When no party at all was favored by U.S. fiat, resentment from close friends would come directly. Even if certain allies, say, the United Kingdom or Japan, fared well, nothing would prevent begrudging vassals from angling for a better deal as circumstances warranted. Within a few years, the United States could again find itself stuck in the thankless role of beleaguered sheriff, enforcing property rights that no other party viewed as legitimate.

An alternative policy to reduce subsequent risks and costs of international law enforcement is to negotiate the initial allocation of property rights.[45]

Emerging space nations have clear economic interests in joining such a regime, as long as initial endowments of electromagnetic spectrum represent an improvement for them over the present, highly skewed distribution of power. The central question would be how the state parties should balance power and equity considerations. Although economic experts may have a formula or a bargaining principle for doing this, game-theoretic solutions to the problem rely upon finite, comprehensible stakes and preferences that for negotiators can be parceled into distinguishable, fixed categories of private versus common information.

Science as a cosmopolitan enterprise, the global market of ideas sustained by individual, self-regarding nation-states, is already involved in the bargaining game at GEO. Nationally sponsored science is the font for *technologies* that expand the size of the pie, allowing competing satellite operators to increase the amount of useful information that may be squeezed through the "pipeline" of a designated frequency band. While this technical contribution to international harmony and general prosperity is very important, in the long run, it may not matter as much as the civilizational influence scientific excellence has on the international allocation of property rights.

The substantive point behind the U.S. slogan of congested, contested, and competitive space is that the international space community's free-range approach—in either LEO or GEO—will soon run its course. Publicized concerns about alternative timing and navigation signals from a Chinese, Russian, or European-Galileo constellation interfering with the U.S. GPS platforms at middle earth orbit foreshadow analogous spectral crowding in the high-frequency communication bands transmitted from GEO.[46] The global commons at high earth orbit is on the cusp of a new era when good fences will make better neighbors, but high stakes questions as to just how GEO slots and parcels of high-frequency spectrum will be allocated loom large.[47]

While the scientific ethos, even if exemplified by the hegemon, is unlikely to transform leaders of self-regarding states into pliant altruists or pool the identities of hard-bitten sovereigns, Science may yet raise the prospects of multilateral cooperation. Rational actors enmeshed in a mixed motive game need to assess their partners, and any hegemon among them most of all. Much of the common information—what everyone understands to be the widespread benefits of cooperation at GEO as well as the distributional consequences of acquiring rights to one frequency band over another—comes from scientific knowledge. Although this knowledge stems from a cosmopolitan enterprise, the contributions of participating states are rarely equal, and for space science, especially with regard to instrumentation, the United States historically has held the clear lead. In order to assess their predicament and optimize strategies based on a common information set, states of the international space community have to accept the results of science produced elsewhere, in this case disproportionately by the hegemon.

In other words, even if the preferences of states were autonomously constructed so that health of the international community entered not at all in formation of individual preferences, a certain amount of trust could creep into the game if it were embedded in information priors—operational beliefs about costs and benefits of certain policy options, which are necessary in order to calculate rationally even on stubbornly selfish desires. As they sift through possible strategies, moreover, states must form some sense of what lies behind the curtain of private information. Other players must ask, for example, how the United States assesses the value of monopolizing access to space so as to gain *short-term* military and economic advantages versus the value of a broadly beneficial, sustainable international order for the utilization of outer space over the long haul.[48] International Relations scholar John Ikenberry and others have argued that under conditions of increasing interdependence, whether a hegemon opts for a logic of rules or a logic of power resources using a divide and conquer scheme depends on leadership as much as structure.[49] Indeed, in the transition from George W. Bush to Barack Obama the rhetoric of U.S. space policy changed from power dominance to promotion of responsible order— faster than the material structure of capabilities would admit.

When follower states assess the risks of entering into a rule-based regime with the hegemon for future utilization of outer space, they cannot rely on common information about structure—that is, the relative quality of space programs or the likely benefits of technology sharing; they must also assess U.S. intentions, especially at GEO, where so much of the preliminary maneuvering that sets up future frequency crowding is currently unobservable to emerging space actors. In lieu of a smoking gun, potential partners involved in permanent, multilateral solutions with significant distributional consequences—such as initial allocation of property rights for geostationary slots and spectrum— might focus their attention on circumstantial evidence.

Diplomatic negotiations at GEO invite theatrics not because statesmen for civilizing space place moral qualms above their government's interests but because multiple agreements with the hegemon are possible, clustered around the logic of coercion or the logic of rules. When the United States pursues the scientific ethos in space and elsewhere, when the hegemon demonstrates its dedication to a cosmopolitan enterprise, investing certain resources that might have gone directly into more capabilities for interstate competition instead toward a greater understanding of Nature for all mankind, this, indeed, may give ordinary states pause. Combined with the uncertainties and risks involved in defying the hegemon, Science offers a reason for follower states to hold steady and see if a more lucrative, cooperative deal pays off.[50]

Meanwhile, the hegemon walking hand in hand with Science is more likely to see and act upon its enlightened self-interest. In the example of geostationary orbit, the long-term pattern of technological diffusion and international development is such that the hegemon may end up better off in terms of commercial gains from telecommunications services and fewer losses from security competition, once there has been a principled negotiation rather than power soaked imposition of property rights for satellite operations. To the extent that more science rather than advanced technology would raise the likelihood of a cooperative outcome versus raw competition at GEO, in simple policy terms, the state should, despite conventional wisdom and political claims to the contrary, dedicate its next policy dollar toward science.[51]

Sharing Space Technology

Alongside scientific excellence, there are complementary ways for the hegemon to signal its willingness to cooperate and its confidence in a vision of transnational stewardship that eschews any atavistic impulse to conquer space. Several of these signals involve technology sharing. Whether this openness involves hardware design, data distribution, or operational capacity on a space platform, sharing is easier with a strong foundation in science.

The most obvious and yet politically fraught mode of technology exchange requires the hegemon to deliver hardware for performing critical space functions to countries that might, within a few years, turn around and compete against the United States economically or militarily. Understandably, as the commercial value of space increased and military operations embraced greater reliance on space sensing, command, and control, the United States shrank from the possibility of giving away its technological edge.

During the 1990s, scandals surrounding satellite sales of major U.S. companies to China forced a defensive crouch from Congress. Several categories of space component technologies were shifted from the Commerce Department's control list to the State Department's U.S. Munitions List (USML), which mandated far more onerous approval protocols before a foreign sale could take place.[52] Over the ensuing decades, American space companies and industry analysts observed the bite of International Traffic in Arms Regulations (ITAR) as satellite manufacturing know-how diffused to emerging space powers. "The share of commercial and government satellite manufacturing averaged over 60 percent of the total during the period from 1996 to 1999, but had dropped to less than 30 percent by 2008."[53] Arnold and Hays were able to quote commanders of U.S. Strategic Command and Air Force Space Command expressing concern over how the current export control regime was affecting America's industrial base for space.

When it came to high-tech components for satellite manufacturing, the United States appeared to have fallen into a Gilpinesque trap from *War and Change* (1981): key military and economic technology naturally diffused; a strategic arena for the Great Powers became more congested, contentious, and competitive; the hegemon reacted by desperately trying to hang on, but the more it scrambled to protect its markets and the tighter it clutched its possessions—accoutrements of its power—the more it motivated innovative challengers and the deeper it sank into stagnation of its own national capabilities.[54] The very policy to preserve American superiority in space by cutting off technology flows pushed U.S. companies out of the global market and exacerbated the crisis in American leadership.

The fate of U.S. space companies is tied to American hegemony not simply because the commercial value of space related products and services is expected to contribute to GDP growth in the coming decades, but several technologies enabling remote sensing and global communications are dual-use, enhancing military operations as well. The importance of dual-use becomes clear in the statistic reported for U.S. military communications in Iraq. After the initial combat phase, some 40 percent of information traffic used by deployed troops traveled on commercial bandwidth.[55] While missions in Iraq and Afghanistan had major political significance at home and, many believe, for the future of American hegemony, they were still small compared with the number of service members and amount of equipment that would be mobilized in a major war.

After an initial defense buildup in response to 9/11, mounting concern about the growing national debt eventually curtailed congressional desire to prosecute a Global War on Terror with further troop deployments and additional

U.S.-led interventions. By 2011, with the rise of Tea Party Republicans in Congress, numbers of fighter aircraft and active-duty soldiers were on the chopping block. Yet, even with the advent of budget sequestration it was beyond dispute that future operations, whether they were directed against nonstate networks, a rogue regime, or a Great Power challenger, would be information intensive. Military satellite programs largely avoided the budget ax, and defense planners continued to reach for some portion of the growing commercial capacity in traditionally military, high-frequency bands.[56]

Military use of commercial satellite capacity means that space companies in general not just defense contractors are tied to the hegemon's national security. With regard to the space telecommunications sector, the defense industrial base for practical purposes covers the entire industry. Analysts are still wrestling with what capacity sharing across civilian and military applications implies for deterrence and defense, creating an extraordinarily awkward situation in which military procurement officers race to purchase critical twenty-first-century assets—for example, the rights to high throughput channels, without their service quite knowing how to protect them in time of either war or peace.[57]

Considering alternative modes for sharing technology, exchanging hardware or selling hardware as previously mentioned are remarkably intensive, incurring a substantial amount of risk to the hegemon's technological edge. Sharing mere data is easier because the powerful supplying state maintains such strict control over future flows of information. It may be the case that nearly all technologies of importance to the state diffuse internationally with time, mimicking the famous S-curve of innovation theorists referencing the free market, but data sharing, assessed as a form of technology exchange, highlights how time is a proxy for other variables actually governing the pace of diffusion.[58] There is something inviscid about data with respect to underlying technology such that even though one of the original American uses of space in the 1960s was to capture high-resolution images from low earth orbit, fewer governments today can independently access space images at 0.1 meter resolution than can manufacture their own nuclear weapons. Such constraints on technology diffusion via data exist despite the fact that 1.0-meter resolution images of the earth are widely available on the open market, and, at lower resolutions, say, 15–100 meters, freely provided by U.S. and European governments for scientific use in environmental management and international development.[59]

Unlike equipment, data can, relatively easily, be cleaned and thrown over the transom to partners, so they benefit from the information without having a way to reverse engineer the process and build their own reconnaissance platforms. This is an important reason why data sharing—transferring appealing intelligence morsels sanitized of savoir faire—has been a reliable legitimizing tactic by the American hegemon for over half a century.[60] The Kennedy administration, for example, effectively employed U-2 photographs at the UN Security Council in order to isolate Cuba during the 1962 Missile Crisis, and the W. Bush administration shared limited intelligence (as well as war plans) with Saudi Arabia before launching a politically, if not militarily, risky invasion of Iraq in 2003.[61]

Yet, for at least two reasons, the venerable practice of sharing technology by disseminating only its fruits—without the seeds—is coming under pressure. The complexion of American hegemony is changing as the international distribution of power, or, as important, its perception, shifts from unipolarity to asymmetric multipolarity. Costs and benefits of multilateralism are shifting as well, so that the hegemon finds advantages in "leading from behind," as critics have it, but this more accurately amounts to coordinating increasingly interdependent operations on behalf of international security with more than symbolic participation from other military powers.[62] As security operations become more intertwined and burden sharing ratios increase, the trust threshold for effective cooperation with the hegemon climbs: the old stratagem of spitting out what must in the end be sanitized data no longer quite convinces wary partners of the hegemon. The year 2003 saw a U.S.-led coalition conquer Iraq in less than a month, but hegemonic leadership turned out to be inadequate to the postcombat task of stabilizing the new regime. The American-centered posse assembled to enforce previous UN resolutions was neither broad nor durable enough in part because prior to invading, the United States torched much of its social capital with other states in a flawed data presentation before the UN Security Council on the WMD threat from Saddam Hussein's Iraq. Comparing the hegemon's Cuba presentation in 1962 with the 2003 indictment of Iraq, it is easy to see the limitations of technology sharing via data transfer. The Iraq dossier in many ways was more detailed, more dazzling, and more revealing of U.S. intelligence collection capabilities; yet, unlike the 1962 case, it destroyed rather than built trust for the hegemonic maneuvers that lay ahead.[63]

In addition to demand pull for independent production of national intelligence, the second impulse undermining the power play of controlled data sharing relates to supply push. Despite the U.S. export control regime, sophisticated space technology has made its way to independent-minded state actors with desire to redeem their rightful access to the global commons and shoulder international agenda items in their preferred direction. One of the ratcheting effects of shedding classic diplomacy in favor of benign hegemony and rule-through-rules is that it opens up issue areas, such as stewardship of space, where stakeholders do not need to amass rival capabilities or literally balance U.S. power in order to drive a hard bargain with the hegemon. The United States can do very little, for example, when the European Commission plays by mutually agreed rules and still stuns the international community by offering open access to medium resolution radar and multispectral imaging from the upcoming Copernicus system, part of its state-of-the-art Sentinel series of earth observation satellites.[64]

As the sophistication of nationally provided open access data increases, anticipated effects on commercial space are twofold: both undercut the vulgar appeal of U.S. data sharing. First, governments, including that of the United States, are making earth observation data available because high-tech companies contributing to national income and corporate taxes profit from selling information based on the original data. The real money, business associations advise, is in value-added services that are seeded by publicly available data.[65] Unfortunately for controlled sharing, or gating strategies to maintain U.S. hegemony, images from LEO, it turns out, are much like books and media at the public library—far better for the community and local economy if patrons enjoy open access. The global policy movement toward building international stacks filled with images from space at ever higher standards of resolution pressures the United States most of all to lower barriers and grant access to greater shares of its data collection.

A second source of competition comes from those few companies, mainly in the United States and Europe, that are trying to survive in the market for commercial imaging. Not only is the resolution of open access data improving over time, firms like Digital Globe of Boulder, Colorado, testify that their plan for business growth involves competing with aerial cameras delivering 30-cm images, though over relatively narrow patches of ground. Technological innovation in industry has advanced such that companies build LEO payloads capable of 25-cm resolution, but U.S. law currently prohibits commercial sale of space images at this level of acuity.[66] Because of proliferating sources for open access data, accompanied by rising global demand for related information services and increasingly sophisticated commercial imagery from space, the technolog-

ical window through which the U.S. hegemon can buy international cooperation with mere data sharing is closing rapidly.

Now, the United States may enjoy a safer technological lead in the area of
signals intelligence, but exploitation of this advantage has cost the American
hegemon in unanticipated, if predictable, ways. Given the penetration and
sheer breadth of U.S. National Security Agency (NSA) eavesdropping on international telecommunications and the fact that the real dimensions of signals
espionage were not widely understood until a twenty-nine-year-old NSA con-
tractor downloaded the proof and defected to Russia, few allies or partners are
likely close to having the capacity for this caliber of intelligence enterprise.[67] Indeed, reactions of friendly governments in the realm of international scientific
research, including defense-related projects and encompassing Mexico, Brazil,
Spain, France, and Germany, rocked the American foreign policy agenda.[68] Not
only would it become increasingly costly to harvest useful communications
against the wariness and political objections of fellow states, certain avenues of
future cooperation, among them controlled data sharing, were narrowed now
for lack of trust. Even close partners enjoying intimate intelligence-sharing arrangements with the United States such as the United Kingdom, Australia, and
Japan scrambled to revalidate their states as reliable, discrete confidants of the
hegemon.[69] Technologically asymmetric and tactically brilliant, the U.S. signals
intelligence program ultimately did not deliver enduring strategic control for
the hegemon.

In fact, surveying three arenas connected to geostrategic competition in
space where the United States has enjoyed technological superiority—slots
in low earth orbit; spectral bands in geosynchronous (and semigeosynchronous) orbit; and finally intentional sharing, including hardware, satellite capacity, and data—there have always been two paths for the hegemon. The first
is the most obvious: hang on to the technological advantage by circling the
wagons, severely regulating information flow, and maximizing possibilities
for exploiting the vulnerabilities of others. This approach is akin to Ikenberry's rule-by-relationships, in which the hegemon attempts to control its environment and maintain its position through punishment and bribery, simple sticks and carrots that are easy to communicate and work by virtue of the
lead state's seemingly permanent power advantage. The second path is more
complicated and involves novel elements of risk. Hegemonic engagement for
stewardship of space immediately grants autonomy, so follower states become
full-fledged partners instead of mere pawns. Engagement is akin to Ikenberry's

rule-through-rules and involves genuine bargaining; the hegemon concedes autonomy in order to convince other states to remain inside the rules. Trust takes on importance, for while the hegemon may remain first among equals under engagement, control of the environment and predictability of international behavior is now the responsibility not only of the superior power but all participating states.

Negotiating rule through rules leaves the hegemon with less authority, but rule by coercive relationships is more sensitive to sudden reverses in the lead state's power advantage. As has been widely accepted across the ideological spectrum, American superiority since costly expeditionary wars in Iraq and Afghanistan has receded on several dimensions. Except for, perhaps, U.S. technological feats in signals intelligence, which prompted their own political challenges, deterioration in the realm of space power—in key orbits and critical space functions—proceeded apace for all to witness. As engagement appears more and more the prudent strategy, science should receive greater weight relative to technology among factors in preserving U.S. hegemony. While the economic and military benefits of scientific achievements are less direct and less measurable than changes in technological performance, pure science as human enterprise has certain civic, diplomatic, and transnational by-products, what have been referred to as civilizational benefits. These are indeed useful, serving as a kind of global social capital, filling reservoirs of good will when states of diverse capabilities come to the table and begin bargaining over how a common resource like outer space shall be governed for the long-term benefit of all.

Scientific Shortcomings of Space Policy

The biggest problem jeopardizing engagement, rule-through-rules, or a global governance approach to strategic challenges posed by space is not that state parties avert their gaze from evolving circumstance, refusing to face consequences of technological diffusion or to acknowledge genuine opportunities for mutual gain.[70] Nor are those states likely to imbibe some newfangled cocktail of idealism that blinds them to the dangers of security competition, including the possibility of a hostile stratagem against sovereign space operations that would spoil important U.S. military advantages. The difficulty besetting a democratic hegemon in particular, is in seeing how to square the circle, how to leverage interdependence and break down barriers to technological cooperation while simultaneously reinforcing capability gaps related to economy and national security, areas of constant preoccupation for fellow states' competitive instincts. Precisely, here, in formulating the optimal mix of policies so that the hegemon can be indispensable—the benign provider of public goods—without conceding its preeminent power position in the system, is where science as distinct from technology makes the difference.

In space, as in other transnational arenas, the same physical phenomena, the very same actions taken by governmental or subgovernmental actors, admit of widely different interpretations. If a satellite collision occurs or a communication signal suddenly goes inoperable, how are victims to discern the real threat? Even the United States employing its vaunted space situational awareness capabilities might take days to determine with confidence whether the destruction of its national security asset resulted from hostile action or what amounts to a traffic accident.[71] Longtime analyst Joan Johnson-Freese of the U.S. Naval War College pointed out how the U.S. government viewed the Chinese debris-creating ASAT test of 2007 very negatively compared with its "responsible" use of missile defense capability when the United States knocked its own ailing satellite out of the sky.[72] The American justification that an antimissile missile was necessary to prevent the spill of hydrazine fuel as USA 193 came crashing through the atmosphere did not wash publicly. Potential partners in transnational space cooperation perceived *both* the Chinese and American actions as provocative.

Beyond threat assessment, policy-makers must also decide how to judge consequences of developments in space for national capabilities and the balance of power. The 2011 *National Security Space Strategy* (NSSS) reported that the Chinese ASAT test and the unintentional collision between a Russian Cosmos and commercial Iridium satellite contributed substantially to the number of objects tracked by U.S. terrestrial radars.[73] A denser or wider debris field at first blush imposes a cost on all space-faring nations in LEO, an absolute loss for the transnational community of space actors. At the same time, the U.S. fields the most space assets in LEO and relies on them most for augmenting military operations. In the near term, a more formidable debris field could offer a relative gain to China or other potential military challengers to the hegemon. Similarly, when the United States improves its open-access timing and navigation signal from semigeosynchronous orbit, it provides an immediate gain for all users in the transnational community. During an international crisis, however, with allies and possibly some adversaries relying on that U.S.-controlled signal for critical functions such as financial transactions, utilities management, or national transportation, GPS modifications over the long haul could deliver *relative* gains to the hegemon. The general difficulty in anticipating pivotal events or sudden policy reversals, what they imply about economic competition, security threats, or future balance of capabilities, exposes two holes in the hegemon's plans for engagement in space.

Regardless of promising expressions in the hegemon's public policy documents, extending cooperation in orbit will not be possible without trust. Trust is the first ingredient lacking from a viable plan to shape global governance structures that would also reinforce the hegemon's leading influence. Three prominent issues in policy circles relating to the commons of space and the widening call for global utilities demonstrate how central trust is to the hegemon's hopes of establishing itself as the lead steward of global resources.

For avoiding collisions in LEO, the United States possesses by far the superior network of ground radars, but without trust, who can say during a crisis whether the United States would share its tracking information as openly or notify the community comprehensively of American satellite locations? Under a sharp security threat, any sovereign would make changes, but the magnitude of collective punishment, or the amount of degradation in global utilities, would depend on how much the sovereign trusted neutral states and on the hegemon's long-term commitment to global institutions. Similar questions attend cooperation at GEO. How far would the hegemon have to be pushed before it violated international rules on spectrum allocation, before it stopped sharing information on missile warning, or before it interfered with commercial telecommunications channels? Finally, at semigeosynchronous orbit, the hegemon has to worry on the margins whether foreign partners might pull their supplemental constellations from an integrated timing and navigation system, but in the near term the American GPS will supply the core utility. The rest of the world must gauge, or trust, the U.S. hegemon will retract its service only under the direst conditions.

American hegemony and America's willingness to supply global public goods may facilitate collective action for the transnational stewardship of space, but asymmetric power inherent in hegemony complicates trust, which lies at the foundation of global governing institutions and international integration of technological systems. Building trust under trying circumstances is where science—the civilizational impulse of science—spares the engagement strategy, rescues the hegemon from rule by relationships, and stays hegemony's secular decline.

Basic science is a competitive arena, linked to technological innovation, but science is just as surely a cosmopolitan enterprise. National commitment to Science and desire to cooperate internationally on scientific research sends a credible signal of commitment to the community. Scientific achievement registers the hegemon's down payment for the future robustness of global institutions, a clear sign a leader will stick with the long-term plan and not defect at the first opportunity to exploit technological advantage for economic or military coercion. Science usefully sheathes a hegemon's raw power, demonstrating the leader's discipline and self-restraint, giving follower states tangible reason to trust a hegemon's judgment. Hegemony as a concentration of resources makes global governance more practicable; yet, in order for hegemony and global governance to coexist, national science expresses to state and nonstate audiences alike the center will hold under pressure—the leader will accept some risk to its own position, pay a fair price in freedom of action in order to obey agreed rules and preserve a system that provides substantial absolute gains for all.

Science has long been recognized as an elixir of civilization. Less often has it been appreciated for its potential as an especially fungible form of social capital, the elusive glue that permits decentralized institutions to manage conflicts of interest without inviting violent collapse of cooperation. Benefits of Science as a cosmopolitan enterprise with implications for national capabilities move easily across the sovereign boundaries distinguishing traditional levels of analysis in international relations. If global order, hegemonic or otherwise, is to endure, it must endure at three levels—transnational, international, and civic.[74]

Science helps make this happen, adding foundations for trust simultaneously at all three levels. A Scientific State has a chance at least to negotiate a favorable set of rules for stewardship of space and have other sovereigns comply through their consent and acquiescence to the transnational regime's legitimacy. The possibilities for state-to-state cooperation between the hegemon and a rising power—say, Brazil—on sensitive issues such as sharing military technology, reducing barriers to free trade, or preserving the Amazon rain forest expand if there is already a thriving relationship between the sovereigns based on joint science. Finally, the United States as hegemon is more secure at home, in a way that permits greater generosity, patience, and sagacity abroad, when its consumer-oriented, liberal democracy is tempered by a serious national commitment to Science as a human enterprise, a civilizational good relating mankind to Nature through philosophical advancement rather than a national economic input for technological innovation.

The true value of scientific excellence for sustaining the hegemon's influence goes underappreciated because powerful states have difficulty seeing scientific research as anything but the topsoil for advanced weapons and sophisticated exports. Democratic hegemons are no exception. In fact, democratic accountability, to public opinion and organized interests agitating party competition, aggravates the shortsightedness of policy-makers. Philosophical abstractions and theoretical constructs of a more humane world order struggle in vain to draw voters who prefer government policies and programs that deliver short-term, concrete results. Democratic enlightenment, a form of civic virtue characterized by scientific awareness, is the secret ingredient missing from any American plans to extend U.S. hegemony through engagement at the transnational level.

With regard to the hegemon's policy in space, recent documents show U.S. policy-makers have begun to recognize the contradiction lying at the heart of hegemonic engagement but have little sense of how to cultivate deeper partnerships and global norms for stewardship of space while simultaneously fortifying U.S. leadership and technological advantage. Three official policy statements telescope from American grand strategy to specific Department of Defense (DOD) responsibilities on space stewardship: the White House *National Security Strategy*; the White House *National Space Policy*; and the *National Security Space Strategy* authored jointly by the Defense Department and the Director of National Intelligence (DNI).[75]

The Obama administration's 2010 *National Security Strategy* (NSS), like its predecessors and indeed, like the Preamble of the U.S. Constitution, held aloft traditional high-valence goals of territorial security, prosperous trade, and promotion of justice consistent with American values. Apart from the change in tone toward negotiation and burden sharing, the 2010 NSS added a fourth strategic objective to the Bush administration document from 2006. If the Bush-era strategies had been famous for fusing preemptive and preventive war, Obama's version declared a U.S. security interest in ensuring benign international order.[76]

Here was a nod toward global governance without, of course, surrendering the right of self-defense. Reserving room for unilateral action—when U.S. policy-makers deemed it necessary—meant that the NSS raised the ideal of rule-through-rules without specifying conditions under which the U.S. hegemon would constrain its own freedom of action. The White House grand strategy articulated broad goals but avoided discussion of ways and means, leaving unanswered the central strategic question of whether the United States would risk its present position of international influence in order to respect and thereby strengthen international order based on strictures that applied globally.

Both the tonal shift and avoidance of difficult trade-offs were predictable, not just because the previous administration had paid unexpectedly high costs for U.S.-led military missions in Iraq and Afghanistan. At home, the nature of American constitutional democracy, with warring parties and separation of powers, all but compelled the incoming Democratic president to distinguish his *National Security Strategy* from the Republican version published four years earlier, without alienating constituencies tied to supplying ways and means, constituencies that could someday turn specific NSS claims about what might work for U.S. foreign policy into political broadsides against the president.

Moving to the narrower question of national space policy, the Obama administration responded to some of the same pressures it sensed at the grand strategic level. The previous policy under the Bush administration had stressed rejection of arms control or any multilateral arrangements that impinged on freedom of access while improving U.S. capabilities to deny exploitation of space by a hostile power.[77] Consistent with the *Space Policy* goal of "extending human presence across the solar system," President Bush had also proposed a spectacular manned mission to Mars.[78] By contrast, the *National Space Policy* (NSP) document of June 2010 appeared to rein in vastly expensive prestige projects such as the human voyage to Mars in favor of less costly, safer robotic exploration that had some hope of leading to commercial returns.[79] The sober, pragmatically austere tone sounded as soon as the opening epigrams. The first, from Eisenhower, promised to support peaceful uses of outer space. The implication in the late 1950s, when only the Soviets and Americans were racing to outdo each other's achievements, was that the United States, for one, would exercise self-restraint and not rush to deploy space weapons. The Eisenhower quotation also suggested a sacred appreciation for the human longing to touch the hem of Heaven, "to explore the mysteries of outer space." President Obama's response, fifty years later, was profane by comparison. The opportunity to "learn" in space shoehorned into a commercial litany: "work . . . and operate and live safely beyond the Earth." All this activity would indeed pay off "not only" in extending "humanity's reach." Deepening man's communion with the divine might have taken second to strengthening "America's leadership here on Earth."[80]

This prioritization makes sense in terms of raw democratic politics: the people and their representatives in Congress demand security and commercial benefits from U.S. leadership on earth. Rallying congressional support for spending on space, then, binds government expenditures of taxpayer money rhetorically to waxing American political influence. Yet, crass democratization of U.S. aspirations in space, boiling down expected returns so they appeal mainly to immediate desires of the electorate, raises long-term difficulties. This political maneuver to sell policy abandons any effort to educate the public and with it any pretense to visionary leadership. Cutting manned missions and running science proposals through commercial cost-benefit criteria could save tens of billions of dollars over the next decade, but scientific leadership—conducting experiments or observations in space in order to test theoretical knowledge cultivated by the international scientific community—would not cost the same as manned spectacles or industrial research and development.[81] Although news headlines without President Bush's Mars project might be less favorable, or technological developments without President Obama's pragmatism less profitable in the near term, either approach to space bypasses an opportunity to shore up U.S. hegemony over the long haul. The most important challenge for the United States in space, indeed across the global commons, is to negotiate a set of rules, a scheme for global governance, that raises the likelihood of transnational stewardship at the least cost to U.S. freedom of action or potential to dominate the domain during an existential crisis. Fashioning governance through rules that generate global public goods and simultaneously reinforce America's hegemonic position will require mutual trust and an extensive list of responsible stakeholders. Although it is not articulated in either the 2010 *National Security Strategy* or the companion *National Space Policy*, the prerequisites for successful hegemonic engagement are easier to discover when the hegemon has the clear lead in Science.

With the central contradiction between burden sharing and hegemonic advantage already ignored in the White House's *National Security Strategy* and *National Space Policy*, it was difficult to imagine how the *National Security Space Strategy* (NSSS, January 2011), authored by the Department of Defense and the Director of National Intelligence, could somehow resolve the paradox. In fact, the NSSS demonstrates how acute the scientific shortcomings of U.S. space policy are.

Just as the Defense Department implements policy according to presidential directives, the NSSS putatively followed from the White House's *National Space Policy*, and indeed, the 2010 NSP along with other guiding documents is quoted by the *Space Strategy*. On the issue of U.S. cooperation with other powers in space, however, the NSSS, signed by Republican defense secretary Robert Gates, remarkably reverted back to language of the Bush administration in 2006. Whereas the Obama White House "renews its pledge of cooperation" and set a goal to "expand international cooperation" for space utilities, the 2011 NSSS rather hedged like the 2006 NSP, committing only to "seek" cooperation without offering much indication as to whether or where the Americans would find it.[82]

In terms of analysis that clearly distinguished science from technology in S&T policy, the NSSS was more forthright than the 2010 NSP about the excruciating trade-off between hegemonic control and hegemonic engagement. While the guiding NSP did mention national security priorities, including defending against an attack on U.S. space assets should deterrence fail, the NSSS more clearly demonstrated how national security necessity would limit technology and information sharing by the hegemon. Thus, under "Strategic Approaches" in the NSSS, in order to meet "national security space objectives," the United States will "partner with *responsible* nations, international organizations, and commercial firms" (my emphasis).[83] At this point in the document, national security space objectives have been identified and listed as (1) safety, stability, and security in space; (2) enhanced national security advantages afforded to the United States by space; and (3) an energized industrial base that supports U.S. national security.[84]

As in the cases of domestic competition among special interests or state-to-state diplomacy, in the global commons, extending a hand of partnership while maneuvering aggressively to outcompete and dominate the same interlocutors is likely to bring disappointing returns. The NSSS, in essence, warns not to expect too much from hegemonic cooperation in space. After promising to "promote *appropriate* cost-sharing and risk-sharing partnerships to develop and share capabilities," DOD-DNI advise: "Decisions on partnering will be consistent with U.S. policy . . . and consider cost, *protection of sources and methods*, and effects on the U.S. industrial base" (my emphasis).[85] The NSSS wistfully declares: "We will *pursue* increased interoperability, compatibility, and integration of partner nations" before lowering the boom: "*At the same time,* U.S. military and intelligence personnel will ensure the appropriate review and release of classified information" (my emphasis).[86]

The larger point is not that the NSSS walked back policies of enlightened accommodation in 2010 to the dark aftermath of 9/11 when America was besieged by fear—tentatively sharing only when its competitive advantage was already secure and cooperating only in modes that avoided meaningful restrictions on freedom of action. The 2011 NSSS was less recidivist: it did not grasp at imperial control as much as admit that hegemonic engagement compels the lead state to accept real risk against its dominant power position. Opposite from *matryoshka* dolls gradually unmasking the craftsman's true skill with each iteration, U.S. nested strategy documents on space successively show how impoverished American statesmen really are, how ill equipped to strike a practicable balance between coercion of other states through asymmetric power relationships and engagement of fellow stakeholders through a system of universally acceptable rules. Finding the right balance between coercion and engagement—in the case of space stewardship and other transnational issues broaching the question of international organization—will be increasingly salient relative to internal balancing of guns versus butter (and entitlements at home) for rejuvenating the core of U.S. influence and extending American hegemony in a globalizing world.[87] Whatever special ingredient or source of influence helps American democracy manage a complex, mixed policy will soar in value. Science establishes a basis for trust as well as admiration across cultures, and the pervasive effects of scientific achievement—unlike those of, say, an army division, a fighter wing, or a hunter-killer satellite— turn more potent with greater global intercourse and technological diffusion. Science ultimately involves more than a farsighted wager on future research and development, more than a visible manifestation of human artifice; it may well be the sought-after tonic to revive prospects for a Second American Century.

7   Science, Grand Strategy, and Prospects for American Influence

In the transnational arena—as in the bilateral diplomacy and domestic arenas of previous chapters—U.S. policy-makers did not wield sufficient raw power to dictate political solutions for all of civilization. Considering how the U.S. hegemon might shape international order in the unfolding domain of space, this book argued that no amount of feasible investment in science and technology (S&T) programs could generate enough weapons for the United States to sustain dominance—that is, to guarantee safety of its own intelligence and communications satellites while denying, on demand, access to space by any potential competitor. Far more enduring would be rule-through-rules, cast in a philosophy of stewardship over the expanding global commons and designed to avoid destructive competition.

The grand bargain, the glue holding such arrangements together against the ambitions of competing sovereigns, is John Ikenberry's appeal from *Liberal Leviathan*, or the small-group analysis from Mancur Olson's *Logic of Collective Action*: the hegemon provides public goods, such as the Global Positioning System (GPS) timing signal, in return for cooperation from follower states that reinforces system stability and hegemonic influence.[1] The net benefit of rule-through-rules depends on the level of technology on offer from the hegemon, but influence could fluctuate at least as much relative to the level of trust attending the hegemon's commitments. While scientific research frequently leads to development of advanced technology, there is a separable element of Science, as a cosmopolitan enterprise to understand Nature, that more reliably builds trust among politically independent communities. Rather than transform the world according to American lights, Science spares the hegemon's engineers and maintenance crews by lubricating the international system as it is, allowing its existing mechanisms to run somewhat more smoothly.

Republican science, distinct from imperial technology, cultivates more trust, which increases productivity of ongoing negotiations between the hegemon and follower states, and stabilizes international cooperation according to rule-through-rules. Yet, for all this, a deeper question remains. A Westphalian, state-centric, order aims at civilization through mutual recognition—peace and prosperity through a Good Neighbor policy. Divisive creeds founded on Natural Law, inalienable rights, or divine revelation are set aside as internal matters, and states agree merely to acknowledge that good fences, indeed, sovereign boundaries, imply certain restraints on their behavior toward other states.[2]

Twentieth-century critics of Westphalia such as Hedley Bull and John Ruggie actually reached further back to Europe's *original* interstate system surrounding the Aegean Sea to take a page from Thucydides.[3] While appreciating the advantage of a spare, largely procedural system that would allow powerful human communities to agree to disagree on profound moral issues beyond the reach of economics or technological reasoning, paleo-constructivists also recognized that if system rules were enforced by balancing of power, the rules themselves could be constitutive.[4] Powerful states with shared interest in decentralized order that worked to preserve their individual sovereignty would mobilize to support rules of the system, and if these rules functioned more effectively at less cost when embedded in certain norms, well then, suddenly, the hard-won Westphalian cure to chronic holy war confronted a terrible obstacle: no peace without setting values aside and suppressing through diplomatic protocol sovereigns' fight for Truth beyond their borders, and at the same time, no effective protocols without embedding them in common values!

A response, then, to Ruggie, Ikenberry, and constructivist liberals considering a global, as opposed to exclusively European, community of states is that Science rather than liberalism per se may have greater convening power across cultures in support of system rules. Science, as a leavening influence, in addition to inborn Western advocacy for free markets and democratic institutions, could be the heretofore neglected ingredient in a prescription of ideas having cosmopolitan appeal—for navigating the Westphalian paradox.

Science and Transactional Leadership

Still, managing, a problem is not necessarily resolving it. Americans, perched atop a neo-Westphalian, global order, even if they eventually figure out how science, as distinct from technology and consumption, could extend U.S. influence for a second century, must wonder if their decline, contra Thucydides, may be put off forever. Another way of asking this is whether national science is transformational; can the hegemon's commitment to scientific excellence alter the Westphalian order of competing state jurisdictions and create a world constitution that would freeze the distribution of power in place, finally breaking the classic cycle of rise and fall among Great Powers, which Thucydides the historian and many since found so hazardous to human civilization?[5] It is worth recalling that Robert Gilpin in *France in the Age of the Scientific State* (1968) boldly answered in the affirmative: once the United States captured the *scientific* lead after World War II, it was simply too difficult for its main adversary, the Soviet Union, or its allies in Western Europe, to catch up.[6]

Young Gilpin's argument prefigured a central claim of the dominant unipolarity school some forty years later that economic and military indicators for the United States finally climbed to such a superior level, not even a plausible combination of other states could balance against the U.S. hegemon.[7] Both arguments, it turns out, were nearsighted, concentrating almost entirely on the obvious, technological capability, and resolutely tying future growth to the size of current stock. The apogee of influence for both claims lasted somewhat less than a decade, about as long as it took for the unchallengeable hegemon to insert itself into an overseas quagmire and discover the limits of material power bereft of legitimacy.

The first notion, then, that science is transformative of the Westphalian order based on competing nation-states—scorpions in a bottle, cooperating only at the rudimentary level of withholding attack in order to survive—rests heavily on conventional understanding of the technological innovation cycle. Accordingly, science provides the wherewithal for a hegemon to extend its technological lead, ad infinitum, so not all the scorpions are any longer functionally equivalent; none of them, once one of their number has been technologically transformed, can compete, economically or militarily, with the alpha member in the system.

By contrast, this book holds that human scientific activity affects international order on multiple dimensions, which cannot be encapsulated by the familiar innovation cycle. While interdependence between science and technology is compelling, and President Kennedy's deputy national security adviser, Carl Kaysen, was wise to incorporate it into national policy, now nearly fifty years after young Gilpin announced the birth of the Scientific State, technology production by the hegemon appears nowhere close to transforming Westphalia into some bland administration of the world under stable unipolarity; S&T policy has simply been inadequate to that task.

What about the trinity of civilizational mechanisms from national science featured here? In addition to inspiring technological advances, scientific achievement modulates our worldview as a species. It encourages moderation at the *domestic level*, the kind of self-abnegation democracy needs to avoid hyperconsumption, profligate fiscal policies, and a crushing debt burden. Science, in contrast to technology transfer, opens opportunities for *bilateral cooperation* with rising powers in ways conducive to expansion of human capital and accelerated natural development, without directly aggravating threats to the U.S. hegemon's economic or military position. Finally, science can also help legitimize an asymmetric distribution of power and reinforce the lead state's influence by burnishing the hegemon's credentials as a reliable provider of public goods in the *transnational* arena.

At all three levels, though—domestic, interstate, and cosmopolitan—science works within the basic parameters of the Westphalian order. It may reduce incentives for rising states to challenge established norms, but it will not implant American values in every world culture; it will not eliminate fundamental conflicts of interest among independent sovereigns desiring to preserve their way of life. Science may cool the ardor with which challenger states wager what they have, including their independence, to wrest power from the hegemon, but it does not displace mechanisms of diffusion and power convergence among competing polities, which have governed international systems since Thucydides. Science, ultimately, is transactional rather than transformational.[8] Americans may get a second century if they play their cards well, but nothing is guaranteed as much as the need, someday, to prepare the country for a power transition.[9]

Science and American Grand Strategy

That science is transactional, that it can improve the Westphalian system—make cooperation among states run more efficiently to produce greater shares of peace and prosperity—but not, in the end, break Thucydides' trap, or achieve Dante's ideal unified kingdom here on earth profoundly affects how Americans should think about grand strategy. From America's founding, from its first thoughts about its proper role in the world, strategy has adhered more or less to the plot lines of the American Epic.[10] Settlers in the New World of the seventeenth and eighteenth centuries, as if by Providence, had been granted an opportunity to remake civilization in the wilderness. They were close enough to Europe to borrow scientific and philosophical ideas from the Enlightenment, yet far away enough to be free of Old World corruption. As George Washington asked his countrymen after the first presidency under the new Constitution, "Why forego the advantages of so peculiar a situation? . . . Why . . . entangle our peace and prosperity in the toils of European ambition, rivalship, interest, humor or caprice?"[11] The answer, the happy ending according to the American Epic, was that once American democratic institutions matured and U.S. power grew, the champion of the New World would recross the Atlantic in order to redeem the Old.[12] In the journal *International Security*, summarizing his research on the American foreign policy tradition, Jonathan Monten concluded that democracy promotion, either through exemplarism or vindicationism, was woven into American national identity.[13] If, indeed, Calvinism, Enlightenment ideas about human progress, and the functional imperative to bind together one society from many diverse peoples, as Monten argued, etched world transformation in the American psyche, there was bound to be cognitive dissonance with respect to national science. American statesmen will naturally insist on using science and especially technology to unify the world through determination and hard work, but science, as it has been discussed here, is more effective at helping states of the world, sovereign as they are, find common ground for negotiations, consistent with each of their particular and enduring interests. Should the dissonance between American instincts and scientific reality be resolved through willful denial, the United States may awake from its reverie to find it squandered the opportunity for a Second American Century.

The United States, however, could choose a different path, one that probably increases its chances for extending its benign influence over other powers and over the functioning of the international system as a whole. To do so, Americans will have to resist impulses flowing from their national identity and their democratic institutions. Like Odysseus, they will have to suppress their first instincts in order to learn the siren calls of hegemony and still pass through this extraordinary trial with their way of life intact. Attempting to transform, more precisely redeem, the Westphalian compromise and found a New World Order for the ages in America's image is certainly appealing, holding out the tantalizing possibility of a permanent solution to problems of foreign affairs and the vigor of perpetual youth for the United States. Yet, coming to terms with Science, understanding the influence of this common endeavor on human civilization, demands that statesmen turn a classical Periclean epiphany on its head. At the moment of crisis, the Athenian commander-in-chief, Pericles, rallied citizens by persuading them, "What you are fighting against is . . . also the loss of empire . . . what you hold is, to speak somewhat plainly, a tyranny . . . to let it go is unsafe."[14] Now, struggling against the early stages of senility, perhaps, what the United States as an ailing Great Power fights is the loss of hegemony, a process within a multipolar system of sovereign states as natural and inevitable as death for an individual political leader. What the United States holds, to shout over siren calls to power, is not a celestial empire but a secular stewardship. To let it go is dangerous and frightening but also necessary, and before it is too late, appropriate provisions should be made in preparation for the next hegemon: states may live forever in classical Hellas, modern Westphalia, or contemporary global governance, but hegemons, if they are wise, must find a policy that permits them to fade away with dignity, grace, and empathy for the world they will someday leave behind.

Grand Strategy and IR Theory

Planning for retirement is, however, more difficult for leading states than it is for powerful individuals. In addition to greater variability and thus greater uncertainty as to when a hegemon's time on stage will run out, there is the well-founded fear for states under anarchy that granting serious consideration to a postimperial or post-American world will demoralize the citizenry, a source of power in its own right, and hasten the demise of peaceful and prosperous order. Fortunately, in the case of Great Powers, again unlike retirement financing for individuals, strategizing as if one will live forever conduces to comfortable and peaceful sunset years. Moreover, this is especially serendipitous for a democratic power, since no prime minister or president can hope to maintain political support by prophesying the collapse of his own nation's position in the world.[15]

Statesmanship

Those who study grand strategy have elaborated two basic answers to the question of how a hegemon can stay on top forever. The first is statesmanship, and the second is doctrine. Statesmanship as a program for effective foreign policy requires a rigorous education in philosophy and history.[16] It tracks closely with Aristotle's practical wisdom and finds its apotheosis in the crisis diplomacy of Richelieu, Metternich, or Kissinger. Building capacity for states-manship involves cultivating good judgment, what Machiavelli—in a near tau-tology—referred to as virtú, exploiting the logic of power among sovereigns while thriving amid the uncertainty and unavoidable trade-offs of supreme command. If hegemons would exercise their influence while dampening re-sistance from other states, they must balance considerations of interest and justice. This is one of the crucial themes contemporary scholars glean from Thucydides' history of Athens' rise and fall; indeed, it is the central foreign pol-icy message of George Washington's Farewell Address to the United States in 1796. Both Thucydides and Washington pressed a second theme: in order to maximize influence abroad, statesmen must guard against internecine warfare at home. This lesson has held special poignancy for powers of wildly divergent ideological dispositions—for example, Weimar Germany after defeat in World War I and the United States after withdrawal from Vietnam.

Great Powers deprecate the value of statesmanship at their peril. Yet, dem-ocratic states are prone to denying its importance. World-class strategists pose the same problem for republics that so many professions present: they exacer-bate the gap between national security and foreign policy institutions on the one hand and democratic ideals on the other.[17] Ordinary citizens cannot know practical wisdom when they see it. The people are just as likely to elect a dema-gogue as a savant to high office, the difference being opaque to all until foreign policy is implemented and the last game is caught. Thucydides, once again, was instructive, here. His subtle treatment of Pericles in the opening acts of the great war highlighted the spiral of mistrust alienating statesmen from their democracies. Pericles "was enabled to exercise an independent control over the multitude—in short, to lead them instead of being led by them . . . what was nominally a democracy was becoming in his hands government by the first citizen."[18] Consequently, under the stress of war, any error or misfortune suf-fered by the city became the responsibility of Athens' leading statesman. Peri-cles, knowing this, manipulated public opinion, shaded the truth, in order to remain in power, and the Athenians, sensing the darker domestic requirements of Periclean statecraft, were less likely to abide by his policy through all adver-sity. Athenian democracy benefited from Pericles' strategic judgment for about as long as the general lived. As in the classical case, modern democracies cannot rely on statesmen, alone; almost by definition, they cannot outsource statecraft to an unaccountable elite, a "first citizen," or a unitary executive.

Unipolarity

The second alternative for formulating grand strategy adopts a theory, or doctrine, based on a mechanistic explanation for how the world works. It is probably easier for citizens of a modern democracy to place their trust in professional scientists and engineers than statesmen. Advanced technology, in the perceptions of the majority in society, has made life healthier and easier, and these obvious accomplishments would not have happened without scientific bureaucrats—technocrats—who may still be held accountable by political authority embodied by the people's representatives in government. By contrast, superdiplomats, in the eyes of the *demos*, appear above the bureaucracy as aristocrats. Like the case of archcapitalists floating outside society's grasp, different or no rules of accountability apply.

In this context, the realist doctrine of unipolarity emerging out of American fin de siècle International Relations scholarship captured widely shared, post–Cold War illusions in a double sense. First, the stripped-down versions of political power and polarity were easy to measure and easily accessible. Arcane debates about the nature of power and polarity in the centuries-old international system were abruptly cleared aside to make way for commonplace economic charts that any generally educated layman could read. In this way, unipolarity was democratic—obvious to all. Second, unipolarity was something the American public wanted to be true. It was also democratic, then, in the sense that an overwhelming power imbalance seemed to eliminate the need for statesmen. Objective system parameters, primarily the distribution of power, pointed toward stability, so Americans had no need to concentrate authority in the hands of aristocrats of the national security establishment—cabinet secretaries, generals, and intelligence agency directors who were not really of the people.

The "peace of illusions," as Christopher Layne called it, nonetheless fooled few leading realists of International Relations theory.[19] Although the 9/11 terrorist attacks highlighted U.S. dominance in its global share of material resources as the American military-industrial complex swung into action, once sharp military victories in Afghanistan then Iraq had passed in quick succession, the unipolar illusion seemed less convincing. Political power under the Constitution was already flowing, in desperation, to the American executive, and George W. Bush transformed from a CEO president with delegatory, unassuming foreign policy to decider-in-chief, an American war president prepared to defend (or deny) freedom anywhere. As the United States became more engaged in the world, as it attempted to mobilize dominant resources and actualize its influence, Iraq then Afghanistan spun out of control; the American economy sank, setting off a global financial crisis; China and Iran became more assertive; and early into a new American administration, North Africa and the Middle East caught fire with revolutions that unfolded without any apparent concern for the magnetic pull of U.S. unipolarity.

Even so, unipolarity, despite its mounting problems over time, was not ridiculous as a model for attempting to understand the post–Cold War world. Rather, any theoretical construct, even one with much to recommend it, would still be incomplete for producing grand strategy. While International Relations theory can offer a coherent world view that makes formulation of strategy more transparent and comprehensible for ordinary voters in a democracy, because such models of state behavior will not anticipate many strategically significant events, they do not eliminate the need for statesmanship, a species of practical wisdom that like the figure of Pericles himself inhabits a plane above democracy and remains only imperfectly accountable to the people.[20] Conversely, persuasive theory helps adapt freewheeling statesmanship for a democratic power. As Henry Kissinger pointed out during the Cold War, appropriate foreign policy doctrine based on a useful explanation of how the world usually works, frees the democratic statesman to focus on the most difficult and surprising challenges.[21] The noble diplomatist can consequently husband his unique powers, which also economizes the amount of trust, the leaps of faith, he must petition, every time with trepidation, from a great people jealously guarding their sovereign prerogatives.

International Relations theory, still far from perfect in its ability to predict outcomes, remains quite useful for a democratic power. If a case can be made that the United States has neglected to address a genuine trade-off between science and technology, that its strategic investment in both has been out of balance with respect to the goal of extending hegemony in a multipolar world, then for this argument to have traction with the broad electorate, which would play a part in shifting national budgets, the case for a policy shift needs to follow some plausible theory about how the world works.

Three IR Schools and New Institutions

Today, there are three main schools of thought for how the world works.[22] Realism focuses on how states exercise power on other states, as Thucydides reminded his readers, out of fear, honor, and interest, or, as the Preamble of the

American Constitution put it when creating a federal union of once independent states, in pursuit of the common defense, justice, and the general welfare. Liberal institutionalism, also in the tradition of the Constitution, emphasizes that sovereign states under anarchy must cooperate as well as compete. International institutions providing reliable monitoring functions and communication channels can alter the incentives for self-regarding, nonaltruistic states, encouraging them to stick with agreements—as in trade, environmental protection, or arms reduction—that accrue significant mutual benefits over the long term. Finally, constructivism, in its policy implications, also tends to favor liberal values. The social construction of new norms over time, involving powerful state actors, international institutions, and nongovernmental organizations of a global civil society, can change state preferences, and probably has on issues such as ozone depletion, universal human rights, and climate change. Cooperative interventions that would not have been possible, indeed, not even conceived of, without evolution in nation-state identities lie outside the scope of realism and institutionalism, which John Ruggie critiqued as IR theory's squatters, too narrow and neoutilitarian to explain real transformation of the international system.[23]

Ruggie's critique notwithstanding, advocates of a greater role for science in the life and grand strategy of a liberal hegemon will find the most theoretical support for requisite policies and government investment within the middle course discussed, here, liberal institutionalism. Institutionalism as developed by Robert Keohane, Lisa Martin, and later G. John Ikenberry incorporated many of the key provisions of realism.[24] This body of theory allowed for progress—new vistas for cooperation in international affairs without abandoning cyclical power dynamics and the enduring competition for hegemony vividly portrayed in International Relations by compelling realist briefs such as Gilpin's *War & Change in World Politics* (1982). The reason why Robert Gilpin alone does not justify how science can increase a powerful state's influence and extend its hegemony is Gilpin's realism offered no exit ramp from the pathway of Great Power decline, and his early work on the *Scientific State* (1968) included only those mechanisms by which national science improved a nation's technological capability, not the *civilizational* ties by which science reinforced constitutions—and therefore cooperation—at the domestic, interstate, and transnational levels.[25]

Now, instead of liberal institutionalism, why not resort just as much to IR's third school, the constructivism of Alexander Wendt, John Ruggie, Martha

Finnemore, and Michael Barnett, in order to explain how a norm of respect for science, distinct from technology, could become instantiated among powerful states?[26] The answer is, the Republic of Science already exists. Scientific excellence already carries legitimacy across cultures, both through its role early in the cycle of technological innovation and in its ties to progress of civilization. What S&T policy lacks is enlightened *institutional* reform to help self-regarding states, the hegemon in particular, realize the full benefits from a vigorous commitment to cosmopolitan Science. There is no reason to believe that dramatic construction of a new identity is necessary for the hegemon and follower states to increase their commitment. Rather, states in a multipolar system, as both Keohane and Gilpin described it already during the 1980s for economic issues, instinctively appreciate the possible gains with increasing global social capital.

A key question pops up where Keohane articulated it in *After Hegemony* (1984). How can states build the trust that enables mutually beneficial cooperation on environmental issues, human rights, trade and investment, or arms control? Keohane asked this with America's post-Vietnam decline on just about everybody's mind, but of course, the opposite happened in the 1990s, at least in terms of economic measures. Nevertheless, a major defect from relentless reification of national power in economic statistics, and thus of polarity as easily measured stock ratios of dollar value, was that these simplifications did not account for changes after the Cold War in the medium through which the purported metropole, or unipole, had to project power in order to maintain minor states in its gravitational pull.

Following Chapter Three, the problems with unipolarity as a system concept were not merely theoretical, overwriting Waltz's (1979) claim, *by definition*, that two (viz., bipolarity) was the minimum—and most stable—number of major powers under anarchy. Whether or not the new unipolarists explicitly changed the organizing principle of the international system, their predictions ran opposite from traditional realists who interpreted the so-called unipolar moment essentially as a return to asymmetric multipolarity.[27] Unipolarists, for example, did not expect balancing behavior, so active resistance to *Pax Americana* ought to have declined, and in a throwback to young Gilpin's predictions regarding the Scientific State, the distribution of power should have become static, or perhaps featured a widening gap between the lead and follower states. Almost as soon as these claims were made in the 1990s, however, U.S. authority as the guarantor of world order was challenged.

The United States might claim a bare tactical victory in Kosovo and avoidance of utter humiliation in Somalia. During the first fifteen years of the twenty-first century, though, the vaunted U.S. military appeared overextended in Afghanistan and Iraq; the U.S. economy struggled to recover from a global financial crisis, which began by most accounts with a housing bubble collapse at home; and finally, perceptions of U.S. will and competence to lead in world affairs declined. The self-proclaimed sole remaining superpower and indispensable nation stuttered and stumbled on a host of issues. After Libyan regime change; Iranian nuclear deception; North Korean missile and warhead testing; Syrian civil war; expanding Chinese air defense identification zones; and Russian moves in Eastern Europe, including annexation of Crimea, to say the United States as hegemon and unipole was having its way in the world because of hopelessly concentrated economic and military power fumbled the facts and diverged further, with each alarming frustration, from the global public's common sense. Although the United States remained by far the largest economy according to currency exchange rates, with the greatest per capita product of any large state, and the largest expense on future power resources such as the military and research and development, few regions, indeed, very few governments, followed predicted orbits in a unipolar world or carried out tasks according to the hegemon's preferred plan for international order.

More important for gauging the potential of science in extending American hegemony during a second century, genuine unipolarity and the lack of serious competition against hegemonic influence should have made the task of institution building easier for the United States. Keohane's great problem in *After Hegemony* (1984) had been how to detect and take the measure of international institutions that could go on functioning after their most important sponsor, the U.S. hegemon, lost the margin of power necessary to persuade its taxpayers to foot the bill for providing global public goods. With more power concentrated in U.S. hands during the 1990s and 2000s, the kind of lopsided distribution one would expect for a unipolar system, the United States should have been able to steer follower states toward acceptable agreements rather easily. While the margin of surplus power was great, the U.S. hegemon could afford to be generous, offering substantial carrots to more than meet follower states' participation constraints. At the same time, surplus power could be used to punish states for defection or for attempting to relitigate rules in directions less favorable to the hegemon.

Unipolarity should have made Keohane's institutional concern easier to address, global social capital being less important in the presence of raw, concentrated power. On this point, John Ikenberry's call for institutionalism, *Liberal Leviathan* (2011), got it wrong, or at least omitted important constraints, apparently because of his commitment to describing the world as unipolar rather than one of asymmetric multipolarity.[28] Why did the W. Bush administration after 9/11 rely so heavily on rule-by-relationships rather than rule-through-rules? Ikenberry concluded that unipolarity made coercion seem easy and efficient since resistance against priorities of the sole significant state was clearly futile. This conclusion, though, discounted the fact that little coercion of follower states was required to execute initial operations in Afghanistan. As the United States requested more assistance and increased burden-sharing for stabilizing the Karzai government against remnants of the Taliban; isolating Saddam Hussein and forcing regime change in Iraq; advancing the Doha Round of international trade negotiations; establishing a Free Trade Area of the Americas (FTAA) in the hegemon's home region; even coordinating naval action to support the Proliferation Security Initiative, the rational incentives to resist American power, the real magnitude of U.S. sacrifices required in order to transform or create new international regimes, and the hegemon's dearth of legitimacy in a multipolar world were truly felt.

Recognition that polarity measures must take into account the global medium, the context through which economic or military power is exercised, leads to a stronger case for the continuing relevance of both realism and institutionalism. The realists need not expect that minor powers will follow predictable arcs of policy according to the hegemon's desires simply because stock measures of economic capacity and military technology are concentrated. In order for those stocks to translate into polarity, they must be put in play or pass through physical and cultural geography. The actual concentration of power and the relative margin of superiority may be less than what they appear from resource stocks alone, and realists may find more robust predictions once they replace unipolarity with John Mearsheimer's concept of asymmetric multipolarity.[29] Similarly, institutionalism or institutional regime theory predicts that states will search for ways to approach the Pareto Frontier, increasing resource stocks for all. Along the way, however, they will try to get the best deal possible, fighting distributional battles and maximizing gains for themselves.[30] Institutionalists may see more predictions of expanding cooperation come to fruition when the system leader carefully cultivates global social capital. Increased legitimacy and the value of trust are fully appreciated when the would-be hegemon properly conceives of itself in a multipolar world.

After 9/11, Koehane's challenge for states to build institutions that work for all while continuing to reflect the asymmetric distribution of power became *harder* not easier. Despite American resources and dramatic revival of its will to project power, other states across the seas in Europe, Asia, and the Middle East retained independence to chart their own course with respect to matters of war and peace, trade, and cosmopolitan justice. Because the United States devoted so much energy to Afghanistan and Iraq, even the effects of polarity in its home region dampened, so poorer states with far smaller economies such as Brazil, Argentina, and Venezuela found ways to alter the track of the United States (and U.S. corporations), not always the other way around. Building international institutions in a multipolar world is much harder than under a unipolar distribution of power. The negotiations under multipolarity are substantive; the hegemon's continued influence is on the line, as the more powerful other states become, the more public goods and the less favoritism for the patron they may demand from rule-through-rules. In a multipolar world, a hegemon interested in sponsoring institutionalized order needs all the help it can get: success in this type of bargaining is vital for its grand strategy.

Institutions, Identities, and Science

If the United States indeed confronts the strategic problem highlighted by institutionalist theory, national science can be a timely part of the solution. Through selective case studies, this book has shown how a national commitment to exploring Nature can operate at three different levels of analysis simultaneously to build trust for a democratic hegemon seeking to sponsor a benign international order. First, democracy on the world stage labors under a historical reputation for impetuosity. Frequent elections mean that statesmen face unremitting pressure to give the people what they want, and the people want more than anything to consume. Democracy unbound leads to government by, for, and of, the appetites. Since individual appetites conflict, especially across different sectors of society, partisan bickering and gridlock at home, after it is broadcast for all to witness by global media, transmits a clear signal that the state pretending to construct a new order abroad cannot discipline vulgar desires at home.

Investment in scientific discovery apart from technology development binds Odysseus's hands to the mast by countering democracy's penchant for avarice. Potential foreign partners, considering whether to enter into negotiations with the lead state from a position of relative weakness, can observe the hegemon's excellence in science. Almost regardless of cultural dissonance or civilizational differences, follower states respect scientific knowledge, would like to advance their own scientific capacity, and can take confidence in the presumption that a democratic hegemon willing to defer mass gratification for higher purposes within its S&T policy will also discipline its imperial ambition in order to sow a sustainable, purposeful, and mutually beneficial international order. A review of S&T policy since World War II with a focus on the Department of Defense's Office of Naval Research showed that the relatively decentralized federal bureaucracy has great potential for nurturing groundbreaking scientific work. However, the disparate mission agencies and their patrons in Congress rarely resist for long the strident calls from constituents. These urge policy-makers to forgo basic science and spend taxpayer dollars instead on pushing new technologies from the laboratory bench to the field where they can contribute directly to meeting military or commercial objectives.

Inability to maintain a balance between science and technology investments undercuts the U.S. appeals for collaboration at the international level. A hegemon attempting to build an enduring, highly institutionalized order must find a method for channeling the effects from shifts in the distribution of power: the hegemon's system must accommodate rising powers, offering them space to grow while avoiding accumulation of resentments, which could lead to a violent challenge against system rules that are the hallmark of hegemonic success.

Today, the American hegemon operates in a world of several rising states. A review in this book of the diplomatic relationship between the United States and Brazil, a power, notably, presenting one of the lowest direct security threats among rising states, showed how trust is still necessary to optimize cooperation in policy areas such as health, agriculture, and outer space. Trust, unfortunately, is difficult to nurture through technology sharing. Technology diplomacy between the United States and Brazil historically has strained the patience of both sides, with Brazilian leaders remaining understandably sensitive to patronizing attitudes and assistance that results in increased dependence on American know-how. During the fight to eradicate tropical diseases before the *Estado Novo*, the green revolution of the 1960s, and the initiative to develop a satellite launch capability for Brazil in the 1980s, Brazil essentially responded to American technology offers by erecting barriers to contain U.S. political influence—either bringing in competing technology partners or working furiously to set up independent technology institutes controlled by Brazilians.

As in the case of other rising powers, Brazil can claim a proud tradition of scientific competence emanating from its best universities. Indeed, the United States recently reached out to Brazil as part of a broad academic exchange program, "100,000 Strong in the Americas." Yet, such efforts are very often under-resourced to have much positive effect, scientifically or diplomatically. Educating a professional cadre to pursue basic science takes even longer than training engineers. Legislators on both sides struggle to hold together coalitions that will support even modest public funding amounts over multiple election cycles; the science cadre is inevitably swamped by "private investment" and other incentives to disband, so they can serve Brazil instead by entering the ranks of well-connected big business. This result, of course, shifts the focus of Great Power diplomacy from inspirational cooperation on behalf of mankind, solving the mysteries of Nature, to habitual interstate technology competition punctuated by commercial ambition and hypernationalism.

Greater attentiveness to Science within S&T diplomacy might very well improve profitability of relations for both the rising state and the status quo hegemon, with cosmopolitan Science in the role of Keohane's international institutions: reducing the fear of exploitation, bringing new opportunities for joint action into view, and reducing costs for communication, monitoring, and verification of agreements. Yet, U.S. efforts to support Science in its diplomatic relations have devolved into stratagems to capture more engineering and technology. Science-cum-technology spending follows rather than leads other dimensions of hegemonic diplomacy. Revelations, for example, that the United States exploited its technological advantage to collect signals intelligence on the leaders of partner states, including Brazil, confirmed Brazil's darkest suspicions regarding technology sharing with the Americans, through either official or private sector initiatives. Science as a cosmopolitan enterprise stands a greater chance of demonstrating its resilience in the midst of occasional diplomatic imbroglios as the hegemon attempts to both preserve its influence and cultivate legitimacy for the system it sponsors against the natural impatience of rising powers.

Although the American hegemon by some measures is less dependent on other states than previous Great Powers of Europe, if America succeeds in sustaining its international influence deep into the twenty-first century, it will have directed some of its energies toward organizing and sponsoring new institutions for the expanding transnational space in world politics. Pursuing security, prosperity, and justice—those Enlightenment values corresponding to Thucydides' ancient list of motivations, fear, glory, and honor—contemporary states find themselves jostling with new types of actors. State bureaucracies have become professionalized so that subgovernmental units dealing with issues such as military training, trade in services, or international human rights reach common understandings with one another, within their field of expertise but crossing sovereign boundaries. Some transnational knowledge is sufficiently rich to inspire epistemic communities, which in turn shape further relationships, between subunits and central authorities as well as among states themselves. The rising profile of issue expertise and technical advice in interstate bargaining has also created maneuvering room for specialized nongovernmental organizations (NGOs) to influence the formulation and implementation of global rules for state behavior in areas from military intervention and humanitarian operations to intellectual property rights and climate change. Finally, the process of globalization—less expensive and thickening lines of communication for information, goods, and services among states and a burgeoning cast of nonstate actors—has elevated the importance of new international concerns relating to the global commons and global utilities.

A review in this book of dilemmas confronting the United States as it attempts to influence multilateral discussions on the future use of outer space showed that in the transnational arena, the lead power must find a balance. In the global commons, it cannot afford to enforce property rights unilaterally and maintain something like space dominance against all comers. Even if, or in part because, it can claim space superiority, the United States also competes against other states under a handicap of space vulnerability, especially against asymmetric strategies. Creating a space debris field, for example, tit-for-tat against an adversary, could end up harming the U.S. hegemon more than the challenger. On the other hand, the Americans cannot afford to play the pure benign hegemon, providing massive amounts of public goods and giving away technology in order to entice follower states into an American-run system for employing critical orbits in space. Such arrangements would increase the size of the pie for all players but have distributional consequences as well, and if the United States lost its technological and economic advantages, it could expect severe challenges from blocks of participating states demanding changes in governance. With regard to space, a strategy imbalance in the transnational arena between coercive threat and generous sponsorship (sticks and carrots) could eventually jeopardize hegemony, the position of international leadership such strategies were designed to preserve.

Leadership in science can play a helpful role, once again, at the transnational level, easing the hegemon's trade-off between provision of goods and services for the international system and preserving a technological edge over potential rivals that are benefiting and growing within this same system. In the case of space governance, the contributions of scientists in epistemic communities, advising policy-makers on the ultimate consequences of proposed rules and regulations, are especially salient. Scientific students of Nature, specializing in the extraordinary space environment, have unique insight on the strategic opportunities—and dangers—to be encountered in space operations. Even so, science's most important contribution is likely not in the form of specialized knowledge for engineers, program managers, or multilateral treaty negotiators. When the United States supplies a global utility such as the GPS timing and navigation signal or reliable updates on space situational awareness, follower states, as they invest in space systems, must have confidence that the hegemon will not deploy its superior technology to deny them access to space at some point in the future as a method of coercion. The hegemon's national commitment to cosmopolitan Science, its record of scientific achievement and encouragement of joint research with other nations, gives a hard indication of how the lead state balances the benefits of long-term cooperation against short-term exploitation.

In fact, current U.S. policy documents on space such as the *National Space Policy* (2010) and the *National Security Space Strategy* (2011) declare simultaneously the hegemon's intentions to expand cooperation and data sharing while maintaining superior capability for unilaterally securing space. This fundamental tension is unlikely to disappear from U.S. space policy or from the American hegemon's approach in general to global governance. Emergent problems such as unintentional satellite interference, spreading air and water pollution, climate change, and even criminal networks do not respect sovereign boundaries and cannot be resolved without willing international cooperation. The United States, by virtue of its superior resources, is in position not to rule the world but to earn legitimacy abroad through effective global contributions and leadership on these issues. Contradictory impulses, toward multilateral organization versus exclusive dominance of common geopolitical space, threaten to undermine these efforts at benign hegemony. Because the United States must manage unavoidable tensions between supplying the infrastructure for collective progress on transnational challenges and preserving hard power to enforce international order—that is, between benign and classical hegemony—

the United States has a unique interest in building its global social capital, in getting others to trust it will balance system versus national obligations in ways that benefit all. Science, a type of nonthreatening, attractive, cosmopolitan idiom, can place what otherwise might be perceived as hypocritical—or schizophrenic—behaviors on the part of a Great Power in a coherent and reassuring context. A multipolar system of sovereign states has a better chance of addressing transnational challenges, navigating cultural diversity, and getting past unequal distribution of power when the lead state can sustain and persuade other several sovereigns to freely join the most effective international institution of them all, an overarching Republic of Science.

The Way Forward

The case for a hegemonic turn toward Science, for distinguishing it from technology and directing more intellectual and financial energy toward it, rests on the persuasiveness of liberal institutionalist theory. Science also appears poised to pay empirical dividends for the theory, revitalizing interest in the capacity of international institutions, work of human ingenuity, to channel the course of world politics toward greater security, prosperity, and justice for vast tracts of humanity. This enthusiasm has waned in recent decades despite an unbroken stream of data on GDP and military spending showing America yet possesses the wherewithal to support and upgrade organizational frameworks that have undergirded international order for more than sixty years. Part of the problem may inhere in runaway expectations after the Free World's victory in the Cold War, which Americans hoped would usher in a novel epoch of international comity—a grand mobilization of latent or previously misdirected global resources to combat insecurity, poverty, and injustice for the least powerful, most vulnerable human beings. Yet, one by one, premier institutions of the old Western, liberal-democratic bloc buckled under the weight of twenty-first-century challenges.

NATO struggled to maintain its cohesion during out of area missions in the Balkans and later in Afghanistan and Libya. For all the blood and treasure sacrificed, it remained far from clear whether fragile democratic governments in Kosovo, Kabul, or Tripoli could survive without consistent infusions of Western aid. In addition, NATO balked at calls from the United States for assistance in Iraq and more tellingly from Eastern Europeans to intervene beyond the Atlantic Alliance's frontiers in Georgia and Ukraine. The famed Bretton Woods institutions emerging from the aftermath of World War II apparently ran out of answers for the global economy in the early twenty-first century. Global trade talks stalled over agriculture protections in Europe as well as the United States, while international financial institutions fumbled their response to crucial developments such as the rise of the BRIC countries from the periphery and rich countries' insistence upon a mutually draining combination of local austerity packages and reluctant multilateral bailouts. With respect to the highest-order concerns over environmental sustainability and cosmopolitan justice, both the UN Intergovernmental Panel on Climate Change and the International Criminal Court barely managed to stay one step ahead of withering criticism attacking their competency and their reputation for independence from inappropriate ideological or regional preconceptions. Liberal institutionalists never promised to create a Garden of Eden out of the old Westphalian compromise; interdependence did not mean that sovereign nation-states, born of diverse civilizations and competing for survival, could set aside their fears of being exploited. Yet, on the part of many Americans and some Europeans—the so-called Atlanticists—there burned the hope that overwhelming U.S. power advantages could be cleverly employed to strengthen institutions against atavistic predilections. An even bigger problem for the architects of twenty-first-century liberal order than the drumbeat of security, economic, and legal shortcomings was the overarching message that the liberal internationalists were running out of time. Functioning institutions to meet the most pressing challenges of interstate conflict and global governance would not be in place before democracy in America lost the popular will—or its material surplus—to provide necessary support in the form of global public goods.

Throughout our three-dimensional analysis of the international system, and the dimensions correspond to Kant's constitutions—civic, diplomatic, and cosmopolitan, national science relieves the pressure, buying time for the ailing American hegemon by adding social capital to the mix. At each level, the hegemon's genuine vocation for science modulates self-destructive impulses: wanton consumerism fanning flames of domestic faction; primal desire for domination of rival states crippling diplomacy; and lust for imperial control spoiling multilateral regimes before they begin to address transnational problems. Of course, in order to avail itself of this elixir of civilization, heaven-sent insurance against exclusion and parochialism in the administration of awesome global power, the lead state must craft a policy. Until now, through a century of material dominance when the U.S. homeland had enjoyed unique impregnability from military attack, a balanced policy advancing both science and technology has hovered just out of reach. Farsighted officials in every era realize that basic science is like seed corn for the subsequent harvest of superior technologies. Yet, along each dimension of system analysis, at every juncture so important for maintaining legitimacy and sustaining international leadership, Americans indulged Eros, grasping for more technology, rather than patiently consulting Minerva.

America has from its founding fortified itself against the worst excesses of the old-style Athenian hegemony: the U.S. Constitution, a prototypical international organization in conception, impeded the concentration of power in any single pair of hands that could deliver the nation to a false god. Nevertheless, great undertakings, especially ones in which the United States ventured out into the world to redeem the old Westphalian system of warring states, led the American president to forge and maintain consensus across numberless and sprawling constituencies. Not surprisingly, these constituencies ordinarily pursued diverse, if overlapping, objectives. Coalition building at home for U.S. grandeur—at domestic, international, and transnational levels—meant delivering on a range of promises through herding a plethora of bureaucracies and organizations animated by their sense of mission.

Mission accomplishment, then, drove government and civil society's unceasing demand for *technology* while science, by contrast, satisfied neither Democratic nor Republican party platforms. The public at large did not insist on more rapid *scientific* discovery. Instead, the masses cried for less expensive and higher quality products and services. Meanwhile, their representatives at the head of national districts, state governments, or social movements wanted concrete progress on their priority issues before the next election. Science, once the dauntless herald of democracy to monarchs of early-modern Europe, has, in American national life, unwisely been swept aside, as a quaint pursuit suitable for eccentric savants and their unmistakably aristocratic patrons.[31]

Reviving science, bringing it back to center stage, consistent with ambient conditions under an American-led liberal order but short of an existential crisis like the race for the atomic bomb during World War II or the apparent missile gap after *Sputnik*, will test the mettle of democratically accountable policy-makers.[32] During a time of spiraling security challenges overseas and sluggish economic performance at home, significant S&T budget increases or transfers from technology pots to pure scientists carrying out basic research are not in the cards. However, there are two significant policy initiatives that might be explored, even under tight, or highly competitive, budget restraints.

Since much of federal support for science with the partial exception of the National Science Foundation is driven by the agendas of decentralized mission agencies, and these organizations tend to be insulated from immediate political pressures on the president, reforms to expand federal government concern for pure science could begin at the leadership levels of these semiautonomous bureaus. Like civic-minded parishioners on Sunday, broad-minded units within the executive branch have the discretion to tithe. In a religious context, the first dollar wrung from daily labor, a contemporary echo of the unblemished calf from ancient times, goes not toward consumption but to charity for the glory of God—a type of power distinct from and transcendent of the state.[33] While liberal democracy must take care to avoid persecuting minority faiths, there are no parallel compunctions against favoring the scientific method as a universal doctrine for respecting and appreciating Nature. More to the practical limits on formulating policy, most good ideas in pure science or basic research demand fewer dollars than technology development projects; science rather requires more budget discipline than technology when protecting dollars on the margin. What has been happening of late is budget legerdemain: cooption of dollars earmarked for prediscovery or blue sky work by urgent, mission-oriented demand for advanced technology. Mission agencies could instead strive harder to be upstanding members of civil society in the cosmopolitan Republic of Science, using their first dollars to draw crucial attention toward worthy projects that might otherwise languish in obscurity. In essence, America's S&T policy agencies could perform better at what they already claim to be doing: reserving a small portion of taxpayer provided resources to identify and promote excellence in basic research.

The president of the United States already accepts a certain amount of autonomy for agencies under him within the vast executive branch. The president, therefore, is unlikely to raise serious objections if mission-oriented technology sponsors within the government were to devote less than 1 percent of their budget to facilitating communications through conferences and travel funds, supplementing foundation or university grants, and possibly lending existing laboratory equipment or personnel for essentially humanitarian projects— where this pro bono work would be dedicated to the mind and soul of the citizenry and mankind in general more than sustenance of the national body. Relevant committee members in Congress, who tend to be closer to individuals and businesses within their districts served by technology, would, however, notice the incremental shift in S&T policy. Unlike the situation with congressional earmarks, lawmakers would have a harder time seeing the benefits from such spending. A hundred thousand dollars going to a private university here or a research foundation there without regard to equity across different parts of the American republic presents a reelection threat for the majority of members. Thus, the requisite autonomy to balance properly science and technology in the government's S&T portfolio will likely be in short supply, unless, that is, participants on both sides of this principal-agent divide can be educated.

American scientists, the new agents in this age of STEM reforms, could use more civic education that would cover the evolution of debate over core American values, particularly the balancing of freedom versus equality in national life, and provide insight into the ubiquitous dilemmas liberal democracy must navigate in order to benefit from, without being consumed by, the modern professions.[34] Although the old metaphor of a marriage between science and the sovereign remains problematic, there is a sense in which Americans, as a sovereign people, must reciprocate and learn to love science for Science's sake. The title of Hans Morgenthau's famous essay to Americans at a moment of self-doubt comes close to describing the relationship that would best support American success, domestically and in foreign affairs: *Science: Master or Servant?* ends in a question because the answer is both. Science is the handmaiden of *technē*, the instrumental knowledge that makes every American combatant commander and every U.S.-led task force arbiter of the conventional military situation in whichever area of responsibility (AOR) it appears. Yet, Science is, at the same time, party to the creation of human civilization and a deep well for latent social capital, good at home and abroad for tempering Eros in human nature and restraining American hegemony from metastasizing into self-destructive imperialism.

At this moment, when Americans stand near the precipice, peering over the edge and contemplating the consequences of U.S. decline in the world, there is no better time for this people to consider whether the Last Man will not only be democratic man or self-made man, but scientific man as well. In her essay on co-production, Science & Technology Studies (STS) professor Sheila Jasanoff hit on the right idea: tech savvy Americans almost intuitively understand the potential for "facts and artifacts to reconfigure nature," so, unsurprisingly, American scientists and policy experts help set the agenda while contributing lead voices in the global discourse over transnational causes such as climate change and space situational awareness.[35] Yet, co-*discovery* in place of co-production would be more useful for sustaining American influence in the twenty-first century. Co-production, of course, illuminates how technology embedded in new products alters our structure of preferences and lifestyle as consumers. While this is certainly an important sociological question, going forward, the world historical issue of "American hegemony, *quo vadis?*" will likely turn on somewhat different ground—whether American democracy can lead other states and societies in understanding co-discovery, the capacity for national scientific progress to reconfigure human values in ways conducive to a secure, prosperous, and just international order.

Notes

Chapter 1

1. Robert Gilpin, *War and Change in World Politics* (Cambridge: Cambridge University Press, 1981), 211.

2. Robert Kaplan, *Warrior Politics: Why Leadership Demands a Pagan Ethos* (New York: Random House, 2002); Victor Davis Hanson, *The Father of Us All: War and History, Ancient and Modern* (New York: Bloomsbury Press, 2010); Colin Gray, "War—Continuity in Change, and Change in Continuity," *Parameters* Vol. 40, No. 2 (Summer 2010): 5–13. See also the recent edited volume in tribute to Robert Gilpin's contributions, Wolfgang Danspeckgruber, ed., *Robert Gilpin and International Relations: Reflections* (Boulder, CO: Lynne Rienner, 2012).

3. W. Robert Connor, *Thucydides* (Princeton: Princeton University Press, 1984), 154–59.

4. Peter Paret, ed., *Makers of Modern Strategy from Machiavelli to the Nuclear Age* (Princeton: Princeton University Press, 1986); Michael Smith, *Realist Thought from Weber to Kissinger* (Baton Rouge: Louisiana State University Press, 1986); Charles Hill, *Grand Strategies: Literature, Statecraft, and World Order* (New Haven: Yale University Press, 2010).

5. Robert Keohane and Joseph Nye, *Power and Interdependence: World Politics in Transition*, 2nd ed. (Glenview, IL: Scott, Foresman, 1989), excerpted in Richard Betts, ed., *Conflict after the Cold War*, 2nd ed. (New York: Pearson Education, 2005), 139–45.

6. Michael Doyle, *Ways of War and Peace: Realism, Liberalism, and Socialism* (New York: W. W. Norton and Co., 1997).

7. Alexander Wendt, "Anarchy Is What States Make of It: The Social Construction of Power Politics," *International Organization* Vol. 46, No. 2 (Spring 1992): 391–425; Martha Finnemore, "Constructing Norms of Humanitarian Intervention," in Peter Katzenstein, ed., *The Culture of National Security: Norms and Identity in World Politics* (New York: Columbia University Press, 1996), 153–85; Martha Finnemore and Kathryn Sikkink, "International Norm Dynamics and Political Change," *International Organization* Vol. 52, No. 4 (Autumn 1998): 887–917.

8.   Setting a realist baseline then assessing the residuals, that is, the anomalies left unexplained, has underwritten important projects across a range of international relations research agendas and methods. See Stephen Walt, *The Origins of Alliances* (Ithaca, NY: Cornell University Press, 1987); Robert Keohane, "Institutionalist Theory and the Realist Challenge after the Cold War," in David Baldwin, ed., *Neorealism and Neoliberalism: The Contemporary Debate* (New York: Columbia University Press, 1993), 269–300, esp. 271; James Fearon, "Rationalist Explanations for War," *International Organization* Vol. 49, No. 3 (Summer 1995): 379–414.

9.   Thucydides, "The Peloponnesian War," trans. Rex Warner, intro. M. I. Finley (New York: Penguin Books, 1983 [1954]).

10.   Robert Gilpin, *France in the Age of the Scientific State* (Princeton: Princeton University Press, 1968).

11.   Robert Keohane, *After Hegemony: Cooperation and Discord in the World Political Economy* (Princeton: Princeton University Press, 1984).

12.   Robert Kagan, *Of Paradise and Power: America and Europe in the New World Order* (New York: Vintage Books, 2004); Randall Schweller, *Unanswered Threats: Political Constraints on the Balance of Power* (Princeton: Princeton University Press, 2006); Thomas Mowle and David Sacko, *The Unipolar World: An Unbalanced Future* (New York: Palgrave Macmillan, 2007); Stephen Brooks and William Wohlforth, *World out of Balance: International Relations and the Challenge of American Primacy* (Princeton: Princeton University Press, 2008).

13.   Hubert Védrine, "Into the 'Twenty-First,'" speech at the opening of the IFRI Annual Conference, Paris, November 3, 1999; Dominique de Villepin, *Toward a New World* (Hoboken, NJ: Melville House, 2004).

14.   Raymond Aron, *Peace and War: A Theory of International Relations* (New York: Doubleday and Co., 1966), esp. ch. 2; Niall Ferguson, *Colossus: The Price of America's Empire* (New York: Penguin Press, 2004); Stephen Walt, *Taming American Power: The Global Response to U.S. Primacy* (New York: W. W. Norton and Co., 2006); Francis Fukuyama, *America at the Crossroads: Democracy, Power, and the Neoconservative Legacy* (New Haven: Yale University Press, 2007); Parag Khanna, *The Second World: Empires and Influence in the New Global Order* (New York: Random House, 2008); Fareed Zakaria, *The Post-American World* (New York: W. W. Norton and Co., 2008); Christopher Layne, "The Waning of U.S. Hegemony—Myth or Reality? A Review Essay," *International Security* Vol. 34, No. 1 (Summer 2009): 147–72; Charles Kupchan, *No One's World: The West, the Rising Rest, and the Coming Global Turn* (Oxford: Oxford University Press, 2012); Dale Copeland, *Economic Interdependence and War* (Princeton: Princeton University Press, 2014); Paul Voitti, *The Dollar and National Security: The Monetary Component of Hard Power* (Stanford: Stanford University Press, 2014).

15.   Former Columbia University provost Jonathan Cole touched on this idea in *The Great American University* (2009), acknowledging the link between knowledge pro-

duction and national preeminence in global affairs and distinguishing investments in fundamental knowledge from products and technology. His emphasis, however, was the fate of the American research university, not the arc of U.S. hegemony (Jonathan Cole, *The Great American University: Its Rise to Preeminence; Its Indispensable National Role; Why It Must Be Protected* (New York: Public Affairs, 2009), esp. ch. 14, "Trouble in Paradise?" 451–510).

16. Carl von Clausewitz, *On War*, ed. and trans. Michael Howard and Peter Paret (Princeton: Princeton University Press, 1984 [1976]), 184. I take "moral elements" and "moral power" as concepts that go beyond casual usage of "morale." Here, morale of an army, morality (or character) of its officers and men, and, ultimately, the legitimacy of state authority are indeed connected.

17. See www.bartleby.com/73/1213.html, accessed June 23, 2010.

18. Robert Kagan, "America's Crisis of Legitimacy," *Foreign Affairs* Vol. 83, No. 2 (March/April 2004): 65–87; Joseph Nye, Jr., *Soft Power: The Means to Success in World Politics* (New York: Public Affairs, 2005).

19. "And do not imagine that what we are fighting for is simply the question of freedom or slavery: there is also involved the loss of an empire and the dangers arising from the hatred which we have incurred in administering it" (Pericles to the Athenians, Thucydides [1954]: II, 63, p. 161). "(T)hose who still preserve their independence do so because they are strong . . . by conquering you we shall increase not only the size but the security of our empire" (Athenians to the Melians, Thucydides [1954]: V, 97, p. 403). Dimitri Simes, "America's Imperial Dilemma," *Foreign Affairs* Vol. 82, No. 6 (November/December 2003): 91–102.

20. Frank Oliveri, "Military Takes Aim at New Weaponry," *CQ Weekly*, June 14, 2010, 1428–29.

21. Mark Brawley, *Political Economy and Grand Strategy: A Neoclassical Realist View* (Abingdon: Routledge, 2010), ch. 7, "The Consequences of Mismanagement: Soviet Grand Strategy in the 1980s," 117–37.

22. Joseph Nye, "Gorbachev and the End of the Cold War," *New Straits Times*, editorial, April 5, 2006, available from Harvard University, John F. Kennedy School of Government, Belfer Center website: http://belfercenter.ksg.harvard.edu/publication/1531/gorbachev_and_the_end_of_the_cold_war.html, accessed September 22, 2010. Nonstate actors chipped in as well: see Thomas Risse-Kappen, "Ideas Do Not Float Freely: Transnational Coalitions, Domestic Structures and the End of the Cold War," *IO* Vol. 48, No. 2 (Spring 1994): 185–214.

23. Cathleen Campbell, "Chapter 16: Science and Technology," in *A Country Study: Soviet Union (Former)*, Library of Congress, Federal Research Division (Washington, DC: LOC, 1989), available at http://rs6.loc.gov/frd/cs/sutoc.html#su0421, accessed May 18, 2015; Linda Weiss argued that U.S. success in S&T derived not only from the unmatched size of the U.S. economy and its Research & Development investment but also

from creative organization, which reconciled the need for government financial and managerial support of S&T with the American national ideology of *antistatism*. Linda Weiss, *America Inc.? Innovation and Enterprise in the National Security State* (Ithaca, NY: Cornell University Press, 2014).

24. George Kennan, "The Sources of Soviet Conduct," *Foreign Affairs* Vol. 25, No. 4 (July 1947), available at www.historyguide.org/europe/kennan.html.

25. Ibid.

26. Ibid. This was the last line in Kennan's famous essay.

27. Joseph Nye, Jr., *The Paradox of American Power* (New York: Oxford University Press, 2002); Joseph Nye, Jr., "The Decline of America's Soft Power: Why Washington Should Worry," *Foreign Affairs* Vol. 83, No. 3 (May/June 2004): 16–21; Nye (2005).

28. Joseph Nye, "Donald Rumsfeld and Soft Power," Project Syndicate, April 24, 2006, available at www.project-syndicate.org/commentary/nye32/English, accessed June 28, 2010.

29. Joseph Nye, "Smart Power," *Huffington Post*, November 29, 2007, available at www.huffingtonpost.com/joseph-nye/smart-power_b_74725.html, accessed September 23, 2010.

30. Thomas Ricks, *The Gamble: General David Petraeus and the American Military Adventure in Iraq, 2006–2008* (New York: Penguin Press, 2009); Peter Feaver, "The Right to Be Right: Civil-Military Relations and the Iraq Surge Decision," *International Security* Vol. 35, No. 4 (Spring 2011): 87–125.

31. James Baker III and Lee Hamilton, cochairs, *Iraq Study Group: The Report* (Washington, DC: USIP, December 2006), available at www.usip.org/isg/iraq_study_group_report/report/1206/index.html, accessed September 23, 2010.

32. Leslie Gelb, *Power Rules: How Common Sense Can Rescue American Foreign Policy* (New York: HarperCollins, 2009).

33. Ibid., xi.

34. Daniel Drezner, "Machiavelli Revisited, Review," *National Interest*, March/April 2009, available at http://nationalinterest.org/bookreview/machiavelli-revisited-3037.

35. One of the most influential International Relations scholars and a leading realist published a book just before 9/11, highlighting how difficult it would be for the United States to hold on to its unique status and control the system, even when no peer competitor was immediately obvious after the dissolution of the Soviet Union. John Mearsheimer, *The Tragedy of Great Power Politics* (New York: W. W. Norton and Co., 2001).

36. Recall Thucydides' observation on what motivates state actors: he reported the Athenians justifying to rival Sparta Athens' acquiring of empire the result first of fear, then *honor* and interest (Robert Strassler, ed., *The Landmark Thucydides: A Comprehensive Guide to the Peloponnesian War* (New York: Free Press, 1996), 43/I.75).

37. There are no guarantees here. Admiral Yamamoto studied and worked in the

United States, understood its power potential, but nevertheless designed and executed the Japanese attack on Pearl Harbor. Still, awe makes aggressors hesitate before challenging the leader, and Machiavelli felt that over the long run, Fortune rather favors the bold (Niccolò Machiavelli, *The Prince*, trans. and intro. Harvey Mansfield, Jr. (Chicago: University of Chicago Press, 1985), ch. XXV.

38. Peter Haas, "Introduction: Epistemic Communities and International Policy Coordination," *International Organization* Vol. 46, No. 1 (Winter 1992): 1–35.

39. Roger Pielke featured the IPCC in his discussion of science advice and the politics of climate change in *The Honest Broker* (Cambridge: Cambridge University Press, 2007).

40. Immanuel Kant, *Perpetual Peace and Other Essays*, trans. and intro. Ted Humphrey (Indianapolis, IN: Hackett, 1983 [1795]). On Kant's legacy, see Doyle (1997). For Johns Hopkins scholar Francis Fukuyama, the apparent end of cycles in the early 1990s meant the end of History (*The End of History and the Last Man* [New York: Avon Books, 1992]). One of the reasons why Keohane's *After Hegemony* (1984) had a lasting impact on the modern study of international relations was that it built a plausible case for predicting prosperous cooperation covering the greater part of the world and not subject to the vicissitudes of Great Power rivalry or decline.

41. Henry Luce of *Life* magazine coined the triumphant phrase "The American Century" in the midst of U.S. material and diplomatic preponderance after World War II.

42. Late in the Cold War, just a few years behind *After Hegemony*, came Paul Kennedy, *The Rise and Fall of the Great Powers* (New York: Vintage Books, 1987). Samuel Huntington, John Mearsheimer, and Robert Kagan consciously riposted against Fukuyama's *End of History* with their own theories and evidence pointing toward more of the same, rising and falling, which would jeopardize the dream of a second American Century. Samuel Huntington, *The Clash of Civilizations and the Remaking of World Order* (New York: Simon and Schuster, 1998); Mearsheimer (2001); Kagan (2004). See also Joseph Nye, *Is the American Century Over?* (Cambridge: Policy Press, 2015).

43. Christopher Layne (2009: 147–72, esp. 168–69) noted the reserve currency issue as he summed up several widely circulated books considering the extent and consequences of American decline. The books reviewed for the journal, *International Security*, were Brooks and Wohlforth (2008); Parag Khanna, *The Second World: How Emerging Powers Are Redefining Global Competition in the Twenty-first Century* (NY: Random House, 2008).; Kishore Mahbubani, *The New Asian Hemisphere: The Irresistible Shift of Global Power to the East* (New York: Public Affairs, 2008); and Zakaria (2008). Layne also referred to the contemporaneous National Intelligence Estimate from the U.S. government: National Intelligence Council, *Global Trends 2025: A Transformed World* (Washington, DC: GPO, November 2008). A burgeoning literature corresponds to the intense interest in faltering American leadership. Layne might have easily been asked to include

the aforementioned *Power Rules*, plus Barry Buzan, *The United States and the Great Powers: World Politics in the Twenty-first Century* (Cambridge: Polity Press, 2004); Peter Katzenstein, *A World of Regions: Asia and Europe in the American Imperium* (Ithaca, NY: Cornell University Press, 2005); Amy Chua, *Day of Empire: How Hyperpowers Rise to Global Dominance . . . and Why They Fall* (New York: Doubleday and Co., 2007); Jeffrey Anderson, G. John Ikenberry, and Thomas Risse, *The End of the West?: Crisis and Change in the Atlantic Order* (Ithaca, NY: Cornell University Press, 2008); and Michael Klare, *Rising Powers, Shrinking Planet: The New Geopolitics of Energy* (New York: Henry Holt and Co., 2008). See also the multibook review by Michael Mastanduno, "Overpowered?" *Foreign Affairs* Vol. 89, No. 3 (May/June 2010): 114–19, in which he cites debt and continued deficit spending by the United States as the chief factor in forcing the last standing superpower to pull back from international commitments.

44. Layne (2009: 170).

45. Charles Kindleberger, "Systems of International Economic Organization," in David Calleo, ed., *Money and the Coming World Order* (New York: New York University Press, 1976), 15–39; Joanne Gowa, "Rational Hegemons, Excludable Goods, and Small Groups: An Epitaph for Hegemonic Stability Theory?" *World Politics* Vol. 41, No. 3 (April 1989): 307–24; G. John Ikenberry and Charles Kupchan, "Socialization and Hegemonic Power," *International Organization* Vol. 44, No. 3 (Summer 1990): 283–315; George Modelski and William Thompson, *Leading Sectors and World Powers: The Coevolution of Global Economics and Politics* (Columbia: University of South Carolina Press, 1996), 51–55.

46. Bruce Russett, "The Mysterious Case of Vanishing Hegemony; or Is Mark Twain Really Dead?" *International Organization* Vol. 39, No. 2 (Spring 1985): 207–31; Stephen Walt, "Alliance Formation and the Balance of World Power," *International Security* Vol. 9, No. 4 (Spring 1985): 3–43; Susan Strange, "The Persistent Myth of Lost Hegemony," *International Organization* Vol. 41, No. 4 (Autumn 1987): 551–74; Nye (2015).

47. Steve Chan, *China, the U.S., and the Power Transition Theory: A Critique* (London: Routledge, 2008).

48. John Ruggie, "What Makes the World Hang Together? Neo-utilitarianism and the Social Constructivist Challenge," *International Organization* Vol. 52, No. 4 (Autumn 1998): 855–85.

Chapter 2

1. Jean-Jacques Rousseau, "Discourse on the Origin of Inequality," in Donald Cress, trans. and ed., and Peter Gay, intro., *Basic Political Writings of Jean-Jacques Rousseau* (Indianapolis, IN: Hackett, 1987), 25–81.

2. Ken Binmore, *Playing Fair: Game Theory and the Social Contract, Volume 1* (Cambridge: MIT Press, 1994); Robert Powell, *In the Shadow of Power: States and Strategies in International Politics* (Princeton: Princeton University Press, 1999); R. Harrison

Wagner, *War and the State: The Theory of International Politics* (Ann Arbor: University of Michigan Press, 2007).

3. Thomas Spragens, *Understanding Political Theory: An Introduction* (New York: St. Martin's Press, 1976).

4. Plato, *The Trial and Death of Socrates*, 3rd ed., trans. G. M. A. Grube, ed. John Cooper (Indianapolis, IN: Hackett, 2000).

5. St. Augustine, *The City of God against the Pagans*, ed. R. W. Dyson (Cambridge: Cambridge University Press, 1998); Edward Gibbon, *The Decline and Fall of the Roman Empire*, ed. Antony Lentin, intro. Brian Norman (Ware: Wordsworth Editions Limited, 1998).

6. John Freely, *Aladdin's Lamp: How Greek Science Came to Europe through the Islamic World* (New York: Vintage Books, 2010).

7. See the first two volumes of Eric Hobsbawm's trilogy on European history. Eric Hobsbawm, *The Age of Revolution, 1789–1848* (Cleveland, OH: World, 1962); *The Age of Capital, 1848–1875* (New York: Charles Scribner's Sons, 1975).

8. John Brehm and Scott Gates, *Working, Shirking, and Sabotage: Bureaucratic Response to a Democratic Public* (Ann Arbor: University of Michigan Press, 1997). For application of the principal-agent problem to civil-military relations, see Deborah Avant, "Are the Reluctant Warriors out of Control? Why the U.S. Military Is Averse to Responding to Post–Cold War, Low-Level Threats," *Security Studies* Vol. 6, No. 2 (December 1996); and Peter Feaver, *Armed Servants: Agency, Oversight, and Civil-Military Relations* (Cambridge: Harvard University Press, 2003).

9. Two classic essays from the twentieth century on how science can preserve integrity despite pressure from the state are Max Weber, "Science as a Vocation," in David Owen and Tracy Strong, eds. and intro., Rodney Livingstone, trans., *The Vocation Lectures* (Indianapolis, IN: Hackett, 2004), 1–31; and Hans Morgenthau, *Science: Servant or Master* (New York: W. W. Norton and Co., 1972). For case studies illustrating the difficulties both authoritarian and democratic governments run in tasking science, and therefore scientists, to shape policy, see H. Lyman Miller, *Science and Dissent in Post-Mao China: The Politics of Knowledge* (Seattle: University of Washington Press, 1996); and Gregg Herken, *Cardinal Choices: Presidential Science Advising from the Atomic Bomb to SDI* (Stanford: Stanford University Press, 2000 [1992]). See also Thomas Hayden, "Scientists and Bush Administration at Odds," *U.S. News and World Report*, June 30, 2005, available at www.usnews.com/usnews/culture/articles/050630/30science.htm.

10. Reinhold Niebuhr, "America's Precarious Eminence" (1960 [1947]), reprinted in *American Defense Policy*, 8th ed., ed. Paul Bolt, Damon Coletta, and Collins Shackelford (Baltimore, MD: Johns Hopkins University Press, 2005), 16–23.

11. Robert Gilpin, *War and Change in World Politics* (Cambridge: Cambridge University Press, 1981); Paul Kennedy, *The Rise and Fall of the Great Powers* (New York: Vintage Books, 1987).

12. Freely (2010).

13. Roger Crowley, *Empires of the Sea: The Siege of Malta, the Battle of Lepanto, and the Contest for the Center of the World* (New York: Random House, 2008).

14. *Francis Bacon: The Major Works,* ed. and intro. Brian Vickers (Oxford: Oxford University Press, 2002 [1996]). The quotation is from Bacon's prior essay on "The Advancement of Learning" (1605), 147–48.

15. For Richelieu as a transition figure, caught between principles of his faith and raison d'état, see Joseph Bergin and L. W. B. Brockliss, eds, *Richelieu and His Age* (Oxford: Clarendon Press, 1992). Evolution of state administration under chief minister Richelieu is covered in Richard Bonney, *Political Change in France under Richelieu and Mazarin, 1624–1661* (Oxford: Oxford University Press, 1978).

16. L. W. B. Brockliss, "The Scientific Revolution in France," in Roy Porter and Mikulas Teich, eds., *The Scientific Revolution in National Context* (Cambridge: Cambridge University Press, 1992), 63. See also the biography by Andrew Trout, *Jean-Baptiste Colbert* (Boston: Twayne, 1978).

17. Jacob Soll, *The Information Master: Jean-Baptiste Colbert's Secret State Intelligence System* (Ann Arbor: University of Michigan Press, 2009). Within ch. 2, "Colbert's Cosmos: The Expert and the Rise of the Modern State," see, esp., the section after "Antiquarians and the Information State" (25–33) on the role of scholars and experts for legitimizing centralized state authority apart from the Church.

18. John Lynn, *The Wars of Louis XIV, 1667–1714* (Harlow: Addison Wesley Longman, 1999), esp. ch. 5, "Violence and State Policy," 160–90.

19. Alexander Hamilton, "Federalist No. 11," in George Carey and James McClellan, eds., *The Federalist* (Indianapolis, IN: Liberty Fund, 2001), 49–55; John Miller, *Alexander Hamilton and the Growth of the New Nation,* intro. A. Owen Aldridge (New Brunswick, NJ: Transaction, 2004 [1959]), 284–85.

20. W. Roger Louis and Ronald Robinson, "The Imperialism of Decolonization," in Walter Hixson, ed., *The American Experience in World War II: American Diplomacy in the Second World War,* Vol. 8 (London: Routledge, 2003), 30–79; D. Cameron Watt, *Succeeding John Bull: America in Britain's Place, 1900–1975* (Cambridge: Cambridge University Press, 1984), 102–10, 129–30. See also Julian Go, *Patterns of Empire: The British and American Empires, 1688 to the Present* (New York: Cambridge University Press, 2011).

21. Geir Lundestad, *The United States and Western Europe since 1945: From "Empire" by Invitation to Transatlantic Drift* (Oxford: Oxford University Press, 2003). For U.S. government reaction to this concern over the decades, see Susan Brewer: *Why America Fights: Patriotism and War Propaganda from the Philippines to Iraq* (New York: Oxford University Press, 2009).

22. Woodrow Wilson, *Constitutional Government in the United States* (1908), reprinted in *Woodrow Wilson: The Essential Writings,* intro. Ronald Pestritto (Lanham, MD: Lexington Books, 2005), 176.

23. Ibid.

24. Charles de Secondat, Baron de Montesquieu, *The Spirit of Laws* (1752), trans. Thomas Nugent, ed. J. V. Prichard, Liberty Library of the Constitution Society, 1998, online text based on G. Bell and Sons, Ltd., London, 1914, available at www.constitution. org/cm/sol.htm, bk. IV.4.

25. Ibid., bk. V.5; religious faith served to discourage outrageous or antisocial behavior (XX.18), making the polity easier to govern. Robert Putnam and David Campbell, *American Grace: How Religion Divides and Unites Us* (New York: Simon and Schuster, 2010).

26. Montesquieu, bk. XXVI.7, 9.

27. Ibid., bk. XX.14, 16.

28. Ibid., bk. XXIV.17.

29. Ibid., bk. XXV.4.

30. Ibid., bk. XXVI.2, 9.

31. Ibid., bk. XXVI.5.

32. Ibid., bk. XXVI.4.

33. Ibid., bk. IV.6.

34. Ibid., bk. XVIII.6.

35. Ibid., bk. XVIII.21.

36. Andreas Osiander, "Sovereignty, International Relations, and the Westphalian Myth," *International Organization* Vol. 55, No. 2 (Spring 2001): 251–87, esp. 272. For an analysis of Thomas Hobbes's attempt to tame religion in *Leviathan*, see Benjamin Milner, "Hobbes on Religion," *Political Theory* Vol. 16, No. 3 (August 1988): 400–425, esp. 415–18. A contemporary application of the idea that political mobilization on religious grounds threatens the peace appears in Michael Devine, "Religion in the Thirty Years' War and Peace of Westphalia: Relevant to Pakistan Today?" *Joint Force Quarterly* Vol. 65 (2nd Quarter 2012): 22–26.

37. Hamilton, "Federalist No. 11"; George Washington, "Washington's Farewell Address" (1796), Yale Law School-Avalon Project, available at http://avalon.law.yale. edu/18th_century/washing.asp: "It will be worthy of a free, enlightened, and at no distant period, a great nation, to give to mankind the magnanimous and too novel example of a people always guided by an exalted justice and benevolence."

38. Walter McDougall, *The Heavens and the Earth: A Political History of the Space Age* (New York: Basic Books, 1985), 160, 210, passim; G. Pascal Zachary, *Endless Frontier: Vannevar Bush, Engineer of the American Century* (New York: Free Press, 1997), 389–92; Jonathan Cole, *The Great American University* (New York: Public Affairs, 2009), 145–48.

39. Richard Evans, *The Third Reich in Power* (New York: Penguin Books, 2006), 318. Having experienced the battlefield in World War I, Hitler and his associates appreciated the potential, for example, of practical medical research.

40. Ibid., 319; Peter Watson, *The German Genius: Europe's Third Renaissance, the*

Second Scientific Revolution, and the Twentieth Century (New York: Harper Perennial, 2010), 658, 666, 689–98.

41. Ibid., 694; McDougall (1985: 44–45).

42. McDougall (1985: 250–52, 280–89). See also Roger Launius, John Logsdon, and Robert Smith, eds., *Reconsidering Sputnik: Forty Years since the Soviet Satellite* (London: Routledge, 2002 [2000]).

43. Stuart Croft, *Strategies of Arms Control: A History and Typology* (Manchester: Manchester University Press, 1996), 36–39; Committee on International Security and Arms Control, National Academy of Sciences, *Nuclear Arms Control: Background and Issues* (Washington, DC: National Academies Press, 1985), 35–38.

44. Loren Graham, *What Have We Learned about Science and Technology from the Russian Experience?* (Stanford: Stanford University Press, 1998).

45. Bertrand Russell "Science and Values," in *The Impact of Science on Society* (London: Routledge, 1998 [1952]), 90–108, esp. ff. 100; Audra Wolfe, *Competing with the Soviets: Science, Technology, and the State in Cold War America* (Baltimore, MD: Johns Hopkins University Press, 2012), e.g. 4–5.

46. David Holloway, "Soviet Scientists Speak Out," and Yuli Khariton and Yuri Smirnov, "The Khariton Version," both in *The Bulletin of the Atomic Scientists* (May 1993): 18–31. See also David Holloway, *Stalin and the Bomb: The Soviet Union and Atomic Energy, 1939–1956* (New Haven: Yale University Press, 1994).

47. Graham (1998: 52–73).

48. Kenneth Heineman, *Campus Wars: The Peace Movement at American State Universities in the Vietnam Era* (New York: New York University Press, 1993), 4–5, and ch. 1 (13–41); Zachary (1997: 393–95). "Federal funding for research and development—a drop in the bucket compared with farm subsidies—has long been in decline. From 1970 to 1995, it fell as a percentage of gross domestic product by 54 percent in physical sciences and 51 percent in engineering." Fareed Zakaria, "How Government Funding of Science Rewards U.S. Taxpayers," *Washington Post*, June 20, 2012, available at http://articles. washingtonpost.com/2012–06–20/opinions/35460033_1_human-genome-project-science-and-technology-farm-subsidies.

49. Ajin Choi, "The Power of Democratic Cooperation," *International Security* Vol. 28, No. 1 (Summer 2003): 142–53. Choi's argument is countered, only partially, by Michael Desch, *Power and Military Effectiveness: The Fallacy of Democratic Triumphalism* (Baltimore, MD: Johns Hopkins University Press, 2008).

50. Fareed Zakaria, *Post-American World* (New York: W. W. Norton and Co., 2008), 256–58; Fareed Zakaria, "Broken and Obsolete," *TIME* Magazine, June 18, 2012, available at www.time.com/time/magazine/article/0,9171,2116713,00.html; James Surowiecki, "The Track Star Economy," *New Yorker* Magazine, August 27, 2012, available at www. newyorker.com/talk/financial/2012/08/27/120827ta_talk_surowiecki.

51. See Gilpin (1981: 185, 191–93) for mechanisms on the diffusion of power in the international system and hegemonic war. Gilpin was influenced by Thucydides' account of imperial overextension in Athens' attempt to conquer Sicily in the *Peloponnesian War* (books VI and VII).

52. Larry Diamond, *Developing Democracy: Toward Consolidation* (Baltimore, MD: Johns Hopkins University Press, 1999), 23, and ch. 6, 218–60. For an evaluation of transparency and accountability in world politics that draws from theory on democracy at the nation-state level, see Ruth Grant and Robert Keohane, "Accountability and Abuses of Power in World Politics," *American Political Science Review* Vol. 99, No. 1 (February 2005): 29–43.

53. John Lukacs, *Democracy and Populism: Fear and Hatred* (New Haven: Yale University Press, 2005); Harvey Mansfield, "Democracy and Populism," *Society* Vol. 32, No. 5 (July/August 1995): 30–32.

54. National Science Board, *Research and Development: Essential Foundation for U.S. Competitiveness in a Global Economy*, a companion to *Science and Engineering Indicators*—2008 (Arlington, VA: National Science Foundation, National Science Board, 2008), available at www.nsf.gov/statistics/nsb0803/nsb0803.pdf, esp. "Basic Research: A Declining National Commitment," p. 2, accessed January 28, 2013.

55. Zachary (1997: 254–56; 353–55); John Brehm and Scott Gates, *Teaching, Tasks, and Trust: Functions of the Public Executive* (New York: Russell Sage Foundation, 2008); Feaver (2003).

56. Samuel Huntington thoroughly explored this tension in the developing world. Samuel Huntington, *Political Order in Changing Societies* (New Haven: Yale University Press, 1968). For his analysis of democracy in the United States, see Samuel Huntington, *American Politics: The Promise of Disharmony* (Cambridge: Harvard University Press, 1981).

57. Margaret Karns and Karen Mingst, *International Organizations: The Politics and Processes of Global Governance* (Boulder, CO: Lynne Rienner, 2010), 57.

58. Grant and Keohane (2005: 29–44). William Easterly, *The Tyranny of Experts: Economists, Dictators, and the Forgotten Rights of the Poor* (New York: Basic Books, 2013).

Chapter 3

1. David Baldwin, "Power and International Relations," in Walter Carlsnaes and Beth Simmons, eds., *Handbook of International Relations* (London: Sage Publications, 2002), 177–91.

2. Amitai Etzioni, *From Empire to Community: A New Approach to International Relations* (New York: Palgrave Macmillan, 2004); Friedrich Kratochvil and Edward Mansfield, *International Organization and Global Governance: A Reader*, 2nd ed. (New York: Pearson Longman, 2006); Alexander Cooley and Hendrik Spruyt, *Contracting States:*

Sovereign Transfers in International Relations (Princeton: Princeton University Press, 2009); Iver Neumann and Ole Jacob Sending, *Governing the Global Polity: Practice, Mentality, Rationality* (Ann Arbor: University of Michigan Press, 2010).

3. Kenneth Waltz, "Structural Realism after the Cold War," *International Security* Vol. 25, No. 1 (Summer 2000): 5–41; John Mearsheimer, *The Tragedy of Great Power Politics* (New York: W. W. Norton and Co., 2001); Stephen Brooks and William Wohlforth, *World out of Balance: International Relations and the Challenge of American Primacy* (Princeton: Princeton University Press, 2008); Fareed Zakaria, *The Post-American World* (New York: W. W. Norton and Co., 2008); Leslie Gelb, *Power Rules: How Common Sense Can Rescue American Foreign Policy* (New York: HarperCollins, 2009); Joseph Nye, "The Future of American Power: Dominance and Decline in Perspective," *Foreign Affairs* Vol. 89, No. 6 (November/December 2010).

4. Daniel Nexon and Thomas Wright, "What's at Stake in the American Empire Debate," *American Political Science Review* Vol. 101, No. 2 (May 2007): 253–71, esp. 268.

5. Kenneth Waltz, *Theory of International Politics* (Reading, MA: Addison-Wesley, 1979), 131.

6. J. David Singer and Paul Diehl, eds., *Measuring the Correlates of War* (Ann Arbor: University of Michigan Press, 1990); Ashley Tellis, Janice Bially, Christopher Layne, Melissa McPherson, and Jerry Sollinger, *Measuring National Power in the Postindustrial Age: Analyst's Handbook* (Santa Monica, CA: RAND, 2000); Thomas Mowle and David Sacko, *The Unipolar World: An Unbalanced Future* (New York: Palgrave Macmillan, 2007); Brooks and Wohlforth (2008).

7. Bruce Russett, *Power and Conformity in World Politics* (San Francisco: W. H. Freeman and Co., 1974), 279–80.

8. G. John Ikenberry, Michael Mastenduno, and William Wohlforth, "Introduction: Unipolarity, State Behavior, and System Consequences," in G. John Ikenberry, Michael Mastenduno, and William Wohlforth, eds., *International Relations Theory and the Consequences of Unipolarity* (Cambridge: Cambridge University Press, 2011), 1–32; ref. also figures 2.1, 2.2; see critics of soft balancing in a special issue of the journal *International Security* Vol. 30, No. 1 (Summer 2005).

9. Waltz (1979: 96–97, 191 para. 3).

10. "States have different combinations of capabilities which are difficult to measure and compare, the more so since the weight to be assigned to different items changes with time" (ibid., 131).

11. Christopher Layne, "The Waning of U.S. Hegemony—Myth or Reality," *International Security* Vol. 34, No. 1 (Summer 2009): 147–72, esp. 170. On the practitioner side, see National Intelligence Council, *Global Trends 2025: A Transformed World* (Washington, DC: GPO, November 2008); and Ed O'Keefe, "Mullen: Despite Deal, Debt Still Poses the Biggest Threat to U.S. National Security," *Washington Post*, August 2, 2011,

available at www.washingtonpost.com/blogs/checkpoint-washington/post/mullen-de-spite-deal-debt-still-a-risk-to-national-security/2011/08/02/gIQAhSr2oI_blog.html.

12. There are alternative interpretations of how instability at home enervated U.S. power in the case of Iraq. Leading realists John Mearsheimer and Stephen Walt, who are generally friendly toward structural realism, noted that the United States was paying unnecessary costs in Iraq because it made a mistake in choosing to fight there—as a result of imbalance among influential interest groups at home. John Mearsheimer and Stephen Walt, *The Israel Lobby and U.S. Foreign Policy* (New York: Farrar, Straus, Giroux, 2007).

13. The text of Kennan's Long Telegram (February 1946) is available online at www.trumanlibrary.org/whistlestop/study_collections/coldwar/documents/pdf/6–6.pdf; George Kennan, "The Sources of Soviet Conduct," *Foreign Affairs* Vol. 25, No. 4 (July 1947): 566–82, esp. 580.

14. Bertrand Russell, *Power* (Oxon: Routledge Classics, 2004 [1938]). Compare E. H. Carr, *The Twenty Years' Crisis, 1919–1939* (New York: Harper and Row, 1964 [1939]); Raymond Aron, *Peace and War: A Theory of International Relations* (Garden City, NY: Doubleday, 1966), ch. II; and Tellis et al. (2000).

15. Russell (2004: 22, 23, 223).

16. Ibid., 19–20.

17. Max Weber, "Science as a Vocation," in David Owen and Tracy Strong, eds., Rodney Livingstone, trans., *The Vocation Lectures: "Science as a Vocation," "Politics as a Vocation"* (1919) (Indianapolis, IN: Hackett, 2004).

18. Hans Morgenthau, *Science: Servant or Master?* (New York: New American Library/Norton, 1972).

19. Hedley Bull, *The Anarchical Society: A Study of Order in World Politics*, 3rd ed. (New York: Columbia University Press, 2002 [1977]); Alexander Wendt, *Social Theory of International Politics* (Cambridge: Cambridge University Press, 1999).

20. Waltz (1979: see, for example, 161, 191).

21. Ibid., 192.

22. Mowle and Sacko (2007); Ikenberry et al. (2011).

23. For example, see Waltz (2000), esp. 27.

24. Waltz (1979: 129–31).

25. William Wohlforth, "The Stability of a Unipolar World, *International Security* Vol. 24, No. 1 (Summer 1999): 5–41, esp. 12, 15, 19.

26. Waltz (1979: 136).

27. Ibid., 126.

28. Ibid., 199–201.

29. Ibid., 201. Kenneth Waltz, "Kant, Liberalism, and War," *American Political Science Review* Vol. 56, No. 2 (June 1962): 331–40. For a comparison of Niebuhr and Waltz

on the prospects of a functional world state, or world government, see Campbell Craig, *Glimmer of a New Leviathan: Total War in the Realism of Niebuhr, Morgenthau, and Waltz* (New York: Columbia University Press, 2003), 164–65, 169–73.

30. Waltz (1979: 201).

31. Ibid., 112, 201.

32. Chris Giles and Paul Rathbone, "Currency Wars Not Over, Says Brazil," *Financial Times* (U.K.), July 5, 2011, available at www.ft.com/intl/cms/s/0/36ee3298-a731–11e0-b6d4–00144feabdc0.html#axzz10G6urzzR, accessed March 5, 2012.

33. T. V. Paul, James Wirtz, and Michel Fortmann, eds., *Balance of Power: Theory and Practice in the 21st Century* (Stanford: Stanford University Press, 2004); "Balancing Acts," *International Security* (Special Issue) Vol. 30, No. 1 (Summer 2005); Ikenberry et al. (2011), chs. by Stephen Walt and Martha Finnemore, along with the Introduction.

34. Parag Khanna, *The Second World: Empires and Influence in the New Global Order* (New York: Random House, 2008); Fareed Zakaria, *The Post-American World*, enl. ed. (New York: W. W. Norton and Co., 2011); Thomas Friedman and Michael Mandelbaum, *That Used to Be Us: How America Fell behind in the World It Invented and How We Can Come Back* (New York: Farrar, Straus, and Giroux, 2011); Zbigniew Brzezinski, *Strategic Vision: America and the Crisis of Global Power* (New York: Basic Books, 2012). For recent scholarly sources, see Charles Glaser, *Rational Theory of International Politics: The Logic of Competition and Cooperation* (Princeton: Princeton University Press, 2010); Charles Kupchan, *No One's World: The West, the Rising West, and the Coming Global Turn* (Oxford: Oxford University Press, 2012); and most interestingly, given his early writings on unipolarity, Stephen Walt, "The End of the American Era," *National Interest*, November/December 2011, 6–16, esp. 7, 10.

35. For rigorous theoretical development from this phrasing, see Mowle and Sacko (2007). I reach a different conclusion from the oligopoly production models because in the current system, actions of the first-mover do not sufficiently constrain follower units, or price taking states.

36. Regarding the pedigree of this idea, that power in the international system cannot be completely divorced from role, Robert Keohane challenged Waltz's separation of the concepts in an edited volume; see "Realism, Neorealism, and the Study of World Politics," in Robert Keohane, ed., *Neorealism and Its Critics* (New York: Columba University Press, 1986), 1–26, esp. 18. Interestingly, despite disagreements on several fundamentals, the volume's discussion of power and capacity for setting system constraints runs quite parallel across the theoretical divide. Compare also Robert Keohane, "Lilliputians' Dilemmas: Small States in International Politics," *International Organization* Vol. 23, No. 2 (Spring 1969): 291–310 with Waltz's (1979) discussion of international poles and price setters in microeconomics.

37. Stephen Walt, "Alliances in a Unipolar World," *World Politics* Vol. 61, No. 1 (January 2009): 86–120, esp. 96.

38. G. John Ikenberry, Michael Mastanduno, and William Wohlforth, "Introduction: Unipolarity, State Behavior, and Systemic Consequences," *World Politics* Vol. 61, No. 1 (January 2009): 1–27, esp. 18.

39. Jane Perlez, "Continuing Buildup, China Boosts Defense Spending More than 11 Percent," *New York Times*, March 5, 2012, A8.

40. John Tirpak, "Washington Watch: China Surpasses—Doubles—Russia's Military Spending," *AirForce-Magazine.com* Vol. 94, No. 10 (October 2011), available at www.airforce-magazine.com/MagazineArchive/Pages/2011/October%202011/1011watch.aspx, accessed March 7, 2012.

41. Waltz (1979: 130, 180–81).

42. Scott Sagan and Kenneth Waltz, *The Spread of Nuclear Weapons: A Debate Renewed* (New York: Norton, 2003). Campbell Craig noted the increase in weight Waltz accorded second-strike nuclear forces for producing international stability as bipolarity waned. Waltz maintained the consistency of polarity as a non-nuclear concept by describing system structure as one important non-nuclear variable but not the only factor that determined stability (Craig 2003: 166–67).

43. Daniel Nexon, *The Struggle for Power in Early Modern Europe: Religious Conflict, Dynastic Empires, and International Change* (Princeton: Princeton University Press, 2009), esp. ch. 9, drew an extensive, well-illustrated parallel between emerging secular governments in seventeenth-century Europe and today's postmodern states, which must reconcile powerful demands from supranational, transnational, and subnational groups.

44. Waltz expressed it this way in a 2003 interview: "(T)here are no checks and balances against that power, so it's free to follow its fancy; its free to act on its whims." "Conversations with History: Kenneth Waltz," an interview with Harry Kreisler, University of California, Berkeley, June 2003, available at www.youtube.com/watch?v=F9eV5g-PlPZg, accessed March 8, 2012.

45. Waltz's post-2000 analysis gets a lot right, but that part tended to be consistent with asymmetric multipolarity. If only he had stuck to his theoretical guns even more, he would not have had to endure twenty years of "world hegemony," quite an awkward anomaly, in the language of his 1979 masterpiece.

46. Robert Keohane, *After Hegemony: Cooperation and Discord in the World Political Economy* (Princeton: Princeton University Press, 1984).

47. G. John Ikenberry, *After Victory: Institutions, Strategic Restraint, and the Building of Order after Major Wars* (Princeton: Princeton University Press, 2001).

48. G. John Ikenberry, *Liberal Leviathan: The Origins, Crisis, and Transformation of the American World Order* (Princeton: Princeton University Press, 2011).

49. Zakaria (2008); Simon Serfaty, "Moving into a Post-Western World," *The Washington Quarterly* Vol. 34, No. 2 (Spring 2011): 7–23.

50. See Tony Smith, "In Defense of Intervention," *Foreign Affairs* Vol. 73, No. 6 (No-

vember/December 1994): 34–46, versus Michael Mandelbaum, "Foreign Policy as Social Work," *Foreign Affairs* Vol. 75, No. 1 (January/February 1996): 16–32.

51. Robert Gilpin, *War and Change in World Politics* (Cambridge: Cambridge University Press, 1981); G. John Ikenberry and Charles Kupchan, "Socialization and Hegemonic Power," *International Organization* Vol. 44, No. 3 (Summer 1990): 283–315; Robert Keohane, "Review Essay: The United States and Postwar Order: Empire or Hegemony?" *Journal of Peace Research* Vol. 28, No. 4 (November 1991): 435–39.

52. Geir Lundestad, *The United States and Western Europe since 1945: From "Empire" by Invitation to Transatlantic Drift* (Oxford: Oxford University Press, 2003); Ivan Ivanov, *Transforming NATO: New Allies, Missions, and Capabilities* (Plymouth: Lexington Books, 2011).

53. The solar system is a unipolar system featuring the sun at the center and functionally differentiated from the planets caught in its gravitational field. Stephen Toulmin saw an indirect influence between the success of Newtonian mechanics and modern political philosophy on a natural arrangement for the state in relation to its citizens. Waltz was not as explicit, but in describing world hegemony as an invitation to *civil war* he conjured a solar system of world politics with the United States at the center. The problem with genuine unipolarity if it did occur was that, unlike the sun, the dollop of humanity alone at the center would commit injustices against the many societies trapped in its orbit. Stephen Toulmin, *Cosmopolis: The Hidden Agenda of Modernity* (Chicago: University of Chicago Press, 1990).

54. Joseph Nye, *The Paradox of American Power: Why the World's Only Superpower Can't Go It Alone* (Oxford: Oxford University Press, 2002); Joseph Nye, *Soft Power: The Means to Success in World Politics* (New York: PublicAffairs, 2005); Stephen Walt, *Taming American Power: The Global Response to U.S. Primacy* (New York: W. W. Norton and Co., 2005); and perhaps most interestingly, Robert Kagan, "America's Crisis of Legitimacy," *Foreign Affairs* Vol. 83, No. 2 (March/April 2004): 65–87.

55. John Mearsheimer, "Hans Morgenthau and the Iraq War: Realism versus Neo-conservatism," *OpenDemocracy.net,* May 18, 2005, available at www.opendemocracy.net/democracy-americanpower/morgenthau_2522.jsp, accessed March 10, 2012; Christopher Layne, "The Unipolar Illusion Revisited: The Coming End of the United States' Unipolar Moment," *International Security* Vol. 31, No. 2 (Fall 2006): 7–41; Richard Betts, "The Three Faces of NATO," *National Interest,* no. 100 (March/April 2009): 31–38.

56. Mearsheimer (2001).

57. Mearsheimer and Walt (2007).

58. William Wohlforth, "Unipolarity, Status Competition, and Great Power War," *World Politics* Vol. 61, No. 1 (January 2009): 28–57, esp. 31.

59. Ian Katz and Cheyenne Hopkins, "Geithner Will Press China on Yuan While Seeking Support on Iran Sanctions," *Bloomberg.com,* January 10, 2012, available at www.

bloomberg.com/news/2012–01–10/geithner-to-seek-china-s-support-on-iran-sanc-tions-while-pressing-on-yuan.html, accessed March 12, 2012.

60. Jacek Kugler and Douglas Lemke, "The Power Transition Research Program: Assessing Theoretical and Empirical Analysis," in Manus Midlarsky, ed., *Handbook of War Studies II* (Ann Arbor: University of Michigan Press, 2000), cited in Wohlforth (2009: 57); Nye (2010: 2–12); Joseph Nye, "American and Chinese Power after the Financial Crisis," *Washington Quarterly* Vol. 33, No. 4 (October 2010): 143–53.

61. Wohlforth (2009: 57).

62. As such, science complements the literary approach to grand strategy, linking significant works and their examination of human nature to insights on diplomacy and war. Charles Hill included philosophical treatises along with poems and novels in his sweeping exegesis. The great stories of science, how theories of Nature were formulated, tested, then validated by societies at large, merit a place in this type of scholarship. See Charles Hill, *Grand Strategies: Literature, Statecraft, and World Order* (New Haven: Yale University Press, 2010), especially the treatment of Aristotle's *Politics*, a work in which early science and philosophy went hand in hand, and the relevance to American exceptionalism on pp. 150–51.

Chapter 4

1. James Glimm, "Congressional Testimony in Support of NSF," *Notices of the AMS* (American Mathematical Society), August 2009, 707, available at www.ams.org/notices/200907/rtx090700797p.pdf.

2. Joseph Stiglitz, "Some Lessons from the East Asian Miracle," *World Bank Research Observer* Vol. 11, No. 2 (August 1996): 151–77, esp. 161–62, points out the reluctance of democracies to permit mistakes by the government and accept the level of risk necessary to make industrial policy work. Robert Atkinson and Stephen Ezell, *Innovation Economics: The Race for Global Advantage* (New Haven: Yale University Press, 2012), 135–41 and fig. 5.1, steer clear of industrial policy as extreme government interference in the market by picking specific "firms/industries/technologies." See also "Picking Winners, Saving Losers," *Economist*, August 5, 2010, available at www.economist.com/node/16741043, accessed September 17, 2012; and Darren Samuelsohn, "GOP Grills Stephen Chu, Keeps Solyndra Affair Burning, *Politico.com*, November 17, 2011, available at www.politico.com/news/stories/1111/68643.html, accessed September 17, 2012.

3. John Jay, "Concerning Dangers from Foreign Force and Influence," *Federalist* No. 2, in George Carey and James McClellan, eds., *The Federalist*, Gideon ed. (Indianapolis, IN: Liberty Fund, 2001), 5–9.

4. Robert Strassler, *The Landmark Thucydides: A Comprehensive Guide to the Peloponnesian War* (New York: Free Press, 1996), bk. II (2.65).

5. Edward Gibbon, *The History of the Decline and Fall of the Roman Empire* Vol. 1 [1776], Liberty Fund Online Library of Liberty, ch. 3, available at http://oll.libertyfund.

org/?option=com_staticxt&staticfile=show.php%3Ftitle=1365&chapter=50991&lay-out=html&Itemid=27.

6. Geoffrey Parker, "The Making of Strategy in Hapsburg Spain: Philip II's 'Bid for Mastery,' 1556–1598," in Williamson Murray, MacGregor Knox, and Alvin Bernstein, eds., *The Making of Strategy: Rulers, States, and War* (Cambridge: Cambridge University Press, 1994), 115–150. See also Geoffrey Parker, *Felipe II* (Madrid, Spain: Planeta, 2010); and Daniel Nexon, *The Struggle for Power in Early Modern Europe: Religious Conflict, Dynastic Empires, and International Change* (Princeton: Princeton University Press, 2009), esp. 185–234.

7. Alice Conklin, *A Mission to Civilize: The Republican Idea of Empire in France and West Africa, 1895–1930* (Stanford: Stanford University Press, 1997). Inspiration for *la mission civilisatrice* came out of the universalizing principles of 1789 and expansion of the Napoleonic Empire. See the review of Conklin's study by Christopher English in *Canadian Journal of African Studies* Vol. 32, No. 2 (1998): 397–400; and Brett Bowden, *The Empire of Civilization: The Evolution of an Imperial Idea* (Chicago: University of Chicago Press, 2009), esp. 94–95, 130, 237 (n. 43).

8. Wilhelm Deist, "The Road to Ideological War: Germany, 1918–1945," in Williamson Murray, MacGregor Knox, and Alvin Bernstein, eds., *The Making of Strategy: Rulers, States, and War* (Cambridge: Cambridge University Press, 1994), 352–92.

9. Theologian Reinhold Niebuhr popularized this insight after the war. Much later, his work haunted the United States as it contemplated intervention in Iraq to remake the Middle East. Reinhold Niebuhr, "America's Precarious Eminence," in Harry Davis and Robert Good, eds., *Reinhold Niebuhr on Politics* (New York: Charles Scribner's Sons, 1960), 269–83; Paul Elie, "A Man for All Reasons," *Atlantic,* November/December 2007, available at www.theatlantic.com/magazine/archive/2007/11/a-man-for-all-reasons/306337/.

10. George W. Bush, "Second Inaugural Address," January 20, 2005, available at www.bartleby.com/124/pres67.html. For critiques of American universalism, see Leslie Gelb, "Necessity, Choice, and Common Sense," *Foreign Affairs* Vol. 88, No. 3 (May/June 2009): 56–72; and Dimitri Simes, "America's Imperial Dilemma," *Foreign Affairs* Vol. 82, No. 6 (November 2003): 91–102.

11. Bowden (2009: 161–214).

12. Samuel Huntington, "American Ideals vs. American Institutions," *Political Science Quarterly* Vol. 97, No. 1 (Spring 1982): 1–37.

13. Niall Ferguson, *Civilization: The West and the Rest* (New York: Allen Lane/Penguin, 2011), ch. 5, pp. 196–255.

14. See the Two Americas theme in John Edwards's speech as the vice presidential nominee at the Democratic National Convention, Boston, Massachusetts, July 2004, available at www.washingtonpost.com/wp-dyn/articles/A22230–2004Jul28.html; Jason Riley, "Obama's Class Warfare Campaign," *Wall Street Journal* Online, April 25, 2012,

available at http://online.wsj.com/article/SB100014240527023047233045773657923641777
50.html.

15. Carl Sagan, *The Demon-Haunted World: Science as a Candle in the Dark* (New York: Ballantine Books, 1996), ch. 2, pp. 24–39. Examples of schools distinguished in science and religion tend to come from the list of private institutions of higher education: Harvard, Duke, Notre Dame, and the like.

16. Samuel Huntington, *The Clash of Civilizations and the Remaking of World Order* (New York: Simon and Schuster, 1996). Huntington included Western, Confucian, Eastern Orthodox, Islamic, Hindu, Japanese, African, and Latin American civilizations, which were loosely based on religious fault lines. For critiques that current U.S. policy is not sufficiently progressive on skilled immigration, see Fareed Zakaria, "The Future of American Power: How America Can Survive the Rise of the Rest," *Foreign Affairs* Vol. 87, No. 3 (May/June 2008): 18–43, esp. "The Gray Zone"; and Niall Ferguson, "America's Problem Isn't Immigration—It's Education," *Telegraph* (U.K.), April 19, 2006, available at www.telegraph.co.uk/comment/personal-view/3624228/Americas-problem-isnt-immigration-its-education.html. They, however, tend to emphasize engineers and business entrepreneurs with clear, short-term benefits to the economy over pure scientists, who would have a distinct relationship to economic growth and a moderating influence on American consumerism.

17. James Fallows, "How America Can Rise Again," *Atlantic,* January/February 2010, available at www.theatlantic.com/magazine/archive/2010/01/how-america-can-rise-again/307839/1/, esp. webpage 6.

18. Gallup, "Confidence in Institutions," *Gallup,* June 2012, available at www.gallup.com/poll/1597/confidence-institutions.aspx, accessed September 29, 2012.

19. David Zucchino, "Unemployment Is a Special Challenge for Veterans," *Los Angeles Times,* April 25, 2012, available at http://articles.latimes.com/2012/apr/25/nation/la-na-vets-unemployed-20120426.

20. Brian Williams, "End of an Era: Richard Lugar Loses," *NBC Nightly News,* May 9, 2012, video available at http://video.msnbc.msn.com/nightly-news/47362793#49217926, accessed September 29, 2012.

21. Roger Pielke, Jr., *The Honest Broker: Making Sense of Science in Policy and Politics* (Cambridge: Cambridge University Press, 2007).

22. Andy Guess, "American Science Plateau," *InsideHigherEd.com,* July 20, 2007, available at www.insidehighered.com/news/2007/07/20/plateau, accessed September 29, 2012; "American Science in Decline," editorial, *Washington Times,* July 17, 2005, available at www.washingtontimes.com/news/2005/jul/17/20050717–093342–2847r/; Donald Braben, *Scientific Freedom: The Elixir of Civilization* (Hoboken, NJ: John Wiley and Sons, 2008).

23. Hans Morgenthau, *Science: Servant or Master* (New York: W. W. Norton and Co., 1972).

24. Max Weber, "Science as a Vocation," in David Owen and Tracy Strong, eds. and intro., Rodney Livingstone, trans., *The Vocation Lectures* (Indianapolis, IN: Hackett, 2004), 1–31.

25. Robert Jervis, *The Meaning of the Nuclear Revolution: Statecraft and the Prospect of Armageddon* (Ithaca, NY: Cornell University Press, 1989), 6; see also the opening of Bernard Baruch's speech at the United Nations: "We are here to make a choice between the quick and the dead." "The Baruch Plan," *NuclearFiles*.org (presented June 14, 1946, c1998 by Nuclear Age Peace Foundation), available at www.nuclearfiles.org/menu/key-is-sues/nuclear-weapons/issues/arms-control-disarmament/baruch-plan_1946–06–14. htm, accessed October 1, 2012.

26. A rich biography that captures the ethos of this era when American society and government became highly professionalized is G. Pascal Zachary, *Endless Frontier: Vannevar Bush, Engineer of the American Century* (New York: Free Press, 1997).

27. Kenneth Meier and Laurence O'Toole, *Bureaucracy in a Democratic State: A Governance Perspective* (Baltimore, MD: Johns Hopkins University Press, 2006); John Brehm and Scott Gates, *Working, Shirking, and Sabotage: Bureaucratic Response to a Democratic Public* (Ann Arbor: University of Michigan Press, 1997).

28. Morris Fiorina and David Rohde, eds., *Home Style and Washington Work: Studies of Congressional Politics* (Ann Arbor: University of Michigan Press, 1989).

29. Joel Aberbach and Mark Peterson, eds., *The Executive Branch* (Oxford: Oxford University Press, 2005); Peter Feaver, *Armed Servants: Agency, Oversight, and Civil-Military Relations* (Cambridge: Harvard University Press, 2003); Deborah Avant, "Are the Reluctant Warriors out of Control? Why the U.S. Military Is Averse to Responding to Post–Cold War Low-Level Threats," *Security Studies* Vol. 6, No. 2 (Winter 1996/97): 51–90.

30. Deborah Avant, "Conflicting Indications of 'Crisis' in American Civil-Military Relations," *Armed Forces and Society* Vol. 24, No. 3 (Spring 1998): 375–87.

31. Risa Brooks and Elizabeth Stanley, eds., *Creating Military Power: The Sources of Military Effectiveness* (Stanford: Stanford University Press, 2007).

32. Eliot Cohen, *Supreme Command: Soldiers, Statesmen, and Leadership in Wartime* (New York: Free Press, 2002); Peter Feaver, "The Right to Be Right: Civil-Military Relations and the Iraq Surge Decision," *International Security* Vol. 35, No. 4 (Spring 2011): 87–125.

33. Ole Holsti, "A Widening Gap between the U.S. Military and Civilian Society? Some Evidence, 1976–1996," *International Security* Vol. 23, No. 3 (Winter 1998/99): 5–42; Jason Dempsey, *Our Army: Soldiers, Politics, and American Civil-military Relations* (Princeton: Princeton University Press, 2010), esp. 29–33, and ch. 9, 177–86.

34. MIT economics professor Carl Kaysen served as deputy national security adviser under President Kennedy. Braben (2008) presents this U.S. R&D problem in much the same terms.

35. The best chronicle of how the ONR came into being is Harvey Sapolsky, *Science and the Navy: The History of the Office of Naval Research* (Princeton: Princeton University Press, 1990). There are remarkable similarities with UCSD (est. 1960), a public institution of science and technology rife with stakeholders that also acted on parochial bureaucratic or private interests. Nancy Anderson, *An Improbable Venture: A History of the University of California, San Diego* (La Jolla, CA: UCSD Press, 1993).

36. This metaphor for the U.S. Science Establishment and the analysis of the Office of Naval Research draws from my previous paper on this subject posted online in 2009 by the Institute for National Security Studies, U.S. Air Force Academy, available at www.usafa.edu/df/inss/researchpapers.cfm.

37. See, for example, U.S. National Science Foundation (NSF) statistics from 2009: universities and colleges performing basic research at a far higher rate than either industry or the federal government; available at www.nsf.gov/statistics/nsf08318/pdf/tab2.pdf, accessed October 1, 2012.

38. Paul Cocks, *Science Policy: USA/USSR*, Vol. II: *Science Policy in the Soviet Union* (Washington, DC: National Science Foundation Division of International Programs, 1980), 305–10. "The scientific imagination cannot accomplish its creative task when it is pinned down by despotic prescriptions . . . . Democracy and science are at one in respect for the capacity of every individual to contribute to the common life according to his native talent, revealed by adequate opportunity (Harold Lasswell, "Science and Democracy," speech delivered at the Conference on Science, Philosophy and Religion, New York, September 11, 1940, available at www.ibiblio.org/pha/policy/1940/1940–09–11d.html, accessed October 3, 2012).

39. Today, this is almost certainly a minority view but one still expressed on occasion in Congress. "The best way to administer science in my book is to find smart people, give them good resources and ample funds, and not have them worry about any other administrative deals" (Subcommittee Chairman Vernon Ehlers, U.S. House of Representatives, "Views of the NIST Nobel Laureates," hearing before the Subcommittee on Environment, Technology, and Standards, Committee on Science, 109th Congress, Second Session, May 24, 2006, 38).

40. Charles Townes, "Early Days of Quantum Electronics and the Office of Naval Research," speech delivered at ONR's Fortieth Anniversary (1986), appearing in *The Office of Naval Research 50th Anniversary*, available at www.onr.navy.mil/about/history, accessed June 30, 2009.

41. Sapolsky (1990: 38).

42. James Leutze, *Bargaining for Supremacy: Anglo-American Naval Collaboration 1937–1941* (Chapel Hill: University of North Carolina Press, 1977). Sapolsky (1990: 49) shows the London Office as the only overseas branch in the ONR organization chart for October 1946. For the birth of the Office of Scientific Research and Development, see the biography of Vannevar Bush (Zachary 1997: 95–139).

43. Robert Conrad, "The Navy Looks Forward with Research," speech delivered at the University of Illinois, Urbana, October 27, 1946, appearing in *The Office of Naval Research 50th Anniversary*, available at www.onr.navy.mil/about/history, accessed June 30, 2009.

44. John Krige, *American Hegemony and the Postwar Reconstruction of Science in Europe* (Cambridge: MIT Press, 2006), 31.

45. Ibid., 32. For Solberg's reluctance to turn over university science projects from ONR to the new National Science Foundation, see "Conversation with Rear Admiral T. Solberg, Director, Office of Naval Research, Memoranda of William T. Golden (January 15, 1951), *American Association for the Advancement of Science*, available at http://archives.aaas.org/golden/doc.php?gold_id=107, accessed September 5, 2012.

46. Emelie Rutherford, "Need Seen for Early-Stage Applied Research Funding in Navy," *Defense Daily*, December 16, 2008 (available to subscribers at http://www.defensedaily.com/need-seen-for-early-stage-applied-research-funding-in-navy/); U.S. House of Representatives, "Hearing on FY2010 National Defense Authorization Budget Request for Department of Defense Science and Technology Programs," hearing before the Subcommittee on Terrorism, Unconventional Threats, and Capabilities, Committee on Armed Services, 111th Congress, First Session, May 20, 2009, statement from Chief of Naval Research Nevin Carr, Jr.

47. ONR's *Naval S&T Strategic Plan* from 2007 (available at www.onr.navy.mil/about/docs/0703_naval_st_strategy.pdf, accessed July 7, 2009) supplied crucial justifications in a democratic context for greater S&T investment, clarifying the connection between Discovery & Invention (categories 6.1 and 6.2) and new capabilities for naval operations. Yet, it also buried 6.1 efforts aimed toward national scientific leadership, those that would simply advance the frontiers of science. If a proposal was not something that looked like it would transition to a valuable product, it was not included in the *Strategic Plan*.

48. U.S. House of Representatives, "Hearing on National Defense Authorization Act FY2006 and Oversight of Previous Authorization Programs," hearing on Defense Science and Technology programs before the Subcommittee on Terrorism, Unconventional Threats, and Capabilities, Committee on Armed Services, 109th Congress, First Session, March 10, 2005, 14.

49. Ibid., 15.

50. U.S. House of Representatives, "Hearing on National Defense Authorization Act FY2006," March 2, 2005, 39–40.

51. Kerr, quoted in Anderson (1993: 236).

52. Office of Naval Research, London, *Selections from European Scientific Notes, 1946–1976*, issued on the occasion of the 30th Anniversary of the Office of Naval Research and Its London Branch Office (London: U.S. Department of the Navy, ONR London Branch, 1976).

53. Harvey Brooks, "The Strategic Defense Initiative as Science Policy," *International Security* Vol. 11, No. 2 (Autumn 1986): 177–84.

54. National Science Foundation, "NSF Information Related to the American Recovery and Reinvestment Act of 2009," 2009, available at www.nst.gov/recovery/, accessed June 30, 2009. For a general critique of NSF and the trajectory of U.S. science after the Vietnam years and defense research controversies of the 1970s, see Braben (2008). Braben was not alone in criticizing the evolution of public accountability toward a risk-avoidant peer review process and older first-time grant recipients at NSF; see Susan Morrissey, "COVER STORY: Elisas A. Zerhouni" [NIH director], *Chemical and Engineering News*, July 3, 2006, available at http://pubs.acs.org/cen/coverstory/84/8427zerhouni.html, accessed September 7, 2012. See also Douglas Melton, "Obama's First 100 Days—Research Funding," *Harvard University Gazette*, April 29, 2009, available at http://news.harvard.edu/gazette/story/2009/04/obamas-first-100-days/, accessed September 7, 2012.

55. Feaver (2003) discussed what should be done to defuse the principal-agent trap with respect to the American officer corps in his conclusion, pp. 298–302.

56. Committee on Prospering in the Global Economy of the 21st Century, Norman Augustine, chair, *Rising above the Gathering Storm: Energizing and Employing America for a Brighter Economic Future* (Washington, DC: National Academies Press, 2007).

57. These ideas were emphasized in Members of the 2005 "Rising above the Gathering Storm" Committee, *Rising above the Gathering Storm, Revisited: Rapidly Approaching Category 5* (Washington, DC: National Academies Press, 2010).

58. Commission on Mathematics and Science Education, Phillip Griffiths, chair, *The Opportunity Equation: Transforming Mathematics and Science Education for Citizenship and the Global Economy* (New York: Carnegie Corporation of New York and Institute for Advanced Study, 2009), available at http://carnegie.org/fileadmin/Media/Publications/PDF/OpportunityEquation.pdf, accessed October 13, 2012.

59. *Gathering Storm, Revisited* (2010: 63); David Sirota, "The 'Education Crisis' Myth," *Salon*.com, January 30, 2012, available at www.salon.com/2012/01/30/the_education_crisis_myth/, accessed October 13, 2012.

60. *Gathering Storm, Revisited* (2010: 50).

61. Ibid.; David Bergeman, "A Break in the Storm: USAFA's K-12 Outreach Center Works to Engage Southern Colorado's Youth," *Checkpoints* (U.S. Air Force Academy), December 2011, 39, available at www1.usafa.org/News-Media/Checkpoints/articles/2011-Dec/19-STEM.pdf, accessed October 12, 2012.

62. Richard Levin, "Top of the Class: The Rise of Asia's Universities," *Foreign Affairs* Vol. 89, No. 3 (May/June 2010): 63–75.

63. Tom Hartsfield, "U.S. Could Have Found Higgs Boson 10 Years Ago" (commentary), *RealClearScience*.com, July 9, 2012, available at www.realclearscience.com/articles/2012/07/09/us_could_have_found_higgs_boson_10_years_ago_106319.html, accessed October 12, 2012.

64. Levin (2010) discouraged spreading the science money around, a frequent consequence of the U.S. federal system and 435 congressional districts competing for national government funds.

65. Vannevar Bush, *Science the Endless Frontier: A Report to the President on a Program for Postwar Scientific Research* (July 1945), reprinted July 1960 by the National Science Foundation (Washington, DC), available at http://archive.org/stream/scienceendlessfr00unit#page/n29/mode/2up, accessed October 12, 2012.

66. Zakaria (2008: 31–32).

67. Adam Segal, *Advantage: How American Innovation Can Overcome the Asian Challenge* (New York: W. W. Norton and Co., 2011).

68. *The Opportunity Equation* (2009: vii).

69. Robert Gilpin, *France in the Age of the Scientific State* (Princeton: Princeton University Press, 1968), 58.

Chapter 5

1. The phrase in the chapter title references Charles Kupchan, *No One's World: The West, the Rising Rest, and the Coming Global Turn* (New York: Oxford University Press, 2012). Parts of this chapter draw upon a minicase on Brazil included in my 2009 working paper sponsored by the Institute for National Security Studies (INSS), U.S. Air Force Academy, available at www.usafa.edu/df/inss/researchpapers.cfm.

2. Robert Strassler, ed., *The Landmark Thucydides: A Comprehensive Guide to the Peloponnesian War* (New York: Free Press, 1996); on "the growth of the power of Athens" and what "made war inevitable," see I.23, p. 16. Robert Gilpin, *War and Change in World Politics* (Cambridge: Cambridge University Press, 1981). Williamson Murray, MacGregor Knox, and Alvin Bernstein, eds., *The Making of Strategy: Rulers, States, and War* (Cambridge: Cambridge University Press, 1994). For widely regarded empirical work testing power transition theory, see A. F. K. Organski and Jacek Kugler, *The War Ledger* (Chicago: University of Chicago Press, 1980); and Jacek Kugler and Douglas Lemke, *Parity and War: Evaluations and Extensions of the War Ledger* (Ann Arbor: University of Michigan Press, 1996).

3. G. John Ikenberry, *Liberal Leviathan: The Origins, Crisis, and Transformation of the American World Order* (Princeton: Princeton University Press, 2011), ch. 3, 79–118, passim (e.g. 90). Science, or theoretical knowledge, is a key ingredient of practical wisdom—good judgment under the circumstances, which permits one to prosper while doing good by others. See Sharon Ryan, "Wisdom," *Stanford Encyclopedia of Philosophy*, Summer 2013 ed., ed. Edward Zalata, available at http://plato.stanford.edu/archives/sum2013/entries/wisdom/, accessed July 18, 2013; see para. 3, "Wisdom as Knowledge."

4. As an example of the United States descending into the role of international enforcer, Jorge Domínguez and Rafael Fernández de Castro cite continued securitized relations between the United States and Latin America despite soft diplomatic rhetoric

from the Obama administration; see Domínguez and Fernández de Castro, eds., *Contemporary U.S.–Latin American Relations: Cooperation or Conflict in the 21st Century?* (New York: Routledge, 2010), 13.

5. Adrian Hearn and José Luis León-Manríquez, *China Engages Latin America* (Boulder, CO: Lynne Rienner, 2011).

6. For a range of views on the nature and prospects of the balance of power crisis with China, see John Mearsheimer, *The Tragedy of Great Power Politics* (New York: W. W. Norton and Co., 2001); Aaron Friedberg, *A Contest for Supremacy: China, America, and the Struggle for Mastery in Asia* (W. W. Norton and Co., 2011); Henry Kissinger, *On China* (New York: Penguin Press, 2011); Steve Chan, *Looking for Balance: China, the United States, and Power Balancing in East Asia* (Stanford: Stanford University Press, 2012); David Shambaugh, ed., *Tangled Titans: The United States and China* (Lanham, MD: Rowman and Littlefield, 2013); and Graham Allison, "Thucydides's Trap Has Been Sprung in the Pacific," *Financial Times* (U.K.), August 21, 2012, available at www.ft.com/intl/cms/s/0/5d695b5a-ead3-11e1-984b-00144feab49a.html#axzz2ZhqHozeN, accessed July 21, 2013.

7. For analyses of the U.S.-Brazil relationship in global perspective, see Mônica Hirst, "Brazil-U.S. Relations: Getting Better All the Time," in Domínguez and Fernández de Castro, eds., *Contemporary U.S.–Latin American Relations: Cooperation or Conflict in the 21st Century?* (New York: Routledge, 2010), 124–41; and her book *The United States and Brazil: A Long Road of Unmet Expectations* (New York: Routledge, 2005). See also Britta Crandall, *Hemispheric Giants: The Misunderstood History of U.S.-Brazilian Relations* (Lanham, MD: Rowman and Littlefield, 2011); and Joseph Smith, *Brazil and the United States: Convergence and Divergence* (Athens: University of Georgia Press, 2010).

8. Hirst (2010: 127, 128–32); Economist Staff, "The Cancun Challenge," *Economist*, September 4, 2003, available at www.economist.com/node/2035492, accessed July 21, 2013; Ian Fergusson, *World Trade Organization Negotiations: The Doha Development Agenda* (Washington, DC: Congressional Research Service Report, December 12, 2011), 3–6.

9. World Trade Organization statistics show that some 64 percent of the value of Brazilian exports (compared with 24 percent for U.S. exports) lies in agricultural, fuels, and mining products, with the top two destinations as the EU-27 and China. See World Trade Organization Statistics, Brazil, April 2013, available at http://stat.wto.org/CountryProfile/WSDBCountryPFView.aspx?Country=BR&Language=S, accessed July 22, 2013.

10. Figures for 2011 from CNN Money, "World's Largest Economies," available at http://money.cnn.com/news/economy/world_economies_gdp/, accessed July 22, 2013.

11. Jeb Blount, "Analysis: Brazil's Once-Envied Energy Matrix a Victim of 'Hubris,'" *Reuters*, January 7, 2013, available at http://stat.wto.org/CountryProfile/WSDBCountryPFView.aspx?Country=BR&Language=S.

12. Joe Leahy, "Brazil: The First Big 'Soft' Power," *Financial Times* (U.K.), February 22, 2013, available at www.ft.com/intl/cms/s/2/37685a5c-7bbd-11e2–95b9–00144feabdco. html#axzz2b9vgtUq1 (subscribers only).

13. Blount (2013) on sugar-based ethanol; Juan Forero (for the *Washington Post*), "Brazil's Hydroelectric Dam Boom Is Bringing Tensions as Well as Energy," *Guardian*, February 12, 2013, available at www.guardian.co.uk/world/2013/feb/12/brazil-hydroelec-tric-jirau-dam; on Brazil's oilfields, see Economist Staff, "Back in Business," *Economist*, May 18, 2013, available at www.economist.com/news/business/21578095-strong-bid-ding-exploration-rights-ends-industrys-long-dry-spell-back-business;GlobalSecurity. org, "Brazil Nuclear Weapons Program," September 21, 2012, available at www.globalse-curity.org/wmd/world/brazil/nuke-3.htm, accessed July 23, 2013; on foreign interest in Brazilian nuclear technology, see Tyler Marshall and Henry Chu, "Powell Sees No Nu-clear Red Flags in Brazil," *Los Angeles Times*, October 6, 2004, available at http://articles. latimes.com/2004/oct/06/world/fg-powell6.

14. Joe Leahy, "Brazil Fights Rearguard Action in Currency War," *Financial Times* (U.K.), September 26, 2011, available at www.ft.com/intl/cms/s/0/70dac96c-e85e-11e0–8f05–00144feab49a.html#axzz2ZskIMKoo; Dilma Rousseff, "Brazil Will Fight Back against the Currency Manipulators," *Financial Times* (U.K.), opinion, September 21, 2011, available at www.ft.com/intl/cms/s/0/8871a370-e2aa-11e0–897a-00144feabdco.htm-l#axzz2ZskIMKoo.

15. Gary Duffy, "Brazil Pushes for Bigger G20 Role," *BBC News*, March 26, 2009, available at http://news.bbc.co.uk/2/hi/business/7963704.stm; International Centre for Trade and Sustainable Development, *Technology Transfer and Innovation: Key Country Priorities for Rio + 20*, Information Note (Geneva, Switzerland: ICTSD Programme on Innovation, Technology, and Intellectual Property, March 2012), 4, 6, 9, 10.

16. Ioannis Mantzikos, "The Good Multilateralists: Brazil and South Africa in the New Area of Multilateralism," *Boletim Meridiano* 47 Vol. 11, No. 118 (May 2010): 6–14.

17. Hirst (2010: 133–34).

18. Marshall and Chu (2004).

19. James Reinl, "US Rejects Iran Nuclear Deal Brokered by Turkey and Brazil and Sets up New Sanctions," *National* (UAE), May 20, 2010, available at www.thenational.ae/news/world/us-rejects-iran-nuclear-deal-brokered-by-turkey-and-brazil-and-sets-up-new-sanctions, accessed July 24, 2013.

20. Lydia Polgreen, "Group of Emerging Nations Plans to Form Development Bank," *New York Times*, March 27, 2013, A4.

21. Christopher Layne, *The Peace of Illusions: American Grand Strategy from 1940 to the Present* (Ithaca, NY: Cornell University Press, 2006), 146–47.

22. Alex Sanchez, "Embraer: Brazilian Military Industry Becoming a Global Arms Merchant?" Council on Hemispheric Affairs, September 1, 2009, available at www.coha. org/embraer-brazilian-military-industry-becoming-a-global-arms-merchant/, accessed

July 24, 2013; "Embraer to Modernize Brazilian Navy AF-1 and AF-1A Jets," *Reuters*, press release, April 14, 2009, available at www.reuters.com/article/2009/04/14/idUS206474+14-Apr-2009+PRN20090414; Reuters Staff, "Elbit [ISRAEL], Embraer, Avibras Team up on Unmanned Aircraft in Brazil," *Reuters*, February 6, 2013, available at www.reuters.com/article/2013/02/06/elbit-embraer-avibras-idUSL5N0B63AU20130206; Alexandre Rodrigues, "Porta-aviões São Paulo Volta à Ativa após 4 Anos em Reforma," *O Estado de São Paulo*, July 29, 2009, available at www.estadao.com.br/noticias/impresso,porta-avioes-sao-paulo-volta-a-ativa-apos-4-anos-em-reforma,409999,0.htm; Agence France-Presse, "Brazil to Get Its First Nuclear Subs," *Defense News*, March 2, 2013, available at www.defensenews.com/article/20130302/DEFREG02/303020009/Brazil-Get-Its-First-Nuclear-Subs.

23. John Lindsay-Poland and Susana Pimiento, "U.S. Base Deal for Colombia: Back to the Status Quo," Foreign Policy in Focus, October 8, 2010, available at www.fpif.org/articles/us_base_deal_for_colombia_back_to_the_status_quo, accessed July 24, 2013.

24. Using an idiom that was essentially technological, Brazil signaled the value of trust in its diplomatic relationship with the militarily and economically superior U.S. hegemon when it registered extraordinary protests against the United States for employing secret NSA eavesdropping techniques against Internet and telecommunications in Brazil and several other Latin American countries. Anthony Boadle, "Latin American Nations Fuming over NSA Spying Allegations," *Reuters*, July 9, 2013, available at www.reuters.com/article/2013/07/10/us-usa-security-latinamerica-idUSBRE96900920130710.

25. Renato Dagnino, *Ciência e Tecnologia no Brasil: O Processo Decisório e a Comunidade de Pesquisa* (Campinas, Brasil: Editora da UNICAMP, 2007); Paulo Prada, "Special Report: Why Brazil's New Middle Class Is Seething," *Reuters*, July 3, 2013, available at www.reuters.com/article/2013/07/03/us-brazil-middle-specialreport-idUSBRE9620DT20130703.

26. Simon Schwartzman, *A Space for Science: The Development of the Scientific Community in Brazil* (State College: Pennsylvania State University Press, 1991); Nancy Stepan, *Beginnings of Brazilian Science: Oswaldo Cruz, Medical Research and Policy, 1890–1920* (New York: Science History Publications/Neale Watson, 1976).

27. George Basalla, "The Spread of Western Science," *Science*, new series Vol. 156, No. 3775 (May 5, 1967): 611–22.

28. Stepan (1976: quotation from p. x).

29. Nancy Stepan, "The National and the International in Public Health: Carlos Chagas and the Rockefeller Foundation in Brazil, 1917–1930s," *Hispanic American Historical Review* Vol. 91, No. 3 (August 2011): 469–502, esp. 475.

30. Ibid., 471–74, 500; Nancy Stepan, *Eradication: Ridding the World of Diseases Forever?* (Ithaca, NY: Cornell University Press, 2011).

31. Stepan, "Chagas and the Rockefeller Foundation" (2011: 488).

32. Ibid., 497, 501–2.

33.   Antonio Botelho and Simon Schwartzman, "Growing Pains: Brazilian Scientists and Their Shifting Roles," in Jacques Gaillard, V. V. Krishna, and Roland Waast, eds., *Scientific Communities in the Developing World* (New Delhi, India: Sage Publications, 1997), 336–53, available at www.schwartzman.org.br/simon/growing.htm.

34.   Academia Brasileira de Ciências, "History," March 10, 2011, available at www.abc.org.br/rubrique.php3?id_rubrique=152, accessed July 26, 2013, ff. "Scientific Production."

35.   The Brazilian university names were extracted, in rank order, from the list of the top fifteen universities in Latin America, according to *U.S. News and World Report*, "World's Best Universities 2012/Latin America," *U.S. News and World Report*, 2013, available at www.usnews.com/education/worlds-best-universities-rankings/best-universities-in-latin-america, accessed July 26, 2013.

36.   Simon Schwartzman, "Struggling to Be Born: The Scientific Community in Brazil," *Minerva* (London) Vol. 16, No. 4 (Winter 1978): 545–80, esp. 545, 557–58.

37.   This was the underlying theme of Daniel Hellinger's textbook survey of Latin American politics, *Comparative Politics of Latin America: Democracy at Last?* (New York: Routledge, 2011), esp. parts II–IV.

38.   GlobalSecurity.org, "Brazil—Early Nuclear Program," November 1, 2012, available at www.globalsecurity.org/wmd/world/brazil/nuke-1.htm, accessed July 26, 2013; Otavio Durão, "Planning and Strategic Orientations of the Brazilian Space Program," in Eligar Sadeh, ed., *Space Strategy in the 21st Century: Theory and Policy* (Abingdon: Routledge, 2013), 335–46.

39.   GlobalSecurity.org, "Brazil—Early Nuclear Program" (2012); GlobalSecurity.org, "Brazil—Nuclear Power Program," September 21, 2012, available at www.globalsecurity.org/wmd/world/brazil/nuke-2.htm, accessed July 26, 2013. An initial S&T agreement with China was signed in 1982, and a bilateral space agreement for the China-Brazil Earth Resources Satellite (CBERS) was formalized in 1988 (Durão 2013: 339).

40.   Petrobras, "Our History" (1960s), *Petrobras*, 2011, available at www.petrobras.com/en/about-us/our-history/, accessed July 26, 2013.

41.   Durão (2013: 336).

42.   Embraer, "Timeline" (1970), *Embraer*, 2011, available at www.1.embraer.com.br/timeline/english/, accessed July 26, 2013.

43.   Ministry of Science and Technology (MCT), Brazil, *Action Plan 2007–2010* Summary Document, available from the Ministry of Science and Technology, Brazil, c2008, 16 (available at http://www.access4.eu/_media/Action_Plan_ST_Brazil.pdf).

44.   Stepan, "Chagas and the Rockefeller Foundation" (2011); Dagnino (2007).

45.   John Alic, Lewis Branscomb, Harvey Brooks, Ashton Carter, and Gerald Epstein, *Beyond Spinoff: Military and Commercial Technologies in a Changing World* (Cambridge: Harvard Business Press, 1992). For spin-on and scientific-technological developments in Japan, see Richard Samuels, *"Rich Nation Strong Army": National Security and the*

Technological Transformation of Japan (Ithaca, NY: Cornell University Press, 1994), esp. 26–32; and for attempts at harnessing spin-on in China, see Richard Bitzinger, "Civil-Military Integration and Chinese Military Modernization," *Asia-Pacific Center for Security Studies* Vol. 3, No. 9 (December 2004), available at www.apcss.org/Publications/APSSS/Civil-MilitaryIntegration.pdf.

46. Michael Shifter and Cameron Combs, "Shifting Fortunes: Brazil and Mexico in a Transformed Region," *Current History* Vol. 112, No. 751 (February 2013): 49–55.

47. Thomas Skidmore, *Brazil: Five Centuries of Change*, 2nd ed. (New York: Oxford University Press, 2010), 241–43, 249; Fabiana Frayssinet, "Brazil's Mensalao Trial: Blow to Corruption or Political Ploy?" *Inter Press Service (IPS)*, November 7, 2012, available at www.ipsnews.net/2012/11/brazils-mensalao-trial-blow-to-corruption-or-political-ploy/, accessed July 27, 2013.

48. Robert Levine, "How Brazil Works," in Robert Levine and John Crocitti, eds., *The Brazil Reader: History, Culture, Politics* (Durham, NC: Duke University Press, 1999), 402–7.

49. H.J. ("Americas View" blog), "Untangling the Custo Brasil," *Economist.com*, August 20, 2012, available at www.economist.com/blogs/americasview/2012/08/electricity-taxes-brazil, accessed July 27, 2013.

50. Celso Furtado, "When the Future Arrives," in Ignacy Sachs, Jorge Wilheim, and Paulo Sérgio Pinheiro, eds., Robert Anderson, trans., *Brazil: A Century of Change* (Chapel Hill: University of North Carolina Press, 2009), 291–99, esp. 293. The concessions that ISI was "not sufficient to cause significant changes in the country's occupational structure" and that "the relative importance of the subsistence sector" declined only very slowly are especially poignant coming from prolific, Cambridge educated economist Furtado, who served as planning minister under the ill-fated President Goulart and culture minister twenty years later under President Sarney after democracy returned to Brazil.

51. Stephan Haggard, *Pathways from the Periphery: The Politics of Growth in the Newly Industrializing Countries* (Ithaca, NY: Cornell University Press, 1990), esp. 9–50. For acknowledgment of structural handicaps imposed over time by import-substitution industrialization, even as intriguing qualifications to the economic conventional wisdom are explored, see Albert Fishlow, "The Latin American State," *Journal of Economic Perspectives* Vol. 4, No. 3 (Summer 1990): 61–74; and Emanuel Adler, "Ideological 'Guerrillas' and the Quest for Technological Autonomy: Brazil's Domestic Computer Industry," *International Organization* Vol. 40, No. 3 (Summer 1986): 673–705. For a more recent argument on the importance to development of increasing Brazil's value-added exports, see Gilberto Dupas, "The Challenges of the Globalized Economy," in Ignacy Sachs, Jorge Wilheim, and Sérgio Pinheiro, eds., Robert Anderson, trans., *Brazil: A Century of Change* (Chapel Hill: University of North Carolina Press, 2009), 300–319, esp. 308, 314–17.

52. Blount (2013); Economist Staff (2013).

53. Dagnino (2007); Ana Maria Fernandes, *A Construção da Ciência no Brasil e a SBPC*, 2nd ed. (Brasília, DF, Brasil: Universidade de Brasília, 2000). The Brazilian Society for the Progress of Science (SBPC) offered a democratic alternative to the exclusive Brazilian Academy of Sciences, with special concern for how scientific research might improve the lives of ordinary citizens.

54. The Office of Naval Research history and its evolving influence on sponsorship of scientific activities at home were discussed in Chapter 4. See also Harvey Sapolsky, *Science and the Navy: The History of the Office of Naval Research* (Princeton: Princeton University Press, 1990).

55. James Leutze, *Bargaining for Supremacy: Anglo-American Naval Collaboration, 1937–1941* (Chapel Hill: University of North Carolina Press, 1977). Sapolsky (1990: 49) shows the London Office as the only overseas branch in the ONR organization chart for October 1946. John Krige, *American Hegemony and the Postwar Reconstruction of Science in Europe* (Cambridge: MIT Press, 2006), 31–32.

56. After London, the Tokyo Office for ONR-Global was established in 1974. Office of Naval Research, Science and Technology, "About ONR Global," U.S. Navy, Office of Naval Research, (est.) September 2012, available at www.onr.navy.mil/en/Science-Technology/ONR-Global/About-ONR-Global.aspx, accessed July 29, 2013; Captain Mike Smith (USN), "ONR Naval S&T Partnership Conference & ASNE Expo," October 2012, slide presentation available at www.defenseinnovationmarketplace.mil/resources/ONR_Global.pdf, accessed July 29, 2013, esp. Slide 7.

57. On the positive climate of U.S.-Chile relations at this time, see Claudia Fuentes Julio and Francisco Rojas Aravena, "Chile and the United States 2000–2009: From Elusive Friendship to Cooperative Friendship," in Domínguez and Fernández de Castro, eds., *Contemporary U.S.–Latin American Relations: Cooperation or Conflict in the 21st Century?* (New York: Routledge, 2010), 142–63.

58. Jonathan Wheatley, "Bush and Lula Try to Paper Over Divisions Seen at Summit of Americas," *Financial Times* (U.K.), November 7, 2005, available at www.ft.com/intl/cms/s/0/5550d3b4–4f33–11da-9947–0000779e2340.html#axzz2YkS6yZvF (subscribers only).

59. Geoff Fein, "ONR Lecture Series Focuses on Brazil's Growth in Global Science and Technology," ONR Corporate Strategic Communications, October 22, 2010, available at www.onr.navy.mil/en/Media-Center/Press-Releases/2010/Arrival-Brazil-Panel-Discussion.aspx, accessed August 6, 2013; Rob Anastasios, "Brazil Expo Sets International Stage for ONR Global to Exchange Ideas," ONR Corporate Strategic Communications, April 5, 2011, available at www.onr.navy.mil/en/Media-Center/Press-Releases/2011/LAAD-Brazil-Expo-ONR-Global.aspx, accessed August 6, 2013. The highlighted exposition in the latter news item for exchanging ideas was in fact a defense industry fair, the biannual Latin American Aero and Defence (LAAD) Expo hosted during 2011 in Rio de Janeiro.

60. Soy Stats, "Brazil and Argentina Soybean Production 1986–2010," 2011, available at www.soystats.com/2011/page_31.htm, accessed June 5, 2013. On the "green revolution" and the rise of the Brazilian agroindustrial complex from the 1970s, see Werner Baer, *The Brazilian Economy: Growth and Development*, 5th ed. (Westport, CT: Greenwood/Praeger, 2001), esp. 362–63, 373–74. In praise of Brazilian science emerging out of agronomic research in the 1960s and 1970s and taking on a life of its own, see Larry Rother, "Scientists Are Making Brazil's Savannah Bloom," *New York Times*, October 2, 2007, F3.

61. George Flaskerud, *Brazil's Soybean Production and Impact Report* (Fargo: North Dakota State University Extension Service, July 2003). Jonathan Watts, "Brazil's Amazon Rangers Battle Farmers' Burning Business Logic," *Guardian*, November 14, 2012, available at www.guardian.co.uk/environment/2012/nov/14/brazil-amazon-rangers-farmers-burning. On hydroelectric energy, land use, and disruption of indigenous cultures, see Verónica Goyzueta, "Rousseff Aumenta la Tensión al Enviar Tropas a una Zona en Conflicto con los Indígenas," *ABC* (Spain), June 6, 2013, available at www.abc.es/internacional/20130606/abci-rousseff-aumenta-tension-enviar-201306052144.html. For the as yet unfulfilled mission of Brazil to become international exemplar of tropical science, see Antonio Regalado, "Brazilian Science: Riding a Gusher," *Science* Vol. 330, No. 6009 (December 3, 2010): 1306–12; and Ignacy Sachs, "*Quo Vadis*, Brazil?" in Ignacy Sachs, Jorge Wilheim, and Paulo Sérgio Pinheiro, eds., Robert Anderson, trans., *Brazil: A Century of Change* (Chapel Hill: University of North Carolina Press, 2009), 332–43, 336–38.

62. Nicole Ferrand, "Bush and Lula Sign Agreement on Biofuels," *Americas Report*, March 20, 2007, available at www.theamericasreport.com/2007/03/20/bush-and-lula-sign-agreement-on-biofuels/, accessed July 29, 2013.

63. Office of U.S. Senator Chuck Grassley, "Grassley Seeks Clarification of U.S. Stance on Ethanol Tariff before Nominee," *Senator Chuck Grassley of Iowa*, July 28, 2009, available at www.grassley.senate.gov/news/Article.cfm?customel_dataPageID_1502=22103, accessed July 30, 2013.

64. For example, see John Rush and Ronald Cappelletti, *The NIST Center for Neutron Research: Over 40 Years Serving NIST/NBS and the Nation* (Washington, DC: NIST/U.S. GPO, August 2011). For an argument during the height of post–Cold War industrial competition with Germany and Japan to revisit the NIST charter and rebalance agency efforts toward promotion of U.S. manufacturing, see Alic et al. (1992), esp. 48 (n. 3), 345, 391, 400.

65. U.S. House of Representatives, "Views of the NIST Nobel Laureates on Science Policy," hearing before the Subcommittee on Environment, Technology, and Standards, Committee on Science, 109th Congress, Second Session, May 24, 2006.

66. U.S. Fed News Service, "US, Brazil Publish Compliance Requirement Guides for Selected Industries," *HT Media Ltd.*, November 29, 2012 (available to subscribers at

https://www.highbeam.com/doc/1P3-2827057411.html); UPI Space Daily Staff, "International Effort Takes Critical Steps to Accelerate Growth of Global Biofuels Market," *UPI Space Daily,* February 5, 2008, wire feed.

67. Government of Brazil, "Brazil's Science without Borders Program," press release, December 2011, available at www.brasil.gov.br/para/press/press-releases/december-2011/brazils-science-without-borders-program/br_model1?set_language=en, accessed July 31, 2013.

68. Whitney Eulich, "Brazil's President Rousseff Praises New Study Abroad Program," *Christian Science Monitor,* April 11, 2012, www.csmonitor.com/World/Americas/Latin-America-Monitor/2012/0411/Brazil-s-President-Rousseff-praises-new-study-abroad-program.

69. Ibid.; see also the interview with STEM undergraduate and program participant Felipe Azevedo, bottom of webpage 1.

70. Council on Foreign Relations, "Conference Call Audio," 2013, available at www.cfr.org/about/outreach/religioninitiative/audio.html, accessed July 31, 2013; see the link "Foreign Policy Begins at Home," speaker Richard Haass, May 20, 2013. The citation for Haass's book is Richard Haass, *Foreign Policy Begins at Home: The Case for Putting America's House in Order* (New York: Basic Books, 2013).

71. George Kennan, "Morality and Foreign Policy," *Foreign Affairs* Vol. 64, No. 2 (Winter 1985): 205–18.

72. Hans Morgenthau, *Science: Servant or Master* (New York: W. W. Norton and Co., 1972).

73. World Bank Staff, "Brazil's Largest Environmental Program Leaves Legacy of Preserved Lands and Species," *World Bank,* July 19, 2012, available at www.worldbank.org/en/news/feature/2012/07/19/ppg7-maior-programa-ambiental-brasil, accessed July 31, 2013.

74. Associated Press, "Brazil Loosens Restrictions on Amazon Land Use," *Guardian,* May 25, 2011, available at www.theguardian.com/world/2011/may/25/brazil-loosens-restrictions-amazon-land-use, accessed July 31, 2013.

75. Czech News Agency, "USA to Provide 600,000 Dollars in Support of Czech Science," *Gate2Biotech,* October 31, 2008, available at www.gate2biotech.com/usa-to-provide-dollars-in-support-of-czech/, accessed July 31, 2013.

Chapter 6

1. G. John Ikenberry, *Liberal Leviathan: The Origins, Crisis, and Transformation of the American World Order* (Princeton: Princeton University Press, 2011), 321–25.

2. Immanuel Kant, "To Perpetual Peace: A Philosophical Sketch," in Ted Humphrey, trans. and intro., *Perpetual Peace and Other Essays on Politics, History, and Morals* (Indianapolis, IN: Hackett, 1983 [1795]), 107–43.

3. This is a main theme of *History of the Peloponnesian War,* bk. I, in which Thucydides describes the rise and foreshadows the eventual fall of Athens. See Robert Strassler,

ed., *The Landmark Thucydides: A Comprehensive Guide to the Peloponnesian War* (New York: Free Press, 1996). President George Washington, in his Farewell Address to the nation (1796), justified his unpopular neutrality policy with respect to the wars in Europe, citing a "predominant motive ... to gain time to our country to settle and mature its yet recent institutions, and to progress without interruption to that degree of strength and consistency which is necessary to give it, humanly speaking, the command of its own fortunes." "Washington's Farewell Address, 1796," Avalon Project, Yale Law School, 2008, available at http://avalon.law.yale.edu/18th_century/washing.asp, accessed February 25, 2014. These ideas on democracies' need for tranquil foreign relations are, however, in tension with the notion of restless democracies, in need of expansion and diversionary war to diminish differences that are free to burn and potentially run wild at home. Jack Levy, "The Causes of War and the Conditions of Peace," *Annual Review of Political Science* Vol. 1 (1998): 151–54; Michael Doyle, *Ways of War and Peace* (New York: W. W. Norton and Co., 1997), 77–80, 307–11.

4. "Above all, we are a nation whose strength abroad has been anchored in opportunity for our citizens here at home." Barack Obama, "Remarks by the President on the Way Forward in Afghanistan," June 22, 2011, available at www.whitehouse.gov/the-press-office/2011/06/22/remarks-president-way-forward-afghanistan, accessed May 27, 2014. Richard Haass, *Foreign Policy Begins at Home: The Case for Putting America's House in Order* (New York: Basic Books, 2013).

5. Kenneth Waltz, "Kant, Liberalism, and War," *American Political Science Review* Vol. 56, No. 2 (June 1962): 331–40, esp. 337.

6. In Strassler (1996), for example, see Pericles' arguments in bk. I.142 and bk. II.13.

7. Ibid., "Appendix B: The Athenian Empire in Thucydides," by Alan Boegehold, 583–88, and "Appendix G: Trireme Warfare in Thucydides," by Nicolle Hirschfeld, 608–13.

8. Strassler (1996: 111–18); see Pericles' famous funeral oration, beginning at Thucydides, bk. II.35, esp. II.41.

9. Similar logic drove Joseph Nye's widely read assessment of China, including China's chances for challenging American hegemony: Lack of a republican constitution at home, zero confederative relations with skeptical neighbors in Asia, and a dearth of appeal among opinion leaders in global civil society made it exceedingly difficult for China to sustain near double-digit growth rates long enough to catch the economy of the United States, particularly in terms of per capita GDP, or convert economic success into hegemonic influence across the globe. When the United States lost considerable standing after its 2003 invasion of Iraq and again after the housing collapse and world financial crisis of 2008, Nye argued against a panicked, militarized reaction against fresh Chinese assertiveness in Asia. The key to sustaining American leadership was instead shoring up recent reductions in soft power, and these mainly at the transnational level, the only level where America's edge was increasingly vulnerable. Joseph Nye, Jr., "Amer-

ican and Chinese Power after the Financial Crisis," *Washington Quarterly* Vol. 33, No. 4 (October 2010): 143–53. See also an article from nearly fifteen years earlier: Joseph Nye, Jr., and William Owens, "America's Information Edge," *Foreign Affairs* Vol. 75, No. 2 (March/April 1996): 20–36.

10. Michael Doyle, "Kant, Liberal Legacies, and Foreign Affairs," *Philosophy and Public Affairs* Vol. 12, No. 3 (Summer 1983): 205–35; Waltz (1962).

11. Graham Allison, "Avoiding Thucydides' Trap," *Financial Times* (U.K.), August 22, 2012, available at http://belfercenter.ksg.harvard.edu/publication/22265/avoiding_thucydidess_trap.html, accessed May 27, 2014.

12. The quotation is from Pericles' final exhortation to Athenians, urging them to fight on after a mysterious plague ravages Athens (Strassler 1996: 126/Thucydides II.63.1 and II.64.5).

13. Ibid./Thucydides II.63.2.

14. The authors did not mention it, but part of the appeal of *Power and Interdependence* is literary. They seized upon international outcomes of the 1970s such as cooperation on currency stability and stewardship of the oceans that did not quite fit traditional realist logic by creating a new world, an alternative global narrative that unfolded according to different rules. Their conceit was not unlike Lewis Carroll's in *Through the Looking Glass* (1897). Robert Keohane and Joseph Nye, Jr., *Power and Interdependence: World Politics in Transition* (Boston: Little, Brown, and Co., 1977); Lewis Carroll, *Through the Looking Glass* (Philadelphia: Henry Altemus Co., 1897).

15. Robert Keohane and Joseph Nye, Jr., "Power and Interdependence in the Information Age," *Foreign Affairs* Vol. 77, No. 5 (September/October 1998): 81–94, esp. 81–83.

16. Joseph Nye, Jr., *The Future of Power* (New York: Public Affairs, 2011), e.g. ch. 4, 81–109.

17. Charles Kupchan and Peter Trubowitz, "Grand Strategy for a Divided America," *Foreign Affairs* Vol. 86, No. 4 (July/August 2007): 71–83; Charles Kupchan and Peter Trubowitz, "American Statecraft in an Era of Domestic Polarisation," in Rebecca Friedman, Kevark Oskanian, and Ramon Pacheco Pando, eds., *After Liberalism? The Future of Liberalism in International Relations* (Basingstoke: Palgrave Macmillan, 2013), 117–44; Leslie Gelb, *Power Rules: How Common Sense Can Rescue American Foreign Policy* (New York: HarperCollins, 2009); Haass (2013).

18. Barry Posen, "Command of the Commons: The Military Foundation of U.S. Hegemony," *International Security* Vol. 28, No. 1 (Summer 2003): 5–46; Scott Jasper, ed., *Conflict and Cooperation in the Global Commons: A Comprehensive Approach for International Security* (Washington, DC: Georgetown University Press, 2012).

19. Ikenberry (2011: esp. ch. 5, 159–219); Robert Kagan, *The World America Made* (New York: Alfred A. Knopf, 2012), e.g. 36–39.

20. Objective 4 in the Obama administration's 2010 *National Security Strategy*, supporting a benign international order, is a novel expression of the major, perhaps even

vital, interest of the United States in the global commons. President of the United States, *National Security Strategy* (Washington, DC: The White House, May 2010), available at www.whitehouse.gov/sites/default/files/rss_viewer/national_security_strategy.pdf, accessed May 16, 2014. Joseph Nye, Jr., "The American National Interest and Global Public Goods," *International Affairs* Vol. 78, No. 2 (April 2002): 233–44, esp. 241. See also "Six Vital American Interests," in Adam Lowther and Casey Lucius, "Identifying America's Vital Interests," *Space and Defense* (U.S. Air Force Academy) Vol. 7, No. 1 (Winter 2014): 39–54, available at www.usafa.edu/df/dfe/dfer/centers/ecsds/defense_journal.cfm.

21.   Stephen Krasner, "Global Communications and National Power: Life on the Pareto Frontier," *World Politics* Vol. 43, No. 3 (April 1991): 336–66.

22.   John Mearsheimer, *The Tragedy of Great Power Politics* (New York: W. W. Norton and Co., 2001); Daniel Deudney, *Bounding Power: Republican Security Theory from the Polis to the Global Village* (Princeton: Princeton University Press, 2007); Amitai Etzioni, *Security First: For a Muscular, Moral Foreign Policy* (New Haven: Yale University Press, 2007). Clay Moltz was certainly aware of this trap when it came to twenty-first-century space security. James Clay Moltz, *The Politics of Space Security: Strategic Restraint and the Pursuit of National Interests*, 2nd ed. (Stanford: Stanford University Press, 2011).

23.   Alfred T. Mahan, *The Influence of Sea Power upon History* (Boston: Little, Brown, and Co., 1890). Colin Gray, "The Influence of Space Power upon History," *Comparative Strategy* Vol. 15, No. 4 (October–December 1996): 293–308; Everett Dolman, *Astropolitik: Classical Politics in the Space Age* (London: Frank Cass, 2002); Charles Lutes and Peter Hays, eds., *Toward a Theory of Space Power—Selected Essays* (Washington, DC: Institute for National Strategic Studies, National Defense University, 2011), esp. 5–15, available at www.dtic.mil/dtic/tr/fulltext/u2/a546585.pdf, accessed May 28, 2014.

24.   Robert Putnam, *Making Democracy Work: Civic Traditions in Modern Italy* (Princeton: Princeton University Press, 1993).

25.   An elementary discussion of orbits and associated technological constraints appeared in Martin France and Jerry Sellers, "Real Constraints on Space Power," in Lutes and Hays, eds., *Toward a Theory of Space Power—Selected Essays*, 45–82. See also NASA, "Three Classes of Orbit," NASA Earth Observatory, n.d., available at http://earthobservatory.nasa.gov/Features/OrbitsCatalog/page2.php, accessed May 17, 2014.

26.   Christian Davenport, "Air Force to Award 'Space Fence' Contract to Track Orbital Debris," *Washington Post*, May 6, 2014, available at www.washingtonpost.com/business/economy/air-force-to-award-space-fence-contract-to-track-orbital-debris/2014/05/06/269e5eca-d15b-11e3-a6b1-45c4dffb85a6_story.html. Note: The NASA graphic accompanying this article extended low earth orbit to 1,240 miles and depicted a second "peak area of debris" between 840 and 990 miles altitude. Collision in low earth orbit (at approximately 250 miles above earth) was dramatized in the widely acclaimed movie *Gravity* (Warner Bros. Pictures, 2013). The basic physics formula for kinetic energy, $\frac{1}{2}mv^2$, helps put the danger in context: the energy of a space particle hitting a

satellite goes up directly with mass but increases as the velocity squared—even small particles, of less than a centimeter, can impart damaging amounts of energy to solar panels or space instruments.

27. U.S. Department of Defense and Office of the Director of National Intelligence, *National Security Space Strategy* (Unclassified Summary) (Washington, DC: U.S. Government, January 2011), 1 and fig. 1, available at www.defense.gov/home/features/2011/0111_nsss/docs/NationalSecuritySpaceStrategyUnclassifiedSummary_Jan2011.pdf.

28. *Wikipedia* (unedited and without references), in its article "Satellite Collision," lists ten Artificial Satellite Collisions by year and platform name between 1985 and 2013. The list includes antisatellite tests against previously orbiting research satellites and malfunctions during orbital rendezvous maneuvers (see http://en.wikipedia.org/wiki/Satellite_collision, accessed May 28, 2014). Secure World Foundation (NGO) technical adviser Brian Weeden "charted at least 9 known collisions involving non-secret satellites." Defense Industry Daily Staff, "Don't Touch Their Junk: USAF's SSA Tracking Space Debris," *Defense Industry Daily,* May 12, 2014, available at www.defenseindustrydaily.com/air-force-awards-first-phase-of-next-generation-space-fence-05511/, accessed May 18, 2014.

29. Defense Industry Daily Staff (2014); Davenport (2014); Joan Johnson-Freese, *Heavenly Ambitions: America's Quest to Dominate Space* (Philadelphia: University of Pennsylvania Press, 2009), 125.

30. UN Office for Outer Space Affairs, "Convention on the Registration of Objects Launched into Outer Space," Resolution Adopted by the General Assembly 3235 (XXIX), November 12, 1974, available at www.oosa.unvienna.org/oosa/SpaceLaw/gares/html/gares_29_3235.html, accessed May 28, 2014.

31. Steve Schuster, "US Air Force Space Fence Shutdown Threatens Satellite, Aerospace Industries," *Satellite TODAY,* August 14, 2013, available at www.satellitetoday.com/publications/st/2013/08/14/us-air-force-space-fence-shutdown-threatens-satellite-aerospace-industries/, accessed May 18, 2014. Andrea Mitchell and Erin McClam, "U.S. Coping with Furious Allies as NSA Spying Revelations Grow," *NBC News,* October 28, 2013, available at www.nbcnews.com/#/news/other/us-coping-furious-allies-nsa-spying-revelations-grow-f8C11478337, accessed May 19, 2014. This article does not specify the role of space technology in the NSA spying scandal, but it does illustrate the hegemon's temptation to exploit related technological advantages and government relationships with business to gain control over allies and partners.

32. One hundred new satellites and services worth $17 billion are expected over the next decade according to Optics.org, "Imaging to Drive Remote Sensing Satellite Market," May 31, 2012, available at http://optics.org/news/3/5/43, accessed May 28, 2014.

33. Otavio Durão, "Planning and Strategic Orientations of the Brazilian Space Pro-

gram," in Eligar Sadeh, ed., *Space Strategy in the 21st Century: Theory and Policy* (Abingdon: Routledge, 2013), 335–46, esp. 339.

34. Bruce Linster, "Space and the Economy," and James Clay Moltz, "Russia and China: Strategic Choices in Space," both in Damon Coletta and Frances Pilch, eds., *Space and Defense Policy* (Abingdon: Routledge, 2009), 51–63, esp. 54, and 269–89, esp. 272–74.

35. Andrew Higgins, "Europe's Plan for GPS Limps to Crossroads," *New York Times,* February 7, 2013, A6.

36. Megan Gannon, "China's First Moon Rover Will Launch by End of the Year," *Space.com,* August 29, 2013, available at www.space.com/22580-china-moon-rover-launch-2013.html, accessed <May 28, 2014; Ira Flatow, Jonathan McDowell, and Joan Johnson-Freese, "Will China Blast Pass America in Space?" National Public Radio, June 22, 2012, available at www.wbur.org/npr/155582842/will-china-blast-past-america-in-space?ft=3&f=155582842, accessed May 20, 2014.

37. Eligar Sadeh, "Export Controls of Space Technologies" (editorial), *Astropolitics* Vol. 6, No. 2 (June 2008): 105–11.

38. Ian Sample, "NASA Admits Mistake over Chinese Scientists' Conference Ban," *Guardian,* October 11, 2013, http://timeli.info/item/217922/The_Guardian_Science/ Nasa_admits_mistake_over_Chinese_scientists__conference_ban___Science___ theguardian_com, accessed May 28, 2014.

39. NASA, "Kepler: A Search for Habitable Planets," NASA (updated May 16, 2014), available at http://kepler.nasa.gov/, accessed May 20, 2014.

40. Michael Lipin, "NASA Lifts Ban on Chinese Scientists at US Conference," Voice of America, October 21, 2013, available at www.voanews.com/content/nasa-lifts-ban-on-chinese-scientists-at-us-conference/1773847.html, accessed May 20, 2014; Peter Gwynne, "Astronomers Call off Boycott of NASA Conference," *Physicsworld,* October 30, 2013, available at http://physicsworld.com/cws/article/news/2013/oct/30/astronomers-call-off-boycott-of-nasa-conference, accessed May 20, 2014. Scientists lifted their boycott of the Kepler meeting at NASA AMES once NASA administrator Charles Bolden, upon receiving clarification from Congress, lifted the ban on Chinese researchers. Still, planning delays, international embarrassment, and threats from leading U.S. university astronomers to pull their teams out of the imbroglio illustrate the seriousness of the problem.

41. Federation of American Scientists, "Defense Support Program," Space Policy Project—Military Space Programs, February 2000, available at www.fas.org/spp/military/program/warning/dsp.htm, accessed May 20, 2014.

42. Brian Weeden, "Radio Frequency Spectrum, Interference and Satellites Fact Sheet," Secure World Foundation, June 2013, available at http://swfound.org/media/108538/swf_rfi_fact_sheet_2013.pdf, accessed May 20, 2014. Lawrence Roberts, "A

Lost Connection: Geostationary Satellite Networks and the ITU," *Berkeley Technology Law Journal* Vol. 15, No. 3 (Fall 2000): 1096–1144; Thomas Hazlett and Evan Leo, "The Case for Liberal Spectrum Licenses: A Technical and Economic Perspective," *Berkeley Technology Law Journal* Vol. 26, No. 2 (Spring 2011): 1037–1101.

43. Roberts (2000). The politics behind the International Telecommunications Union was also treated in Peter Cowhey. "The International Telecommunications Regime: The Political Roots of Regimes for High Technology," *International Organization* Vol. 44, No. 2 (Spring 1990): 169–99, esp. 180.

44. NASA, "Space Debris and Human Spacecraft," NASA, September 27, 2013, sections on "Tracking Debris" and "Maneuvering Spacecraft to Avoid Orbital Debris," available at www.nasa.gov/mission_pages/station/news/orbital_debris.html, accessed May 21, 2014; Brian Weeden, "Through a Glass Darkly: Chinese, American, and Russian Anti-Satellite Testing in Space," *Space Review*, March 17, 2014, available at www.thespacereview.com/article/2473/1, accessed May 29, 2014.

45. There is some precedent for this in the reservation of orbital slots for developing nations. As orbits and spectrum become more crowded the "phantom satellites" of small nations are becoming more controversial. Peter de Selding, "Phantom Satellites among Tough Issues Regulators Tackling at WRC," *Space News*, January 30, 2012, available at www.spacenews.com/article/phantom-satellites-among-tough-issues-regulators-tackling-wrc, accessed May 21, 2014.

46. Michael Schmidt and Eric Schmitt, "A Russian GPS Using U.S. Soil Stirs Spy Fears," *New York Times*, November 17, 2013, A1; Simon Rockman, "Russia to Suspend US GPS Stations in Tit-for-Tat Spat," *Register*, May 13, 2014, available at www.theregister.co.uk/2014/05/13/russia_suspends_us_gps_stations/, accessed May 21, 2014. Gunter Hein, Jeremie Godet, Jean-Luc Issler, Jean-Christophe Martin, Rafael Lucas-Rodriguez, and Tony Pratt, "The Galileo Frequency Structure and Signal Design," technical paper by members of the Galileo Signal Task Force of the European Commission, Brussels, 2001–2, available at www2.ulg.ac.be/ipne/garnir/time/galileo/gal_stf_final_paper.pdf, accessed May 21, 2014.

47. Moltz (2011: 335–36).

48. Mark Brawley, *Political Economy and Grand Strategy* (Abingdon: Routledge, 2010). States approach the security dilemma in different ways, and as discussed in Chapter 3, international scholars disagree on the stability of highly skewed distributions of power.

49. Ikenberry (2011: esp. 348–60) argued that a state's willingness to roll the dice and sacrifice freedom of action for a legacy of order that could bring benefits after hegemonic decline depends on leadership as much as structural factors; see also Moltz (2011: 333–53) on "Alternative Futures for Space Security."

50. In the language of International Relations theory, Science offers a potential solution to Rousseau's stag-hunt game, permitting self-regarding states to trust each

other enough to reach a higher, more beneficial equilibrium for all. Robert Jervis, "Cooperation under the Security Dilemma," *World Politics* Vol. 30, No. 2 (January 1978): 167–214; Jean-Jacques Rousseau, "Abstract and Judgement of Saint-Pierre's Project for Perpetual Peace [1756]," in Chris Brown, Terry Nardin, and Nicholas Rengger, eds., *International Relations and Political Thought: Texts from the Ancient Greeks to the First World War* (Cambridge: Cambridge University Press, 2002), 425–27. Transnational space stewardship through commonly accepted rules offers greater security and prosperity than an unfettered arms race in space if the most powerful guarantor of this order, a putatively benign hegemon, can be trusted.

51. Elizabeth Clements, "Crossing the Valley of Death," *Symmetry* Magazine (Fermilab/SLAC), (February 2011, available at www.symmetrymagazine.org/article/february-2011/crossing-the-valley-of-death, accessed May 22, 2014; Committee on Evaluation of U.S. Air Force Preacquisition Technology Development, Air Force Studies Board, Division on Engineering and Physical Sciences, National Research Council, *Evaluation of U.S. Air Force Preacquisition Technology Development* (Washington, DC: National Academies Press, March 1, 2011), e.g. 54.

52. David Arnold and Peter Hays, "Strategy and the Security Space Enterprise," in Eligar Sadeh, ed., *Space Strategy in the 21st Century: Theory and Policy* (Abingdon: Routledge, 2013), 120–58, esp. 141.

53. Ibid., 142.

54. Robert Gilpin, *War & Change in World Politics* (Cambridge: Cambridge University Press, 1981).

55. Sandra Erwin, "Satellite Shortages May Choke Off Military Drone Expansion," *National Defense* (NDIA), April 2013, available at www.nationaldefensemagazine.org/archive/2013/April/Pages/SatelliteShortagesMayChokeOffMilitaryDroneExpansion.aspx, accessed May 22, 2014; Greg Slabodkin, "COMSATCOM Continues to Play Critical Role in Supporting Military," *Defense Systems,* October 25, 2012, available at http://defensesystems.com/articles/2012/10/25/c4isr-2-commercial-satcom-services.aspx, accessed May 22, 2014.

56. Peter de Selding, "Inmarsat Remains Confident Global Xpress Will Be a Hit with U.S. Military," *Space News,* March 6, 2014, available at www.spacenews.com/article/financial-report/39754inmarsat-remains-confident-global-xpress-will-be-a-hit-with-us, accessed May 23, 2014.

57. Roger Harrison, Deron Jackson, and Collins Shackelford, "Space Deterrence: The Delicate Balance of Risk," *Space and Defense* (USAFA) Vol. 3, No. 1 (Summer 2009): 1–30, esp. 20–22, available at www.usafa.edu/df/dfe/dfer/centers/ecsds/defense_journal.cfm. Arnold and Hays (2013: 131–41).

58. Edwin Mansfield, "Technical Change and the Rate of Imitation," *Econometrica* Vol. 29, No. 4 (October 1961): 741–66.

59. Kevin O'Connell, "Game Changers in Remote Sensing," *Space News,* July 7, 2011,

available at www.spacenews.com/article/game-changers-remote-sensing, accessed May 23, 2014; A. J. Clark, "Higher-Res Commercial Satellite Imagery on Hold," *Space News*, April 14, 2014, available at www.spacenews.com/article/opinion/40220higher-res-commercial-satellite-imagery-on-hold, accessed May 23, 2014. NASA Landsat Science, "Landsat 8 Overview," updated May 28, 2014, available at http://landsat.gsfc.nasa.gov /?page_id=7195, accessed May 29, 2014; Copernicus, "Free Access to Copernicus Sentinel Satellite Data," European Space Agency, November 15, 2013, available at www.esa.int/ Our_Activities/Observing_the_Earth/Copernicus/Free_access_to_Copernicus_Sentinel_satellite_data, accessed May 23, 2014.

60. My earlier work explored why this traditional form of information sharing may be nearing the end of its useful life. Damon Coletta, *Trusted Guardian: Information Sharing and the Future of the Atlantic Alliance* (Aldershot: Ashgate, 2008).

61. Ibid., 81–88, 125.

62. Ryan Lizza, "Leading from Behind," *New Yorker*, April 27, 2011, available at www.newyorker.com/online/blogs/newsdesk/2011/04/leading-from-behind-obama-clinton.html; Anne Gearan, Karen DeYoung, and Craig Whitlock, "U.S. Weighs Military Support for France's Campaign against Mali Militants," *Washington Post*, January 15, 2013, available at www.washingtonpost.com/world/national-security/us-weighs-military-support-for-frances-campaign-against-mali-militants/2013/01/15/a071db40–5f4d-11e2-b05a-605528f6b712_story.html.

63. Coletta (2008).

64. European Space Agency, "Copernicus: Observing the Earth," ESA, updated May 28, 2014, available at www.esa.int/Our_Activities/Observing_the_Earth/Copernicus, accessed May 29, 2014.

65. Peter de Selding, "Taking a Cue from U.S. Landsat and GPS Programs, Europe Permits Free Access to Sentinel Earth Observation Data," *Space News*, July 30, 2013, available at www.spacenews.com/article/civil-space/36527taking-a-cue-from-us-landsat-and-gps-programs-europe-permits-free-access-to.

66. Mike Gruss, "U.S. Intelligence Committee Endorses Company's Bid to Sell Sharper Imagery," *Space News*, April 18, 2014, available at www.spacenews.com/article/military-space/40263us-intelligence-community-endorses-company%E2%80%99s-bid-to-sell-sharper-imagery.

67. Deutsche Welle, "A Chronology of the NSA Surveillance Scandal," DW (Germany), October 31, 2013, available at www.dw.de/a-chronology-of-the-nsa-surveillance-scandal/a-17197740, accessed May 24, 2014.

68. Deb Riechmann, "NSA Spying Threatens to Hamper US Foreign Policy," *AP News* Archive, October 26, 2013, available at http://bigstory.ap.org/article/nsa-spying-threatens-hamper-us-foreign-policy, accessed May 24, 2014; Matt Sledge, "NSA Revelations Could Undermine Transatlantic Trade Negotiations," *Huffington Post*, De-

cember 20, 2013, available at www.huffingtonpost.com/2013/12/20/nsa-trade-negotia-
tions_n_4481277.html.

69. Linda Sieg and Kiyoshi Takenaka, "Japan Enacts Strict State Secrets Law Despite
Protests," *Reuters,* December 6, 2013, available at www.reuters.com/article/2013/12/06/
us-japan-secrets-idUSBRE9B50JT20131206; Corinne Purtill, "Among Europe's Leaders,
Cameron Stands Apart on NSA Spying Scandal," *Global Post,* October 28, 2013, available at www.globalpost.com/dispatch/news/regions/europe/united-kingdom/131028/
europe-nsa-british-pm-cameron-spying-surveillance; Joe Cochrane, "N.S.A. Spying
Scandal Hurts Close Ties between Australia and Indonesia," *New York Times,* November
20, 2013, A11.

70. Deborah Avant, Martha Finnemore, and Susan Sell, eds., *Who Governs the
Globe?* (Cambridge: Cambridge University Press, 2010); Nancy Gallagher, "International
Cooperation and Space Governance Strategy," in Eligar Sadeh, ed., *Space Strategy in the
21st Century: Theory and Policy* (Abingdon: Routledge, 2013), 52–76, esp. 53.

71. John Hamre, William Lynn III, Michael Donley, and James Cartwright, "CSIS
Forum on the National Security Space Strategy," U.S. Department of Defense, February
16, 2011, available at www.defense.gov/Speeches/Speech.aspx?SpeechID=1550, accessed
May 24, 2014; see, for example, the first intervention in the transcript by General James
Cartwright, then vice chairman of the Joint Chiefs of Staff.

72. Joan Johnson-Freese (2009: 110–14).

73. *National Security Space Strategy* (2011: 1 and fig. 1).

74. This tripartite division mirrors the structure of this book. More important, the
idea comes from Immanuel Kant's essay on "Perpetual Peace" (1795) in which, on the cusp
of the Napoleonic Wars that would consume Europe, Kant called for three simultaneous
"constitutions"—decentralized, rule-by-rule regimes—at the civic (domestic), international (interstate), and cosmopolitan (transnational) levels of interaction. Kant (1983).

75. Other relevant policy documents include DOD commissioned reports on the
industrial base for U.S. space leadership—for example, Air Force Research Laboratory
(AFRL) and U.S. Department of Commerce, *Defense Industrial Base Assessment: U.S.
Space Industry,* final report (Dayton, OH: AFRL, August 31, 2007), and higher-level guidance such as President of the United States, *National Space Transportation Policy* (Washington, DC: White House, November 21, 2013). Nothing in these additional sources
breaks the official mold discussed here: acknowledgment of the need to cooperate *and*
compete on space while passing over practical tensions generated by attempting to do
both at once.

76. President of the United States, *National Security Strategy* (Washington, DC:
White House, May 2010), 5, 40. Christopher Hemmer, in his evaluation of the *National
Security Strategy,* focused his attention on this change amid other elements of continu-
ity with the earlier Bush strategies. Christopher Hemmer, "Continuity and Change in

the Obama Administration's National Security Strategy," *Comparative Strategy* Vol. 30, No. 3 (July 2011): 268–77.

77. Under "National Security Space Guidelines," the 2006 strategy called for the secretary of defense to "develop capabilities, plans, and options to ensure freedom of action in space, and, if directed, deny such freedom of action to adversaries." President of the United States, "National Space Policy" (unclassified), August 31, 2006, posted by Federation of American Scientists, Washington, DC, available at www.fas.org/irp/offdocs/nspd/space.pdf, accessed May 25, 2014.

78. Ibid., Item 3, "United States Space Policy Goals." Traci Watson and Richard Benedetto, "Bush Proposes Manned Mission to Moon by 2015," *USA Today,* January 15, 2004, available at http://usatoday30.usatoday.com/news/science/2004–01–14-bush-space_x.htm.

79. President of the United States, *National Space Policy of the United States of America* (Washington, DC: White House, June 28, 2010), 4, 10–11.

80. Ibid., 1.

81. Neil deGrasse Tyson, "The Case for Space," *Foreign Affairs* Vol. 91, No. 2 (March/April 2012): 22–33.

82. *National Space Policy* (2010: 2, 4); *National Security Space Strategy* (2011: 4–5).

83. *National Security Space Strategy* (2011: 5).

84. Ibid., 4.

85. Ibid., 8–9.

86. Ibid., 9.

87. Fareed Zakaria and Richard Haass missed the boat, or offered only partial solutions, with their recommendations on infrastructure projects and various stimulus packages at home. Science operates at the home front and in addition facilitates the unavoidable trade-off between coercion and engagement abroad. Fareed Zakaria, "Can America Be Fixed? The New Crisis of Democracy," *Foreign Affairs* Vol. 92, No. 1 (January/February 2013): 22–33; Haass (2013).

Chapter 7

1. G. John Ikenberry, *Liberal Leviathan: The Origins, Crisis, and Transformation of the American World Order* (Princeton: Princeton University Press, 2011); Mancur Olson, *The Logic of Collective Action: Public Goods and the Theory of Groups* (Cambridge: Harvard University Press, 1971).

2. Charles Hill, in *Grand Strategies*, uses an illuminating term, postmetaphysical, to describe the emergent state system in the wake of the Thirty Years' War, which had dashed Catholic Spain's bid for one kingdom on Earth as it is in Heaven. Charles Hill, *Grand Strategies: Literature, Statecraft, and World Order* (New Haven: Yale University Press, 2010), 135, 143–44.

3. S. Sara Monison and Michael Loriaux, "The Illusion of Power and the Disruption of Moral Norms: Thucydides' Critique of Periclean Policy," *American Political Science Review* Vol. 92, No. 2 (June 1998): 285–97.

4. Hedley Bull, *The Anarchical Society: A Study of Order in World Politics* (New York: Columbia University Press, 1977); John Ruggie, "International Regimes, Transactions, and Change: Embedded Liberalism in the Postwar Economic Order," *International Organization* Vol. 36, No. 2 (Spring 1982): 379–415.

5. In their book *Balance: The Economics of Great Powers from Ancient Rome to Modern America* (New York: Simon and Schuster, 2013), Glenn Hubbard and Tim Kane discussed waves of declinism in American discourse. They were mesmerized by the cover art and otherwise impressed by Paul Kennedy's 1987 *Rise and Fall of the Great Powers*, which tied American decline, and every other hegemon's fall, to implacable forces of economic history. *Balance*, like this book, sought policies that would resist the cycle and at least put off the day of reckoning for American hegemony. Hubbard and Kane (2013: 20); Paul Kennedy, *The Rise and Fall of the Great Powers: Economic Change and Military Conflict from 1500 to 2000* (New York: Random House, 1987).

6. Robert Gilpin, *France in the Age of the Scientific State* (Princeton: Princeton University Press, 1968).

7. William Wohlforth, "The Stability of a Unipolar World," *International Security* Vol. 24, No. 1 (Summer 1999): 5–41.

8. Here, I do not distinguish between leadership objectives and style as Joseph Nye, Jr., does in *Presidential Leadership and the Creation of the American Era* (Princeton: Princeton University Press, 2013), 8–13 and Table 1.1. Science better arms the transactional leader to drive favorable bargains within the current system rather than transform international relations in the U.S. image or inspire other states to adopt the hegemon's strategic preferences.

9. A hegemon shrinking from the world, like an army in retreat, is a delicate matter. There are mortal dangers in hanging on too long or withdrawing too quickly. Transactional significance for national science might sound less important than transformational, but nothing is more vital than getting the balance right in American grand strategy. Barry Posen, *Restraint: A New Foundation for U.S. Grand Strategy* (Ithaca, NY: Cornell University Press, 2014); Colin Dueck, *The Obama Doctrine: American Grand Strategy Today* (Oxford: Oxford University Press, 2015).

10. The notion of an American Epic comes from chapter 6 of Charles Hill's *Grand Strategies* (2010: 134–76), "America: A New Idea," in which politically influential renderings of America's purpose are shown to be in dialogue with important literary currents of the time. The actual term, "American Epic," comes from my mentor on the Air Force Academy faculty. On several occasions this former ambassador ruefully recalled how successful policy planning, in the sense of seeing the policy implemented by the bureau-

cracy, boiled down to three key ingredients: a logic of power, a full-throated defense of American values, and a happy ending. All of which could be utter fiction, pure storytelling, with respect to eventual policy outcomes.

11.   George Washington, "Washington's Farewell Address, 1796," Avalon Project, Lillian Goldman Law Library, Yale Law School, 2008, available at http://avalon.law.yale.edu/18th_century/washing.asp, accessed May 6, 2014.

12.   The desire to redeem Europe, teach Europe, or sponsor an international order superior to that of the mother continent consistent with American values is recorded in key American foreign policy documents and speeches from Hamilton's Federalist No. 11, the Monroe Doctrine, the universalist tone of the Roosevelt Corollary, Wilson's Fourteen Points, and Franklin Roosevelt's Atlantic Charter; from the inaugural address of John F. Kennedy in 1961 to George W. Bush's inaugural in 2005; from George H. W. Bush's "New World Order" State of the Union speech in 1991 to Barack Obama's *National Security Strategy* in 2010. Texts of the preceding presidential statements as well as that of Alexander Hamilton are readily available online.

13.   Jonathan Monten, "The Roots of the Bush Doctrine: Power, Nationalism, and Democracy Promotion in U.S. Strategy," *International Security* Vol. 29, No. 4 (Spring 2005): 112–56.

14.   These phrases come from Pericles' famous funeral oration, in which he justifies why free citizens (Athenians) should willingly sacrifice earthly pleasures, to include their very lives, for the triumph of the state in war. Robert Strassler, ed., *The Landmark Thucydides: A Comprehensive Guide to the Peloponnesian War* (New York: Free Press, 1996), 125–26/Thucydides (II.63).

15.   In his book *Limits of Power*, warning Americans of impending imperial overstretch, Andrew Bacevich described the political misfortune of President Jimmy Carter after Carter told the American people the truth about the likely consequences of their profligacy in his "moral equivalent of war" speech (1979). Andrew Bacevich, *The Limits of Power: The End of American Exceptionalism* (New York: Henry Holt and Co., 2008), 32–33.

16.   This is the theme from Charles Hill's *Grand Strategies* (2010).

17.   Samuel Huntington painstakingly described this gap in his important article from the post-Vietnam era, "American Ideals versus American Institutions," *Political Science Quarterly* Vol. 97, No. 1 (Spring 1982): 1–37.

18.   Strassler (1996: 127–28)/Thucydides, bk. II.65.8.

19.   Realists of the late 1990s and 2000s who suspected unipolarity to be nothing more than a will-o'-the-wisp included Kenneth Waltz, "Structural Realism after the Cold War," *International Security* Vol. 25, No. 1 (Summer 2000): 5–41; John Mearsheimer, *The Tragedy of Great Power Politics* (New York: W. W. Norton and Co., 2001); Stephen Walt, "Keeping the World 'Off-Balance': Self-Restraint and U.S. Foreign Policy," in G. John Ikenberry, ed., *America Unrivaled: The Future of the Balance of Power* (Ithaca, NY: Cornell University Press, 2002), 121–54; Walt, *Taming American Power: The Global Re-*

sponse to U.S. Primacy (New York: W. W. Norton and Co., 2006); Christopher Layne, "The Unipolar Illusion: Why New Great Powers Will Rise," *International Security* Vol. 17, No. 4 (Spring 1993): 5–51; and Layne, *The Peace of Illusions: American Grand Strategy from 1940 to the Present* (Ithaca, NY: Cornell University Press, 2006).

20. Carnes Lord, *The Modern Prince: What Leaders Need to Know Now* (New Haven: Yale University Press, 2003), esp. chs. 2–3, pp. 11–32.

21. See Henry Kissinger, *Nuclear Weapons and Foreign Policy* (New York: Harper and Brothers, 1957), ch. 12.

22. When Stephen Brooks and William Wohlforth wanted to explore what IR theory predicts about the costs of unilateralism for a hegemon, they explored the three theoretical lenses discussed here: realism, liberal institutionalism, and constructivism. Stephen Brooks and William Wohlforth, "International Relations Theory and the Case against Unilateralism," *Perspectives on Politics* Vol. 3, No. 3 (September 2005): 509–24.

23. Ruggie's seminal article for establishing the legitimacy, ironically enough, of constructivism among the Big Three schools of International Relations is John Ruggie, "What Makes the World Hang Together? Neo-Utilitarianism and the Social Constructivist Challenge," *International Organization* Vol. 52, No. 4 (Autumn 1998): 855–85.

24. Robert Keohane, *After Hegemony: Cooperation and Discord in the World Political Economy* (Princeton: Princeton University Press, 1984); Lisa Martin, *Coercive Cooperation: Explaining Multilateral Economic Sanctions* (Princeton: Princeton University Press, 1992); Robert Keohane and Lisa Martin, "The Promise of Institutionalist Theory," *International Security* Vol. 20, No. 1 (Summer 1995): 39–51; G. John Ikenberry, *After Victory: Institutions, Strategic Restraint, and the Rebuilding of Order after Major Wars* (Princeton: Princeton University Press, 2001); and Ikenberry (2011).

25. Again, these are the three levels of public right identified by Immanuel Kant as important to address if mankind is to construct a permanent, or self-perpetuating, peace out of the Westphalian system of competing states under anarchy. Immanuel Kant, "To Perpetual Peace: A Philosophical Sketch [1795]," in Ted Humphrey, trans. and intro., *Perpetual Peace and Other Essays on Politics, History, and Morals* (Indianapolis, IN: Hackett, 1983), 107–43, esp. 112–19, 123.

26. Alexander Wendt, *Social Theory of International Politics* (Cambridge: Cambridge University Press, 1999); Martha Finnemore, "Constructing Norms of Humanitarian Intervention," in Peter Katzenstein, ed., *The Culture of National Security: Norms and Identity in World Politics* (New York: Columbia University Press, 1996), 153–85; Michael Barnett and Martha Finnemore, *Rules for the World: International Organizations in Global Politics* (Ithaca, NY: Cornell University Press, 2004).

27. See the discussion of Kenneth Waltz, *Theory of International Politics* (Reading, MA: Addison-Wesley Co., 1979) in my Chapter Three. For commentary on asymmetric, or unbalanced, multipolarity, see Richard Rosecrance, "War and Peace" (review article), *World Politics* Vol. 55, No. 1 (October 2002): 137–66.

28. Ikenberry (2011: 119–56).

29. Rosecrance (2002: 151–53).

30. Stephen Krasner, "Global Communications and National Power: Life on the Pareto Frontier," *World Politics* Vol. 43, No. 3 (April 1991): 336–66. James Fearon, "Bargaining, Enforcement, and International Cooperation," *International Organization* Vol. 52, No. 2 (Spring 1998): 269–305.

31. Aristocratic patrons might sound anachronistic, but it is not an idle characterization. See billionaire science funding concerns that such support could one day substitute, inadequately, for robust federal government commitment to science. William Broad, "Billionaires with Big Ideas Are Privatizing American Science," *New York Times*, March 16, 2014, A1.

32. Sean Kay, "America's *Sputnik* Moments," *Survival: Global Politics and Strategy* Vol. 55, No. 2 (April–May 2013): 123–46.

33. In American democracy, first dollars dedicated in this way are exempt from federal income tax.

34. STEM is the widely used acronym for "Science, Technology, Engineering, and Mathematics."

35. Sheila Jasanoff, ed., *States of Knowledge: The Co-Production of Science and Social Order* (London: Routledge, 2004), 14.

Index

138–45; Kant on, 123–24; science's role in, 154–55, 156–57; trust in, 133, 135, 138, 147, 148, 151, 164; Westphalian order, 155, 156–57, 174. *See also* Outer space, global governance

Good governance, 37

Gorbachev, Mikhail, 7

Goulart, João, 105

Graham, Loren, 33, 34

Great Powers. *See* Hegemony; Polarity; Superpowers

Greece, ancient. *See* Athens

Gross domestic product (GDP), 127

Haass, Richard, 116, 123, 220n87

Hays. Peter, 140

Hegemonic decline: in ancient world, 21, 24, 63, 159; of Athens, 1–2, 3, 14, 20–21, 63; avoiding, 15–16; effects, 165; explanations, 40; managing, 5, 159; science and, 12, 221n9; in space, 145; of United States, 14–15, 55–56, 58, 59, 159, 164–67

Hegemonic state. *See* Scientific State; State

Hegemony: after multipolarity, 54–55, 56; benign, 171–72; as club leadership, 56–57; in future, 56, 59–61, 153, 158–59; global governance and, 122–23, 126–27, 130, 133, 138–45; legitimacy, 15, 40, 57, 122, 166, 171; maintaining, 40, 59–60, 122–23, 159–61, 171–72; meaning, 39–40, 56; in multipolar world, 57, 59–61, 164–67; resistance to, 40; resources, 40, 41–42; rival powers and, 89–90, 92; role of science and technology, 1, 6–7, 16; rule-by-relationships, 144, 145, 166; rule-through-rules, 143, 144–45, 149, 154–55; scientific diplomacy and, 118–21; scientific leadership and, 5–6, 151, 155–56, 157, 167–68, 171, 173–75; Scientific State and, 38, 59–61, 65,

89–90, 148–49; soft power and, 6, 126; technological superiority, 90, 156–57; Waltz on, 49–50, 52, 56, 194n53; world, 49–50, 52, 194n53. *See also* United States hegemony

Hill, Charles, 195n62, 221n10

History, 14

Hitler, Adolf. *See* Nazi Germany

Hume, David, 27

Huntington, Samuel, 53, 67, 75, 83, 120, 197n16

IBSA (India, Brazil, South Africa) group, 93, 96–97

Ikenberry, G. John, 55, 138, 144–45, 154, 163, 166

Imperialism, 24, 27–28, 64

Industrial Revolution, 21–22, 67

Inequality, 66–67, 71–72, 86, 87, 99, 108

Information technology: geographic information systems, 133; for satellites, 136

INMETRO. *See* Instituto Nacional de Metrologia, Qualidade, e Tecnologia

Institute for Advanced Study, 84–85

Institutionalism, 10, 40, 163, 166, 172–73

Instituto Nacional de Metrologia, Qualidade, e Tecnologia (INMETRO), Brazil, 114, 119

Intelligence: data sharing, 141–44; on Iraq's weapons, 142; NSA eavesdropping, 144, 169, 205n24. *See also* Satellites

Intergovernmental Panel on Climate Change (IPCC), 13–14, 173

International Criminal Court, 173

International organizations (IOs), 13–14, 16, 54–55, 58

International partnerships, 13, 24, 91. *See also* Cooperation

International Relations theories: constructivism, 155, 163–64; institutionalism, 10, 40, 163, 166,